Korean Hedges in Spoken Discourse

Korea University Press
82-2-3290-4234 (Tel.) 82-2-923-6311 (Fax)
http://www.kupress.com kupress@korea.ac.kr
145, Anam-Ro, Seongbuk-Gu, Seoul, 02841 Korea

Published May 2016

ISBN 978-89-7641-899-9 93710

PRINTED IN REPUBLIC OF KOREA

KLEAR-RILI Studies in Korean Language and Linguistics

THE KOREAN LANGUAGE EDUCATION AND RESEARCH CENTER &
THE RESEARCH INSTITUTE OF LANGUAGE AND INFORMATION

KOREAN HEDGES IN SPOKEN DISCOURSE

Sociopragmatic and Pragmalinguistic Perspectives

Yeonhee Yoon

KOREA
UNIVERSITY
PRESS
고려대학교
출판문화원

Congratulatory Remarks

I am indeed gratified to see Dr. Yeonhee Yoon's work on Korean hedges in spoken discourse published in the KLEAR-RILI series. My sincere congratulations!

This book is a revised version of Dr. Yoon's University of Hawaii doctoral dissertation in Korean language and linguistics. The gist of the book is a meticulous statistical analysis of the sociolinguistic and pragmatic uses of linguistic hedges that appeared in naturally occurring Korean conversations in Dr. Yoon's corpus data. As chair of her dissertation committee, I confidently say that her dissertation, from which this book derived, is of a superior quality and a significant contribution to Korean linguistics.

Linguistic hedges, both lexical and syntactic, are crucial and indispensable communicative resources for smooth and polite interaction in spoken discourse. Yet, the use of hedges in Korean attracted little scholarly attention before Dr. Yoon's comprehensive and systematic analysis. Dr. Yoon carefully categorized Korean hedges and investigated the frequency of individual hedge items in spoken discourse. She also analyzed Korean hedges empirically in terms of the statistical correlation between hedge use and sociopragmatic factors as well as pragmalinguistic factors.

As summarized in the preface of the book, Dr. Yoon's research, the first of its kind in Korean linguistics, makes several important descriptive and theoretical contributions to general socio-pragmatic studies. For instance, Dr. Yoon discovered that Korean hedges, functioning as interactive strategies, are used more frequently in two-party than many-party conversations and more frequently in personal than impersonal topics. Her study also reveals that hedges are used as both positive and negative politeness strategies and that social situational factors are more influential in affecting hedge use than social structural factors such as gender, age, region, or occupation.

In short, this book is a welcome addition to the KLEAR-RILI series. I enthusiastically recommend it to readers.

Ho-min Sohn
Emeritus Professor of Korean Linguistics
University of Hawaii at Manoa

FOREWORD

Three decades ago, it was difficult to find anyone in America who was interested in learning Korean. Even with its 70 million speakers and its status as one of the world's twenty most spoken languages, few colleges or universities taught it, and almost nothing had been written about it in English. A great deal has changed since then. It is now possible to study Korean at hundreds of post-secondary institutions around the world, state-of-the art teaching materials are widely available, and an ever-increasing amount of research on the language is available in English, ensuring its accessibility to an eager international audience.

A very welcome addition to the literature on Korean is Yeonhee Yoon's account of hedges — the softening strategies that are essential to use of the spoken language. Drawing on meticulously analyzed data from natural spoken discourse, Dr. Yoon takes us beyond vocabulary and grammar into the very heart of Korean, where hedges help speakers manage the delicate complexities of conversation in a culture that values politeness and propriety. Dr. Yoon's findings are invaluable both for the insights that they offer into the intricacies of Korean usage and for their profound usefulness to students of Korean as a second language. This is a pioneering work of scholarship and a fine example of the direction in which researchers should proceed in the years ahead as Korean takes its rightful place among the world's most important languages.

William O'Grady
Professor of Linguistics
University of Hawaii at Manoa

Preface

This book presents an empirical analysis of Korean hedges in contemporary spoken discourse. The data analyzed was drawn from my corpus based on approximately 17 hours of unplanned, naturally occurring conversations. This study classifies lexical and syntactic hedges and investigates the frequency of individual hedge items from the corpus. I provide an analysis of the correlation between hedge use and sociopragmatic factors as well as pragmalinguistic factors.

The results of my statistical analysis reveal that in Korean spoken discourse (i) more hedges are used in two-party conversations than in multiple-party (three or four participants) conversations, (ii) more hedges are used in conversations with personal topics than with impersonal topics, and (iii) hedges are employed as a positive politeness strategy as well as a negative politeness strategy, although hedges have been viewed traditionally as a form of negative politeness.

My study makes several theoretical contributions. First, this study shows that previous sociolinguistic views on the correlation between hedge use and social structural factors such as gender have reflected a tendency for overgeneralization. That is, while hedge use and other tendencies in spoken discourse have been associated with differences in gender, this generalization is not true for Korean spoken discourse. Second, the analysis of this study proposes the importance of social situational factors such as the number of speakers and the topic of conversation for sociopragmatic analysis. The most influential factors affecting hedge use in Korean spoken discourse are not social structural factors such as gender, age, region, or occupation, but social situational factors. Third, this study elucidates the function of hedges as interactive strategies which may facilitate the success of interactions between interlocutors, enhance interpersonal rapport, and establish solidarity in terms of a positive politeness strategy extending beyond the negative politeness strategy. Fourth, this study demonstrates that an analysis that include both sociopragmatic and pragmalinguistic perspectives is necessary and important when analyzing hedges. According to the empirical analysis of Korean hedges in this study, Korean hedge use is affected by contextual factors as well as strategic factors. Thus, my study has broader implications beyond Korean linguistics in suggesting that a multi-layered approach is necessary for analyzing and comprehending the complexity of the hedge.

This book is based on my Ph.D. dissertation that I wrote six years ago. My six years of study at the graduate school of the University of Hawai'i at Mānoa have been the most challenging and precious journey of my life, and the writing of my Ph.D. dissertation required from me a lot of courage and patience. Books are not written alone, and I was fortunate to have extraordinary advisers and colleagues. This study would not have been completed without the support and the encouragement of numerous people. Thus, my sincere gratitude goes to those people who have been so supportive and have made this book possible. First of all, I would like to express my deepest gratitude to my advisor, Professor Ho-min Sohn, who is the most prominent scholar as well as an esteemed educator in Korean linguistics and Korean language pedagogy. Next, I would like to express my sincere gratitude to Professor Seok-Hoon You at Korea University, who encouraged me to publish this book, and Professor William O'Grady, who gave me insightful comments and willingly provided me with references whenever I faced seemingly insurmountable obstacles, and most importantly encouraged me with his warm heart. In addition, my thanks go to Professors Yung-Hee Kim, Dong-Jae Lee, David Ashworth, Mee-Jeong Park, Sang-Yee Cheon who had been supportive and gave me valuable feedback. I also would like to thank the Institute for Scholarship in the Liberal Arts (ISLA) at University of Notre Dame for an Indexing and Copyediting Support grant and the Korea University Press.

Finally, and most importantly, this book would not have been completed without the love and support of my family. Thus, this book is dedicated to my beloved late father, mother, parents-in-law, husband, and daughter. Especially, I would like to thank my parents for their unconditional love and support and my husband, Dr. Kiwoong Yang, a professor of international relations, for his love, support, and advice as an academic mentor. Last but not least, I would like to thank my most precious daughter, Jiyun, for her patience and love.

CONTENTS

LIST OF TABLES

LIST OF FIGURES

LIST OF ABBREVIATIONS (adopted from Sohn, 1998)

AC Accusative particle
AD Adverbial suffix, adverbializer
AH Addressee honorific
APP Apperceptive sentence-type suffix
AUX Auxiliary verb
BLN Blunt speech level or suffix
CAU Causative suffix
CL Numeral classifier (counter)
CONC Concessive
CMP Complementizer suffix
CNJ Conjunctive suffix
DC Declarative sentence-type suffix
DEF Deferential speech level
DM Discourse marker
DR Directional particle
EM Emphasizer
ENDER Sentence/clause ender
EX Exclamatory suffix
FML Familiar speech level or suffix
FUT Future tense
GN Genitive particle
HT Honorific title
IM Imperative sentence-type suffix
IMPFV Imperfective
IN Indicative mood suffix
INF Infinitive suffix
INT Intimate speech level or suffix
NEG Negative
NM Nominative case particle
NOM Nominalizer suffix
PAS Passive suffix
PL Plural suffix or particle
PLN Plain speech level or suffix
POL Polite speech level, suffix, or particle
PR Propositive sentence-type suffix
PRM Promissive sentence-type suffix
PRS Prospective modal suffix
PST Past tense and perfect aspect suffix
Q Question marker (interrogative sentence-type suffix)
QT Quotative particle
RL Relativizer (or adnominal modifier) suffix
RQ Requestive mood suffix
RT Retrospective mood suffix
SH Subject honorific suffix
SUP Suppositive mood suffix
TC Topic-contrast particle
VOC Vocative particle

CHAPTER 1

INTRODUCTION

1.1 Objectives

This empirical study investigates Korean hedges in contemporary spoken discourse. Although hedges as conventionalized illocution-mitigating devices are effective and crucial communicative resources in Korean spoken discourse in terms of politeness, there is little systematic and comprehensive analysis of Korean hedges. Thus, first of all, this study will aim to categorize Korean hedges and investigate the frequency of individual hedge items in spoken discourse. It also analyzes Korean hedges empirically in terms of the statistical correlation between hedge use and sociopragmatic factors as well as pragmalinguistic factors based on statistical methods. The research questions of the current study will be presented in Section 1.2 in detail. Since the study of Korean hedges is a relatively new area, it is my hope that this study, as the first empirical analysis of Korean hedges in spoken discourse, will add to the research in Korean pragmatics as well as contribute to comparative studies in intercultural pragmatics.

According to contemporary views, pragmatics is a broad approach to discourse. As Schiffrin (1994) mentioned, pragmatics deals with the concepts of meaning, context, and communication. Pragmatics is also the study of communicative action in its sociocultural context (Kasper, 1997). Moreover, Leech (1983) and Thomas (1983) proposed dividing pragmatics into *pragmalinguistics and sociopragmatics*. As Kasper (1997) summarized, *pragmalinguistics* refers to the resources for conveying relational or interpersonal meanings and communicative acts. The resources include pragmatic strategies such as indirectness, routines, and various linguistic forms that both intensify and soften communicative acts. On the other hand, according to Leech (1983, p. 10), *sociopragmatics* is the sociological interface of pragmatics, referring to the social perceptions underlying participants' interpretation and performance of communicative actions. Furthermore, as Blum-Kulka (1991) indicates, strategies of communicative actions vary according to context; such variables as social power, social and psychological distance, and the degree of imposition may be involved in a communicative act in terms of sociopragmatics (Kasper & Rose, 2001).

The term *hedge* is used in a complex research area within the fields of pragmatics, discourse analysis, semantics, logic, and philosophy. In each of these research areas, the term hedge is defined in a different way. However, in the field of pragmatics, it is generally said that the concept of a hedge is linked to specific communicative purposes, such as politeness, vagueness, and mitigation in pragmatics (Schröder & Zimmer 1997).

Language use, including use of hedges, varies from culture to culture. Thus, in an intercultural communication situation, cultural differences may cause communication breakdown (Thomas, 1983) and misunderstanding in discourse between native speakers and nonnative speakers. For example, face-threatening acts such as requests or refusals are places where hedges or other pragmatic strategies may be particularly necessary since they are the source of many cross-cultural miscommunications.

In general, Korean hedges are used for mitigating or softening the illocutionary force of speech acts, and are relevant to strategic politeness. According to Sohn (1999b), a hedge is used to tone down or mitigate the illocutionary force of a direct way of speaking by means of various linguistic devices in terms of politeness strategies. In fact, a hedge is an essential resource in communication between interlocutors in Korean spoken discourse.

In the present study, I view the term *hedge* from the pragmatic perspective as a communicative strategy for politeness and mitigation in Korean spoken discourse. Hence, I define a *hedge* as a linguistic device that softens or mitigates the illocutionary force of a proposition as well as expresses a speaker's concern for the addressee's feelings, and as an interactive strategy to protect face for self and/or others as well as to facilitate the success of interactions between interlocutors, enhance interpersonal rapport, and establish solidarity.

1.2 Research Questions

The research questions for the present study are as follows:

(1) How can Korean hedges be classified in spoken discourse?
(2) What is the frequency of the individual hedge item in Korean spoken discourse?
(3) Is there any correlation between hedge use and sociopragmatic factors (social structural factors and social situational factors)?
(4) Is there any correlation between hedge use and pragmalinguistic factors (speech act type and politeness strategy)?
(5) What are the implications of major findings of sociopragmatic analysis and pragmalinguistic analysis?

Let me elaborate my research questions in detail. First, I will classify Korean hedges in spoken discourse based on the classification of the previous studies and my own collected data.

Second, the frequency of individual hedge items will be investigated. The search engine of the *Secong* corpus, *hanmalwu*, will be employed to investigate the frequency of individual hedge items. The data for this study consists of approximately 17 hours of recorded, unplanned, and naturally-occurring conversations which I have collected and developed into a corpus. The classification and frequency of Korean hedges in spoken discourse in this study will provide a basis for more systematic investigation of Korean hedges and for further studies. Thus, the investigation of the frequency of Korean hedges in spoken discourse will be the first contribution of this study.

Third, the correlation between hedge use and sociopragmatic factors will be analyzed in this study. Statistical analysis using t-test, ANOVA, and post-hoc analysis will be conducted. Sociopragmatic factors are divided into social structural factors and social situational factors. Social structural factors include gender, gender composition, age, occupation, and region, while social situational factors include the number of speakers in the conversation, topic of conversation, social power relations between interlocutors, and social distance relations between interlocutors. An empirical analysis of the correlation between hedge use and sociopragmatic factors will be the second contribution of this study.

Fourth, the correlation between hedge use and pragmalinguistic factors will be analyzed in this study. Pragmalinguistic factors include speech act type and politeness strategies. Both quantitative analysis and qualitative analysis will be conducted for the pragmalinguistic analysis of selected hedge items. The empirical analysis of the correlation between hedge use and pragmalinguistic factors will be the third contribution of this study.

Lastly, this study will explain the implications of the major findings of sociopragmatic analysis and pragmalinguistic analysis.

1.3 Organization of the book

The organization of the present study is as follows. In Chapter 2, the definitions, arguments, and major theoretical frameworks presented by previous studies on hedges will be briefly discussed. Chapter 3 introduces the methodology and data collection procedures followed by an overview of the data for this study. More specifically, this chapter introduces how the data was collected, coded, investigated, and analyzed. Furthermore, it presents an overview of the data, such as the distribution of gender, gender composition in conversations, age, region, occupation, and social power relations as well as social distance relations between interlocutors. Chapter 4 will summarize the classification of Korean hedges in spoken discourse and describe the frequency of each hedge item in my data. The data investigated is Yoon's corpus and a total number of 9,962 tokens of hedges were identified. In Chapter 5, I will conduct a sociopragmatic analysis of seven lexical hedge items, which I refer to as interactive sentence enders (ISEs): this quantitative analysis will focus on social structural factors as well as social situational factors. Section 5.1 discusses the results of this analysis of seven ISEs in terms of five social structural factors (gender, gender composition, age, occupation, and region) as well as four social situational factors (number of speakers in the conversation, topic of conversation, social power relations between interlocutors, and social distance relations between interlocutors). Section 5.2 will summarize the findings and results of the sociopragmatic analysis done in Section 5.1. Section 5.3 will re-examine two major findings regarding the number of speakers in the conversation and the topic of conversation. As part of the re-examination, I will conduct an analysis of the correlation between seven auxiliary verbs (AVs) and the number of speakers in the conversation as well as the topic of conversation. Then I will use a contrastive analysis of ISEs and AVs to re-examine the correlation between hedge use and the number of speakers in the conversation and the topic of conversation. Chapter 6 will examine hedge use from a pragmalinguistic perspective. In order to carry out the pragmalinguistic analysis, two interactive sentence enders (ISEs), *-canha(yo)* and *-ketun(yo)* were chosen from seven ISEs and they will be analyzed qualitatively as well as quantitatively. Section 6.1 will examine the development of ISE *-canha(yo)*, summarize the speech act types that are associated with the use of *-canha(yo)*, present examples of these speech acts types, and analyze *-canha(yo)* from the perspective of the politeness. Section 6.2 will examine the development of ISE *-ketun(yo)*, summarize the speech act types that are associated with the use of *-ketun(yo)*, present examples of these speech acts types, and analyze *-ketun(yo)* from the perspective of the politeness strategy. Section 6.3 will compare the results of the analyses in 6.1 and 6.2. Chapter 7 concludes with a summary of the major findings along with the contributions of this work, and discusses pedagogical implications as well as brief suggestions for future studies.

CHAPTER 2

LITERATURE REVIEW

In this chapter, I will discuss the concept, arguments and major theoretical frameworks established by previous studies on hedges.

2.1 The Concept of Hedges

The notion of hedges is viewed differently by various scholars. The concept of hedge was first introduced by G. Lakoff (1972) in his article "Hedges: A study in meaning criteria and the logic of fuzzy concepts." G. Lakoff (1972, p. 195) defined hedge as a word or phrase "whose job it is to make things fuzzier or less fuzzy" from the language philosophy perspective. For example, "sort of" is a hedge as in "a chicken is a *sort of* bird." Zadeh (1972) analyzed English hedges such as *very, much, more or less, essentially,* and *slightly* from the perspective of semantics and logic. In his article "Fuzzy-set-theoretic interpretation of linguistic hedges," he defined hedges as operators that act on the fuzzy set representing the meaning of their operands. In his later study, Zadeh (1975) analyzed written English from the perspective of psycholinguistics.

The concept of hedges has moved far from its origins since the early 1970s and has been adopted by pragmatics and discourse analysis. In more recent approaches, divergent views on lexical and/ or syntactic hedges have been related to pragmatic strategies such as politeness, indirectness, mitigation, and vagueness. Various approaches have pointed to a variety of motives for applying hedges. For instance, Brown and Levinson (1978, 1987) viewed the hedge as a face-saving strategy or expression of negative politeness in the framework of politeness strategies. They defined the term hedge as "a particle, word or phrase that modifies the degree of membership of a predicate or a noun phrase in a set; it says of that membership that it is *partial* or true only in certain respects, or that it is *more* true and complete than perhaps might be expected" (Brown & Levinson, 1987, p. 145). They extend the boundaries of hedges to negative politeness which is used for avoiding threats to the face of the participants.

On the other hand, Fraser (1974) analyzes modal verbs from the pragmatic perspective in his article "Hedged performatives." He considered the effect that modals and semi-modals have on the illocutionary act denoted by a performative verb in performative sentences. For example, *I must advise you to remain quiet* in which the modal *must* relieves the speaker from some of the responsibility. Fraser named the modals *hedged performatives* instead of hedges. Later, he views the hedge from the point of view of its role in mitigation and politeness (Fraser, 1980) and then later as a discourse marker (Fraser, 1990). In the 1980s, more attention was paid to empirical analyses, based on contrastive and cross-cultural approaches. For instance, House and Kasper (1981) classified hedges as a subclass of *downgraders*, which implies a narrower definition. House and Kasper (1981) and Blum-Kulka and Olstein (1984) have discussed hedges as a means of modifying certain types of speech acts such as requests and apologies.

Other researchers have attempted to subcategorize hedges; for instance, Prince et al. (1982) distinguish two types of hedges from the point of view of discourse analysis: one is *approximators* (e.g., His feet were *sort of* blue.) that affect the truth conditions of propositions and the other is *shields* (e.g., *I think* his feet were blue.) that do not affect the truth conditions but reflect the speaker's commitment to the truth-value of the whole proposition. In addition to these subcategories, Rounds (1982) added the notion of *diffusers* that tend to disperse or cut off a source of disagreement or argument. Hübler (1983) in his book *Understatements and hedges in English* makes a distinction between hedges and *understatements*. According to Hübler, hedges concern the speaker's attitude to the hearer regarding the proposition (e.g., It is cold in Alaska, *I suppose*.) while understatements concern the propositional content of the sentence (e.g., It is *a bit* cold in here.). Hübler admits that both understatements and hedges perform the same function of making sentences more acceptable to the hearer.

Further away from the original concept of hedges are those approaches in which hedges are treated as the realization of an interactive communicative strategy called *hedging*. According to Swales (1990), hedges are rhetorical devices used for "projecting honesty, modesty and proper caution in self-reports and for diplomatically creating space in areas heavily populated by other researchers." As G. Clemen (1997) summarized speakers/writers use lexical and/or syntactic devices such as modal auxiliaries (e.g., can/could; may/might; shall/should; will/would; must/ ought to, etc.), hedged performatives (e.g., have to admit; wish to invite; can promise, etc.), impersonal structures (one suggests), conditionals (if this were··· one would···) to mitigate the strength of claims, statements, and utterances while tending to save face to achieve broader acceptance from the recipient, as well as to evade possible criticism. According to Schröder & Zimmer (1997), a hedge is either defined as one or more lexico-syntactical elements that are used to modify a proposition, or as a strategy that modifies a proposition.

In pragmatics, the term hedge is used to refer to the textual strategies of using linguistic means in a certain context for specific communicative purposes, such as politeness (e.g., Blum-Kulka, 1985; Brown & Levinson, 1978, 1987; House & Kasper, 1981; Matsumoto, 1988; H. Sohn, 1996b, etc.), vagueness (e.g., Gruber, 1993), mitigation (e.g., Fraser, 1980). In addition to that, Skelton (1997) argues that the term hedge should be used "very narrowly" and "only for mitigations of responsibility and/or certainty to the truth of a proposition."

2.2 Women's Use of Hedges and Powerless Language

Is a hedge a gender-specific linguistic form? Hedges have often been viewed negatively as being feminine or expressing powerlessness.

Some linguists claim that gender has an influence on the use of hedges; generally, it is assumed that women hedge more than men. For example, R. Lakoff (1975) lists hedges as one of the typical features of women's speech, as one way of indexing their position in society. Also, she classified hedges into three categories: (1) *fully legitimate*, when the speaker is sincerely uncertain about something (p. 53); (2) *justifiable*, when politeness is required to mitigate the possible unfriendliness or unkindness of a statement' (p. 54); and (3) powerless or women's language (p. 54).

Preisler's (1986) study shows that linguistic tentativeness signals are related to both gender and one's interactive role, which is either task-oriented or socioemotional. Preisler's data shows that women use more hedges in general, whereas men lead in linguistic assertiveness. Following Lakoff's (1975) claim, Preisler (1986, p. 288) concludes that men and women have developed gender-specific speech patterns and maintains that women hedge more than men since women's speech is more tentative and less assertive. Mulac et al. (1988) found that women hedged more than men while men hedged more with other men than with women. Carli (1990) found that women used more hedges than men in same-gender and in mixed-gender dyads but only when their interaction partners were males. Grob and Allen (1996) found that women use less certain language and speak more politely than men since they hedged. On the other hand, Grob et al. (1997) found no significant difference between women and men in the use of hedges.

However, Holmes' (1990) findings in her study of gender differences in the use of hedges and boosters disagree strongly with Lakoff's and Preisler's claim. Holmes (1984a) points out that there is probably no women's language. Moreover, Holmes' data shows that hedges are actually frequently used by women "as positive politeness devices signaling solidarity with the addressee" rather than as devices expressing tentativeness or uncertainty (Holmes, 1990, p. 202). Also, Holmes' (1993) analysis of politeness strategies in verbal interaction reveals that women's linguistic behaviors in discourse are contrary to the behaviors proposed by R. Lakoff (1973). Holmes (1995b) analyzed the New Zealand Corpus of English and found few gender differences in the frequency of hedges (e.g., *you know*, *sort of*). However, she found important differences in terms of the functions of hedges. According to Holmes (1995b, p. 91), women employed hedges as positive politeness (Brown & Levinson, 1978, 1987) to fulfill emotional functions and they hedged to soften statements and to show concern for the feelings of others. In other words, Holmes' work finds that men and women use different styles, but does not find that women used hedges because they are insecure. In short, there is no general agreement on women's use of less certain language or evaluation as speaking more politely than men since they use more hedges. Moreover, Holmes (1984c) discussed the multifunctionality of hedges in her study: Hedges are used for (a) attenuating the force of a proposition, (b) modifying the seriousness of a speaker's commitment to a proposition, and (c) protecting speaker and listener face.

According to Baker (1991) and Wood (1996) women often hedge to build rapport with others while men typically use hedges to gain confirmation of their own view. As Grob et al (1997) stated, it is necessary to remember that gender is only one factor in a more complex equation including the interplay of context, social status, roles, and other group interaction factors (p. 296). Hence, gender cannot be analyzed as a "fixed category but needs to be seen as a dynamic social construction" (Holmes 1998, p. 127).

McMullen and Paslovski (1992) investigated the relationship between topic, dyad partner, and the use of hedges, and found that speakers used more hedges when speaking on unfamiliar topics and with strangers. The results of other research (e.g., Coates, 1987; Urbanová, 1996) show the relationship between conversational topic and topic sensitivity. Coates analyzed two natural conversations (female-female and male-male) and found that there was a higher proportion of epistemic modality form in the women's conversation than in the men's. In her data, the women talked about intimate, private issues that involved controversial points such as child abuse and wives' loyalty to husbands (p. 129). On the other hand, in Urbanová's data, the men talked about topics such as home beer making and the complexity of electronic technology (p. 64).

Hence, the topic of conversation should be analyzed in hedge use. Also, research on hedges by scholars such as Adkins and Brashers (1995) and Smith, Siltanen, and Hosman (1998) indicates a relationship between power and speech style and thus these researchers viewed hedges as an indicator of power.

Song (1996) compared gender differences in argumentative conversational strategies in English and Korean. She concluded that Korean women engage in mitigating, less confrontational strategies to avoid conflict, whereas both female and male English speakers engage in direct and indirect strategies in expressing disagreements. Song argues that Korean women engage in mitigating, less face-threatening argumentative strategies as efforts to save face in order to maintain harmonious and respectful interpersonal relationships. In Kim and Seo's (1996) study of gender difference in assessment and understanding check sequences in Korean, they argue that Korean women tend to give empathic assessments, to provide supportive agreement with the others' assessments and to focus on maintaining solidarity, while Korean men tend to display their own assessments and to show their knowledge. These studies illustrate that men's speech is direct, instrumental, competitive, and assertive, while women's speech is indirect, referential, empathic, and tentative. In contrast, Wang's (1999) study of gender differences in disagreement strategies argues that there are no gender differences. Both Korean men and women employ similar politeness strategies although women tend to use more positive politeness strategies than men. However, they use both direct and indirect disagreement strategies according to the type of speech acts.

2.3 Linguistic Politeness and Hedges

Language has essentially two interrelated functions: one is to convey the referential content of the message such as knowledge and information, and the other is to express the social indexical meanings of the message such as establishment, maintenance, and enhancement of social and interpersonal relationships. As Sohn (2001) mentioned, the effective performance of these two functions of language is associated with two opposing sets of principles. The first function of language can be performed most effectively in terms of economy and clarity. For example, Lakoff's (1973) rule of clarity ("be clear") and Grice's (1975) Cooperative Principle (CP) are relevant to the first function of language. On the other hand, the second function of language can be attained in terms of linguistic politeness. That is, the linguistic elements employed for the second function of language have been associated with the term *linguistic politeness*. In short, linguistic politeness is crucial to successful communication for establishing and maintaining human relationships, and thus is consequently sensitive and significant in intercultural communication. Although a number of scholars have different points of view on linguistic politeness, it might be viewed as language use whose purpose is to establish mutual comfort and promote rapport by considering others' feelings or to offer good intentions (Lakoff & Ide, 2005).

It is said that there are two types of linguistic politeness: one is *normative* politeness expressed by grammatical and lexical means such as honorifics, while the other is *strategic* politeness expressed by illocutionary force-modifying devices such as direct or indirect speech acts, hedges, and so on (Cho, 1982; H. Sohn, 1987). Also, other studies on linguistic politeness have identified two types of politeness: discernment politeness (Kasper's social-indexing, 1990) and volitional politeness (Kasper's strategic politeness). The function of discernment politeness controlled by the cultural norms of the society is to index social meanings involved in contexts as well as social variables (e.g., seniority, rank, gender, and education background) involved in interactions. In terms of discernment politeness, Korean exhibits honorifics that are highly systematic, in that sentences can hardly be uttered without the speaker's approximate knowledge of his social relationship with his addressee and/or referents in any of the following categories: age, social status, kinship, and/or ingroupness and outgroupness (H. Sohn, 1999). On the other hand, volitional politeness is to save one's face

(Brown & Levinson, 1987), and it is influenced by interactive speech act situations. In other words, strategic politeness (optional use per volition) is closely associated with pragmatic concerns while normative politeness (obligatory use per discernment) is closely associated with sociolinguistic concerns.

The claims by Brown and Levinson (1987) regarding the universality of politeness systems have been challenged by several researchers. For example, Kasper (1990) makes the point that politeness is not just a strategic device employed to perform "linguistic action in order to reach specific communicative goals··· but also a matter of social indexing" (p.196). Fraser (1990) classified politeness into the social-norm view, the conversational contract view, the conversational-maxim view, and the face-saving view. Kasper (1994) discusses politeness as "proper social conduct and tactful consideration of others and politeness as the pragmatic concept of ways in which relational function in linguistic action is expressed." Also, Janney and Arndt (1992) distinguished between *social politeness* to provide routine strategies in social situations to *coordinate social interaction* and *interpersonal politeness* to support relationships with the function to "preserve face and regulate interpersonal relationships" (p.24).

One universal pragmatic principle involves the assertion that indirect speech acts are more polite than the direct forms. For example, Clark and Schunk (1980) claim that people tend to use indirect interrogative request forms rather than imperatives in order to make a speech act less facethreatening. Furthermore, it is said that the most frequently mentioned motivation for the use of hedges in spoken discourse is politeness, the notion defined by Brown and Levinson (1987). In their view, hedges are mainly used to mitigate the illocutionary force of an utterance for negative politeness. In other words, the motivation for use of hedges is the desire to save the hearer's as well as the speaker's face. In their discussion of politeness the hearer's face-wants are emphasized; however, it is possible to emphasize the importance of hedges for the speaker's own face. It can be claimed that while showing deference to the addressee the speaker tries to protect him/herself from potential face-threatening acts in all communicative situations. House and Kasper (1981) mentioned that both functions (one defensive and ego-oriented, the other protective or alter-oriented) are fulfilled by politeness (p.157). Simon-Vandenbergen (1996) found that politicians used both negative politeness strategies such as avoiding commitment as well as positive strategies to persuade listeners when they have to respond to face-threatening questions. In interaction, hedges are important since they can be used to support the speaker's position as well as to establish speaker-listener rapport.

In Korean there are various linguistic politeness strategies: (i) using hedges (e.g., *ceki, kulssey-yo, com,* etc.), (ii) using ISAs (indirect speech acts[1]), (iii) main clause omission,[2] (iv) using modal suffix *–keyss*, benefactive auxiliary verb *–cwuta*, etc. (e.g., *mwun com yel-e cwu-si-keyss-eyo*? 'Could you open the door?'), (v) using more phatic expressions to show affection and friendliness (e.g., *nalssi ka cham coh-ney-yo.* 'The weather is so good.'; *siksa ha-si-ess-eyo*? 'Did you have a meal?'), (vi) speaker's humbleness (e.g., *pang i tewu-**si**-ci-yo*? (HOST) 'The temperature is hot in this room, isn't it? vs. *tepci anh-ayo*. (**tewusi-ci anh-ayo*.) (GUEST) 'It is not hot in this room.'), (vii) conversational implicature (e.g., *pang i mwuchek tewu-n kes kath-ayo*! 'It seems like that the temperature in this room is so hot (instead of *chang mwun com yel-e cwusey-yo*, 'Please open the window.'), (viii) interrogative with rising tone, (ix) idiomatized indirect speech acts (e.g., *ilum i ettehkey toy-seyyo*? 'What is your name?') (x) modesty (i.e., Korean find it impolite to say "thank you" immediately after compliments , invitation, or receiving a gift). A vital feature of polite communication in Korean

1 If a speech act is not for the benefit of the addressee but for the speaker or somebody else, indirect speech acts are felicitous because direct speech acts are often face-threatening to the addressee's positive self-esteem or to his freedom from imposition. Indirect utterances are used especially when the addressee is a senior or a distant equal or the utterances in question are made for the benefit of the speaker (H. Sohn, 1999b, p. 417).

2 One motivation for omission of main clause is to mitigate the assertiveness of various speech acts in terms of pragmalinguistics. The speaker can give the addressee the option of making the final decision on the basis of the background information expressed in the unomitted clause (H. Sohn, 1999b, p. 418).

is the avoidance of directness, especially with respect to dispreferred speech acts such as commands, requests, refusals, and so on. Korean has language-specific means for indicating different degrees of social meaning such as politeness and distance since Korean is characterized by its highly developed honorifics system. Thus, Korean has its own language-specific structures and means of indicating respect, distance, and humility. For example, a single Korean request can be performed in at least 16 different ways (adapted from Byon, 2006).

(1) *changmwun ye-sey-yo.*
window open-SH-POL
'Open the window.'

(2) *changmwun yel kes –ul myenglyeonghay-yo.*
window open thing-AC order-POL
'I order (you) to open the window.'

(3) *changmwun com ye-sey-yo.*
window DM open-SH-POL
'Please open the window.'

(4) *changmwun com yel-e cwu-sey-yo.*
window DM open-INF give-SH-POL
'Please open the window (for me).'

(5) *changmwun com ye-si-keyss-eyo?*
window DM open-SH-PRS-POL
'Would you please open the window?'

(6) *changmwun com yel-e cwu-si keyss-eyo?*
window DM open-INF give- SH-PRS-POL
'Would you please open the window (for me)?'

(7) *changmwun com yel-e cwu-si-l swu iss-usey-yo?*
window DM open-INF give SH-can-SH-POL
'Could you please open the window (for me)?'

(8) *changmwun com yel-e cwu-si-l swu iss-usi-keyss-eyo?*
window DM open-INF give- SH-can-SH-PRS-POL
'Could you please open the window (for me)?

(9) *changmwun com yel-e cwu-si-ki palay-yo.*
window DM open-INF give-SH-wish-POL
'I wish that you would open the window (for me).'

(10) *changmwun com yel-e cwu-si-myen coh-keyss-eyo.*

window DM open-INF give-SH-if good-PRS-POL
'It would be nice if you please open the window (for me).'

(11) *changmwun com yel-e cwu-si-ess-umyen coh-keyss-eyo.*
window DM open-INF give- SH-if good-PRS-POL
'It would be nice if you would please open the window (for me).'

(12) *changmwun ye-si-lako-yo.*
window open-SH-QT-POL
'(lit. It is quoted that) open the window.'

(13) *changmwun com yel-e cwu-si-ess-umyen hay-yo.*
window DM open-INF give-SH-PST-if do-POL
'I wish that you would please open the window (for me).'

(14) *changmwun com yel-e cwu-si-ess-umyen*
window DM open-INF give-SH-PST if
coh-keyss-nuntey-yo.
good-intend-ENDER-POL
'It would be nice if you would please open the window (for me) but···'

(15) *changmwun-i tathye iss-unikka taptaphay-yo.*
window-NM close-CAU-INF stay-because be stuffy-POL
'Because the window is closed, the room is stuffy.'

(16) *pang-i tto tew-e-ci-ess-kwun-yo.*
Room-NM again hot-INF-become-PST-APP-POL.
'(Oh, I see that) the room has become hot again.'

All of the above sentences except the first two are request forms with different degrees of indirectness in which the speaker asks the listener to open the window. In general, the longer the sentence the more indirect and thus more polite it is since more hedges are included (H. Sohn, 1986).

2.4 Mitigation and Hedges

Mitigation is a set of strategies by which people try to make their speech act more effective. Many scholars (e.g., Fraser, 1980; Faerch and Kasper, 1989) mentioned the notion of mitigation of illocutionary force of utterances. The notion of mitigation is used in pragmatics (Fraser, 1980) and it is opposed and complementary to the notion of *reinforcement*. It reduces participants' obligations, to which the felicity conditions of a speech act belong. Thus, mitigation is functional to smooth interactive management in that it reduces risks for interlocutors at various levels (e.g., risks of request, refusal, conflict, and so on.). House and Kasper (1981) list eleven types of downgraders[3] and six types of upgraders with reference to requests in English. Many devices such as hedges, shields, and approximators express mitigation, which is related to politeness, indirectness, and vagueness in the studies of pragmatics. In the pragmatic context, "to mitigate" is described as the use of "rhetorical devices, which soften the impact of some unpleasant aspect of an utterance on the speaker or the hearer (Martinovski, 2006)."

Mitigation involves reducing the force of an utterance as an expression of courtesy or deference, or as not to give offence. For instance, a *directive*, which is unmitigated (e.g., 'Close the door') may be mitigated (e.g., 'I wonder if you'd mind closing the door'). Mitigation may involve a range of linguistic and other strategies, for example, the use of certain syntactic structures, intonation, and so on. Mitigation is a component of politeness and it also demonstrates a concern for the listener's face.

According to Fraser (1978) and Fraser and Nolan (1981), mitigation is a strategy for softening or reducing the strength of a speech act whose effects are "unwelcome to the hearer" by attempting to make the act more palatable (Fraser, 1980, p. 342). He viewed a hedge (e.g., sort of, kind of) as one of the substrategies of mitigation (p. 344). On the contrary, other researchers such as Holmes (1984, 1986), Brown and Levinson (1978, 1987), and Hyland (1994, 1996) viewed hedges as a broader term including distancing techniques, parenthetical verbs (e.g., guess, think, feel), and tag questions. Mitigation is related to Brown and Levinson's (1978) notion of face-threatening acts in the narrow sense while it is a synonym of weakening, and/or downgrading in the broader

3 The function of downgraders is to modify a request behavior internally by mitigating the impositive force of the request by means of lexical, phrasal, and syntactic choices (Blum-Kulka, House, & Kasper, 1989).

sense (Caffi, 1999).

2.5 The Functions of Hedges

Although many studies on hedges related to gender and power have been investigated, few studies have discussed the function of hedges in a context. However, some linguists realize that hedges have multifunctionality. For example, J. Holmes (1984c) defines hedges as linguistic devices for attenuating utterance and as a part of epistemic modality. She observed that it is essential to make a distinction between two types of functions of hedges: a *modal* function and an *affective* function. The affective function is related to interpersonal relations such as politeness (pragmatic dimension of language), while the modal function is related to the accuracy of propositional content (semantic dimension of language). Her distinction is similar to Leech and Svartvik's (1975)[4] distinctions between logical meaning and pragmatic/interactive meaning in communication. According to Holmes, modal functions represent a speaker's attitude toward the validity of a proposition, corresponding to the concept of epistemic modality.

Holmes categorizes the hedging function as (a) the modal function used for expressing uncertainty, (b) the affective function used for expressing politeness or softening, and (c) the affective function used for building solidarity. She emphasizes that hedges can express not only politeness or the speakers' concern for the addressee's feelings, but also solidarity with or a positive attitude toward the addressee. The speaker is more concerned about the social relationship with the listener than uncertainty about the truth value of the proposition as in the example from Holmes (1984c, p. 49), in which a friend comments on her friend's

4 Leech and Svartvik (1975) classified language function into four categories: (i) conceptual/notional meaning, (ii) logical meaning expressing information, reality and belief, such as judgments about truth and falsehood; (iii) pragmatic or interactive meaning expressing the speaker's emotions and attitudes, and (iv) textual meaning involving the organization of communication.

husband's behavior by saying "*Well I think* George is *a bit er perhaps* foolish." According to Holmes, the italicized hedges are used to express politeness (affective function of a hedge), rather than uncertainty (modal function of hedge).

2.6 Modality and Hedges

One of the most important concepts related to hedges is modality. A functional aspect of modality was suggested by Lyons (1977). He offers an insightful pragmatic aspect of modality as follows: modality, as it operates in a good deal of everyday language behavior, cannot be understood, or properly analyzed, otherwise than in terms of the *indexical* and *instrumental functions* of language, to which its descriptive function is, at times if not always, subordinate (p. 849). In fact, many of the functions of modality are embedded in contexts of social interaction, and cannot be described adequately apart from their contextual discourse (Bybee & Fleishman, 1995).

Three pragmatic approaches have contributed to modality in functional domain: the performative, functional, and politeness approaches. The semantic meanings of modality are not concerned with the *interpersonal* functions of modality. Those semantic meanings are mainly about the relationship between speaker and proposition rather than between speaker and addressee. By contrast, the pragmatic approach views modality as a means of actualizing the relationship between speaker and addressee (Guo, 1995).

First, the performative approach is based on speech act theory, as put forward by Austin (1962) and then elaborated by Searle (1983). A number of linguists (e.g., Lyons, 1977; Palmer, 1990; Perkins, 1983) have employed this theory as a framework for discussing modality as it is related to language use. Lyons (1977) noted the particular relevance of this theory to the nature of modality: "One of the most attractive features of the theory of speech acts··· is that it gives explicit recognition to the social or interpersonal dimension of language behavior and provides a general framework··· for the discussion of syntactic and semantic distinctions that linguists have traditionally described in terms of mood and modality (p. 725)."

Second, the functional approach to modality is rooted in functionalism, advocated by Halliday. The most essential tenet of functionalism is that linguistic forms and structures are motivated to serve certain pragmatic and interactive functions of communication. Halliday (1973, 1985) proposed that a different type of structure is associated with each of the three metafunctions: *interpersonal, textual*, and *ideational.* Among these metafunctions, the *interpersonal metafunctions*[5] are linked to modality. These metafunctions allow *intersubjectivity* between participants. Thus, the linguistic category of modality is viewed as the function of regulating interpersonal relations in social interaction.

Third, a great number of researchers have looked at the functions of modality from the perspective of politeness theory proposed by Brown and Levinson (1987). The face-threatening acts need to be counterbalanced by redressive action, or politeness strategies (Brown & Levinson 1987, Fraser 1990; Kasper 1990). Of the five politeness strategies proposed by Brown and Levinson (opt out, off record, bald on record, positive politeness, and negative politeness), those particularly pertinent to modality are the negative and positive politeness strategies. Hoye (1997) suggests that three strategies of negative politeness (i.e., using hedges, minimizing the imposition, and being pessimistic) can be seen to involve the epistemic modality of uncertainty and doubt. When used as a negative politeness strategy, *modality* functions to soften the illocutionary force of a speech act (e.g., *I think, maybe, perhaps*, etc.). In a similar way, when used as a positive politeness strategy (i.e., exaggerate and intensify interest in the hearer), modality functions to strengthen the illocutionary force of a speech act (e.g., *certainly,* etc.).

5 *Interpersonal metafunctions* refers to language's potential for concern with a speaker's (i) choice of relationship with the interlocutor, consciously acknowledging the rhetorical strategies for stating, questioning, ordering, etc., (ii) judgments of possibility and obligation, (iii) assessments of probability, and (iv) evaluations of phenomena.

Other researchers (e.g. Blum-Kulka, House, & Kasper, 1989; House & Kasper, 1981) categorize such modality as *upgraders* and *downgraders*.

Modality is concerned with a speaker's attitude towards the truth value or factual status of a proposition. Palmer (1986, 2001) classified modality into epistemic and evidential modality: Speakers express their judgments about the factual status of the proposition with epistemic modality, whereas speakers indicate the evidence that they have for its factual status with evidential modality. From Lyons' (1977) definition of epistemic modality, "any utterance in which the speaker explicitly qualifies his commitment to the truth of the proposition expressed by the sentence he utters, whether the qualification is made explicit in the verbal component (···) in the prosodic or paralinguistic component, is an epistemic modal or modalized utterance" (p. 797), we can see its affinity to many of the definitions of hedge.

The basic effect of reducing obligations makes it possible to unify mitigation which relates to deontic modality[6] and mitigation which in turn relates to epistemic modality[7]. Typically, mitigation affecting deontic modality reduces the addressee's obligations, while mitigation affecting epistemic modality reduces the speaker's obligations. Epistemic modality can be used as a hedge by avoiding commitment to a proposition. For example, in Korean the conventionalized illocutionary-mitigating sentence ender *-kes kath-* ('It seems that') functions to attenuate the illocutionary force of refusing and lowers the degree to which the speaker commits himself to the proposition as in the following example (a).

(a)	*Ce-n nayil*	*moim-ey*	*mos*	*ka-l*	***kes kath**-ayo.*
	I -TC tomorrow	meeting-to	cannot	go-PRS	seems-POL

'I think I may not go to tomorrow's meeting'

6 *Deontic modality* is associated with social action of granting permission or imposing an obligation. For example, (a) You *may* go now (permission), (b) You *must* finish reading this article by tomorrow (obligation).

7 *Epistemic modality* conveys the speaker's confidence (or lack of confidence) in the truth of the proposition expressed.

If we define hedges as modifications of the commitment to the truth value of propositions, the English modal auxiliary *may* is a hedge as well as an expression of epistemic modality. Also, deontic modality markers allow for interpretation as hedges; for example, the hypothetical auxiliary *would* in English can be seen as a hedge since it makes an utterance non-categorical (Markkanen & Schröder, 1997). Another concept of modality related to hedges is evidentiality which, is "any linguistic expression of attitudes toward knowledge" (Chafe, 1986). Chafe (1986) uses the term hedge only for expressions that denote "the match between a piece of knowledge and a category may be less than perfect (p. 271)."

The interactive function of epistemic modality in conversational contexts (Bybee et al., 1994) is essential. According to Markkanen and Schröder (1997, p. 6), hedges can be included within the realm of epistemic modality if we accept Stubbs' (1986) view that it is possible to indicate degrees of commitment to three kinds of linguistic items: (i) to propositions, (ii) to illocutionary forces, and (iii) to individual lexical items. Hedges are rather determined by context, speaker's intention, and the situation. Thus, the pragmatic function of hedge is implicit at the level of utterance and not explicit in any lexical unit.

2.7 Speech Acts and Hedges

Speech act theory, developed by the philosophers, John Austin and John Searle, is basically concerned with the functions of language. That is, its fundamental insights emphasize how speech act and meaning are related to language. It is also generally accepted that a speech act is a functional unit in communication (Cohen, 1996). There has been a great deal of research on speech acts since Austin (1962) pointed out that when people talk they not only say things but also do things. According to Austin (1962), all utterances perform speech acts that are comprised of a *locutionary act* (the production of sounds and words with meanings), an *illocutionary act* (the issuing of an utterance with conventional communicative force achieved in "saying"), and a *perlocutionary act* (the actual effect achieved "by saying") (Schiffrin 1994, p. 51). On the other hand, Searle (1969) developed Austin's speech act theory from the basic belief that language is used to perform actions; moreover, he divides utterances into four speech acts; *utterance acts* (the uttering of morphemes and sentences), *propositional acts* (referring and predicating), *illocutionary acts* (acts such as stating, questioning, commanding, and promising), and *perlocutionary acts* (the consequences of illocutionary acts).

Speech acts (e.g., requests, refusals, apologies, compliments, etc.) are included in communicative action. Since a speech act is based on an interlocutor's interaction with another, it is desirable for each interlocutor to protect the other's face by softening or avoiding the impact of face-threatening acts (FTAs). Moreover, speech acts include real-life interactions and require not only knowledge of the language but also appropriate use of that language within the culture. Different cultures may choose different linguistic devices for the same speech acts. Numerous speech acts, such as requests, refusals, or complaints, are prone to be indirect in order to mitigate or soften the illocutionary force.

In Korean, if a speech act is not for the benefit of the addressee but for the speaker, as in the case of requests or refusals, more indirect speech acts are much politer if more hedges are included (e.g., conventionalized apologetic expressions *coysongha-ciman* 'I am sorry but,' discourse marker *ceki*[8] 'well,' diminutive *com*, benefactive auxiliary *-e cwuta*, modal suffix *-keyss*, etc.). Therefore, the cross-cultural study of speech acts is vital to the understanding of intercultural communication. Face-threatening acts such as requests or refusals are particularly important to explore because they are the source of so many cross-cultural miscommunications (Beebe & Takahashi, 1989b).

8 In social interactions which inherently contain a potential for threat to an interlocutor's face, as in speech settings of request, apology, disagreement/argument, and in turn-taking, the employment of the discourse marker *ceki* and its compositional forms preserves and promotes social relationships by softening the potential face threatening acts (Park, 2001).

Some speech acts require a higher level of pragmatic competence than others since they tend to risk the interpersonal relationship of the interlocutors. These speech acts include requests, refusals, complaints, disagreement, disapproval, which are often referred to as face threatening acts (Brown & Levinson, 1978). A face-threatening act tends to risk either the speaker's or the hearer's face. In cross-linguistic or cross-cultural communication, people of different speech communities employ different language uses. When a speech act that entails a high degree of face threat is performed, pragmatic failure (Thomas, 1983) is likely to occur.

2.8 Hedges as a Negative Politeness vs. Hedges as a Positive Politeness

Based on Goffman's (1967) notion of face, Brown and Levinson (1987) suggest universals of politeness strategies and make the assumption that all competent adult speakers of society have face. They categorized the concept of face into two types. *Negative face* is the desire for an interactant to have "his freedom of action unhindered and his attention unimpeded" (p. 129). This can be paraphrased as the addressee's desire to maintain his/her territory and the freedom of action. On the other hand, *positive face* is the desire to maintain a positive self-image or personality and have his/her self-image approved by other interactants (p. 62). Related to these aspects of face, any kind of action which threatens these face-wants is called a *face-threatening act* (FTA). In other words, face-threatening acts are utterances that threaten a person's public self-image.

In their influential study on universal politeness, Brown and Levinson (1978, 1987) claim that superficial cross-cultural diversities can emerge from underlying universal pragmatic principles. Linguistic politeness in the view of Brown and Levinson means recognizing the autonomy of others and avoiding imposition (*negative politeness*) as well as emphasizing solidarity (*positive politeness*). A positive politeness strategy is oriented toward the addressee's positive face and used to minimize the distance between the speakers by expressing friendliness. These all indicate that the speaker is a cooperator or seeks common ground with the addressee. On the other hand, negative politeness strategies may impose on the hearer and intrude on their space, and they assume social distance. It is often pointed out that negative politeness is the most important and sensitive in English-speaking society due to the social value attributed to egalitarianism and individualism (Sohn, 1986).

The use of hedges as mitigating devices is important at the discourse level. Identifying a speaker's motivation for the use of hedges in spoken discourse has concentrated on politeness, as defined by Brown and Levinson (1987). In their view, hedges are mainly used for negative politeness in face-saving. In other words, the motivation for their use is the desire to save face, either the hearer's or the speaker's. While a positive politeness strategy is employed to boost the addressee's "positive face", a negative politeness strategy is employed to minimize the imposition of an FTA and redress the addressee's "negative face."

Holmes (1995) stated that positive politeness strategies are oriented to express solidarity and emphasize equality between interactants while negative politeness strategies are oriented to express social distance and emphasize power distinctions. Hence, positive politeness occurs more in less formal settings while negative politeness occurs more in formal settings and interactions.

However, Meyerhoff (1992) concluded that "a traditional analysis of hedges, solely in terms of deference and negative politeness, is an overgeneralization and does not accurately reflect the way in which they are used" (p. 72). Simon-Vandenbergen (1996) found that on radio shows politicians used both negative politeness strategies, such as avoiding commitment, as well as positive strategies to inspire listener confidence, such as sounding fully committed to the truth value of their claims when they have to respond to face-threatening questions.

In short, a hedge is a mitigating device used to lessen the impact of an utterance. Hedges are intentionally employed since they are crucially important in communication. Hedges help interactants communicate more effectively in terms of the affective function of the hedge to express a speaker's politeness or concern for an addressee's feelings by mitigating the illocutionary force of speech acts.

2.9 Korean Sentence Enders and Discourse Modality

Korean, which is an agglutinative language and SOV language, has a very rich inventory of sentence enders[9] (sentence final suffixes) (M. Park, 2003). Korean sentence enders convey the speaker's attitude or stance as well as speech acts (K. Lee, 1993). According to H. Sohn (1999), sentence enders consists of three slots, (i) addressee honorifics, (ii) mood and modality, and (iii) sentence type and speech level.[10]

Korean sentence-final suffixes express the speaker's attitudes toward or assessment of the proposition described while clause-final suffixes express semantic and/or grammatical relations among clauses and various other parts of the discourse.There have been great attempts to investigate sentence-ender modalities in Korean from a variety of perspectives. In particular, H. Lee (1991) characterized the discourse-pragmatic nature of major sentence-ending suffixes that occur in Korean. He claims that sentence-terminal suffixes used in colloquial Korean differentiate various epistemic modality categories, conveying assimilated information (information that is part of the speaker's

---

9 Different grammarians use different terms to refer to the sentence final verb suffix. K.Lee (1993) and H.Sohn (1999) use the term 'sentence enders', while H.S. Lee (1991) uses the term 'sentence terminal suffix.' (M. Park, 2003).

10 Korean has six speech levels, indicating the speakers' interpersonal relationship with the addressee (H. Sohn, 1994).

	Declarative	Interrogative	Imperative	Propositive
Deferential	-*(su)p-ni-ta*	*(su)p-ni-kka*	-*sip-si-o*	-*(wu)sipsi-ta*
Polite	-*e/a-yo*	-*e/a-yo*	-*e/a-yo*	-*e/a/-yo*
Blunt	-*o*		-*o*	
Familiar	-*ney*	-*na/-nun-ka*	-*key*	-*sey*
Intimate	-*e/a*	-*e/a*	-*e/a*	-*e/a*
Plain	-*ta*	-*ni/-nya*	-*la*	-*ca*

established body of knowledge), unassimilated information, factual realization, and the speaker's belief in the truth of the conveyed information, and informing the hearer of information that has provoked the speaker's consciousness.

According to Suh (1996)'s analysis, Korean expresses modality via sentence enders. Also, modal adverbials (e.g. *amato* 'probably', *pantusi* 'definitely', *hwaksilhi* 'certainly', etc.) may express modality in Korean. The sentence-ender modality is classified into five categories in Korean, depending on the sentence types: declarative, interrogative, propositive, imperative and prommisive (Suh, 1996). Choi (1995) listed the forms and meanings of modalities in Korean as follows. For example, *-ta* is used frequently when the speaker has just perceived something in the present context. The suffix *-kwun* is used for newly acquired information, but often is based on an inference made by the speaker about what he or she has just seen. In addition, *-ci* (certainty of proposition, shared information), *-tay* (reported speech, hearsay/story-telling), *-ney* (information based on factual evidence), *-ni* (Uncertainty and negative bias of proposition) are listed.

Korean *epistemic* modality (speakers express their judgments about the factual status of the proposition) is usually expressed by modal suffix and complement construction. For instance, the modal suffix *-keyss* and *-(u)l(i)* denote the speaker/hearer's attitude or modality toward the content of the sentence (Sohn 1999, p. 360). Two basic meanings of *-keyss* are (i) the speaker/hearer's intention or volition, and (ii) the speaker's presumption or conjecture in declaratives and the hearer's in interrogatives based on immediate information or circumstantial evidence. The basic meaning of the so-called prospective modal suffix *-(u)l(i)* is probability or predictability.

Oh (1998) discusses Korean modal auxiliary *grams* (grammatical morphemes) based on the corpus. According to Oh (1998), the complement construction expresses the *epistemic* modality, such as *-ci molu-* (DN + 'don't know') possibility (weak); *- kes kath-a(yo)* (DN + 'same') 'it seems that…/it is likely that….', strong possibility (subjective); *-tus-ha* (DN + 'do'), strong possibility (objective); *-na po-* (DN + 'see'), inference. *Deontic (Agent-oriented)* modality is expressed by *-(u)l swu iss-* (PROS + 'way'+'exist') 'can'(ability), *-to toy-* (CONC+'become') 'may' (permission), *-ya hay-/toy-* (NEC + 'do') 'have to' (obligation), *-(e/a)ss (u)myen ha-* (PST + COND + 'do') 'want/wish to' (desire), *-(u) lye ha-* (PURP + 'do') 'intend to' (intention), *-koca ha-* (DESR + 'do') 'intend to'(intention). Korean evidential modality (speakers indicate the evidence that they have for its factual status) are usually expressed by the retrospective suffix *-te* (RT) which denotes an act or state as the speaker's past observation or experience (e.g. *-telako*).

While previous studies of the semantic aspect of modality have concentrated on their referential meanings, recent attempts have been made to examine interactive functions of modality/epistemic modality beyond a semantic level to the discourse level. Maynard (1993) distinguishes *discourse modality* from modality which has a narrower sense referring to speaker's opinions and attitudes. Maynard's definition of discourse modality is as follows: *Discourse modality* refers to information that does not or only minimally conveys objective propositional message content. Discourse modality conveys the speaker's subjective emotional, mental, or psychological attitude toward the message content of the speech act itself or toward his or her interlocutor in discourse. Discourse modality operates to define and to foreground certain ways of interpreting the propositional content in discourse; it directly expresses the speaking self's personal voice on the basis of which the utterance is intended to be meaningfully interpreted (Maynard, 1993, p. 38).

There are various functions of epistemic modality in varying contexts: (i) mitigating an illocutionary force, (ii) establishing a good social relationship with the hearer, and (iii) doing the organizational work of projecting a link to the next turn. The present study focuses on the function of the ISEs (e.g., *-canha(yo), -ketun(yo), -nuntey(yo), -telako(yo), -ci(yo), -ney(yo), -tay(yo)*) as an epistemic modality marker since epistemic markers have not only semantic meanings but also pragmatic functions. According to Leech (1983), semantic meaning is defined purely as "a property of expressions in a given language" (i.e., "What does X mean?"), whereas pragmatic meaning is seen as meaning "relative to a speaker or user of the language" (i.e., "What do you mean by X?") (p.6).

Three pragmatic approaches have contributed to our understanding of modality in terms of pragmatics: the performative, functional, and politeness approaches. Despite three approaches' differing theoretical backgrounds, the proponents share a focus on the importance of a speaker's intention. The semantic meanings of modality are not concerned with the "interpersonal" functions of modality. By contrast, the pragmatic approaches view modality as a means of actualizing the relationship between speaker and addressee (Guo, 1995).

CHAPTER 3

Methodology And Data

This chapter introduces the methodology and data collection followed by an overview of the data utilized for this study. In other words, this chapter introduces how the data was collected, coded, investigated, and analyzed. Furthermore, it presents an overview of the data such as the distribution of gender, gender composition in conversations, age, region, occupation, and social power relations as well as social distance relations between interlocutors.

3.1 Data Collection and Methodology

3.1.1 Recorded naturally-occurring face-to-face conversations

It was indispensible for this study to collect authentic conversations within natural speech settings in daily life since hedges are more likely to occur in spoken contexts than in written contexts (R. Lakoff, 1975, p. 59). Also, it is claimed that the best approach is to collect samples of spontaneous speech in natural settings where none of the participants was aware of being observed or studied. Hence, the data collected for this study were unplanned, spontaneous, and face-to-face naturally-occurring conversations. There were 219 participants, all native Koreans who speak either the standard Korean or a dialect of Korean. They are from metropolitan areas such as *Sewul* city and cities in *Kyengki* Province, or non-metropolitan areas including the Korean provinces such as *Kangwen, Cenla, Kyengsang, Chwungcheng*, and so on. A total of 1000 minutes (approximately 17 hours) of recorded data was analyzed. Naturally-occurring discourse in this study was all informal, face-to-face and two-party or multiple-party (three or four) conversations. I asked one hundred students who attend a private university in Korea to record about 10 minute conversations with no restrictions on the topics of conversations and number of interlocutors including himself/herself involved in the conversations. They used the voice recorder I provided or their own equipment such as a laptop computer or iPod for digital recording.

Each conversation has about 10 to12 minutes of recording time which was long enough to develop participants' conversation. A total set of 110 conversations were collected but I selected 100 conversation sets of clear recordings (approximately 1,000 minutes of recording) and excluded 10 conversation sets of unclear recordings. All recorded conversations were transcribed in Korean and each conversation set was saved in its text file (i.e., there are 100 text files). The format of text files[11] was made by *Hankul* 2007 program, which is an optimal program for the search engine *hanmalwu* of *Seycong* Corpus. Then selected excerpts from the conversation were transcribed by Yale Romanization if the data was used for an example. Each line of romanized Korean data has two additional lines; one is a word by word glossary and the other is English translation. In order to obtain the frequency and example of hedge items the search engine *hamalwu* of *Secong* corpus was implemented so that 100 sets of conversation files were searched simultaneously and precisely. Then I checked each marked items using the program manually and decided if those items were appropriate for hedge items. Based on the results of the hedge items search, I investigated the frequency of each hedge item in Chapter 4 and the correlation between hedge items and social structural factors as well as social situational factors in Chapter 5. For the statistical analysis in Chapter 5 individual hedge items were coded individually by the individual interlocutor as well as the individual sociopragmatic factors affecting hedges.

11 All text files can be converted into MS word files.

3.1.2 Classification of Korean hedges in spoken discourse

In order to classify Korean hedges in spoken discourse I adopted Hyland's (1998) categorization. Non-lexical devices, except syntactic devices, are beyond the scope of this work and are not included in this study.

Table 3-1 Classification and Inventory of Korean Hedges in Spoken Discourse

Classification		Inventory
Lexical Hedges	Discourse marker (DM)	1. *com/ccom* 2. *mwe/mo/me; way* 3. *ani* 4. *isscanh-a(yo); iss-ci; iss-cyo* 5. *ce/ceki* 6. *icey/ incey* 7. *mak* 8. *cham* 9. *kunyang* 10. *kuntey* 11. *kulenikka/ kunikka(n)/ ku(n)kka* 12. *kulaykaciko/kulaykacko*
	Interactive sentence ender (ISE)	1. *-canha(yo)* 2. *-nuntey(yo)* 3. *-ketun(yo)* 4. *-telako(yo)* 5. *-ci(yo)* 6. *-ney(yo)* 7. *-tay(yo)*
	Auxiliary verb (AV)	1. *-kes kath-* 2. *-ci molu-* 3. *-tus ha-* 4. *-na po-* 5. *-e/ato toy-* 6. *-e/a cwu-* 7. *-e/a po-*
	Particle (P)	1. *-(i)latunci* 2. *-yo* (floater)
	Filler (F)	*e, a, um, hum, ca, he, i, ku*
	Adverb (Ab)	*amato , yakkan , hoksi , pyello , taycheylo*
	Suffix (Sf)	*-keyss-*
	Phrase (Ph)	1. *-e/a kaciko/kwu* 2. *-e/a kacko/kwu*
Syntactic Hedges	Main Clause Omission	*-e/ase(yo); -ko/kwu(yo)*
	Conditional	*-myen*
	Tag Question	*-ci anha(yo)?* ; *-ci anh-ullay(yo)?*; *-ci anhulkka(yo)?*
	Impersonalization	*ta-tul, wuli* (plural expression)

3.1.3 Statistical methods

Statistical methods, such as *t*-test and ANOVA will be used to analyze the data in this study. A software program called SPSS Statistics 17.0

was employed for the current study in order to use the *t*-test and ANOVA. A brief explanation of the independent *t*-test, one-way ANOVA, and *p*-value follows.

(1) *t*-test : The *t*-test is the most commonly used method to evaluate the differences in means between two groups. Theoretically, the *t*-test can be used even if the sample sizes are very small (e.g., as small as 10; some researchers claim that even smaller n_s are possible), as long as the variables are normally distributed within each group and the variation of scores in the two groups is not reliably different. (http://www.statsoft.com/textbook/basic-statistics/#t-test for independent samples)

(2) ANOVA

In statistics, analysis of variance (ANOVA) is a collection of statistical models, and their associated procedures, in which the observed variance is partitioned into components due to different explanatory variables. In its simplest form ANOVA gives a statistical test of whether the means of several groups are all equal, and therefore generalizes Student's two-sample *t*-test to more than two groups. ANOVAs are helpful because they possess a certain advantage over a two-sample t-test. Doing multiple two-sample *t*-tests would result in a largely increased chance of committing a type I error. For this reason, ANOVAs are useful in comparing three or more means. (http://en.wikipedia.org/wiki/ANOVA)

(3) *statistical significance* (*p*-value)

Technically, the value of the *p*-value represents a decreasing index of the reliability of a result. In many areas of research, the *p*-value of 0.05 is customarily treated as a *border-line acceptable* error level. How to determine that a result is significant? Typically results that yield $p \leq 0.05$ are considered borderline statistically significant, but remember that this level of significance still involves a pretty high probability of error (5%). Results that are significant at the $p \leq 0.01$ level are commonly considered statistically significant, and $p \leq .005$ or $p \leq .001$ levels are often called highly significant. (http://www.statsoft.com/textbook/elementary-concepts-in-statistics/)

3.2 Yoon's Data Overview

3.2.1 Distribution of gender

As shown in Table 3-2, there were a total of 107 male interlocutors and a total of 112 female interlocutors involved in the total conversations, composing 49% and 51% of the total number of participants, respectively. It is considered that the ratio of each gender is ideal for the statistical analysis. Figure 3-1 corresponds to the information presented in Table 3-2.

Table 3-2 Distribution of Gender

Gender	Number	Percentage
Male	107	49%
Female	112	51%
Total	219	100%

Figure 3-1 Distribution of Gender

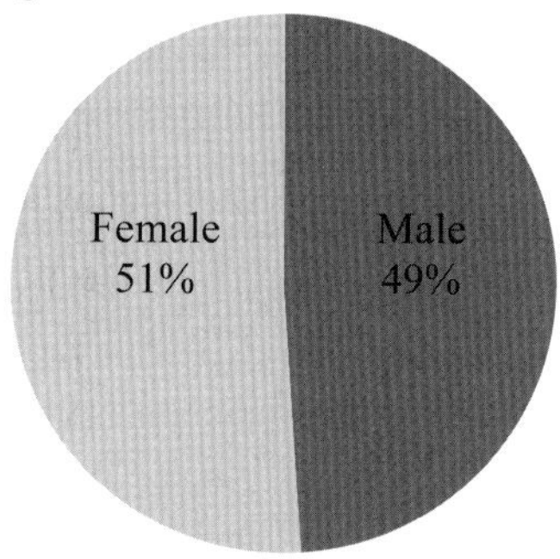

3.2.2 Distribution of gender composition

As shown in Table 3-3, the four types of gender composition groups are female-female (FF), male-female (MF), male-male (MM), multiple gender composition groups such as male-female-male (MFM), female-female-male (FFM), male-male-female, and so on. There are 28 sets of conversation with female-female (FF) gender composition group (28%), 29 sets of conversation with male-female (MF) gender composition group (29%), 28 sets of conversation with male-male gender composition group (28%), 15 sets of conversation with multiple gender composition group involving three or more participants in the conversation (15%). Figure 3-2 is a visual representation of Table 3-3.

Table 3-3
Distribution of Gender Composition

Gender Composition	Set of Conversation	Percent-age
FF	28	28%
MF	29	29%
MM	28	28%
Multi.	15	15%
Total	100	100%

Figure 3-2
Distribution of Gender Composition

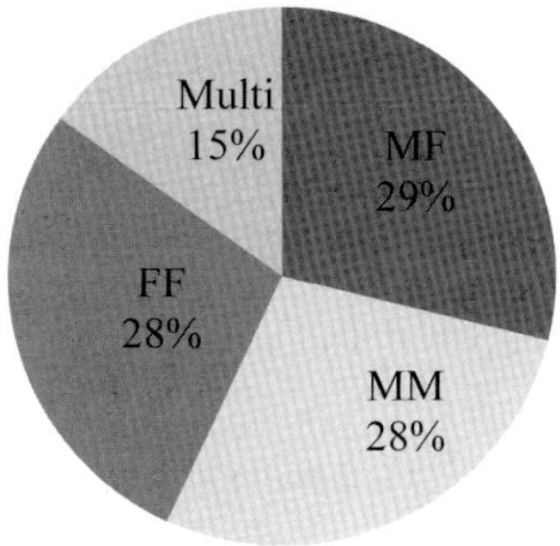

3.2.3 Distribution of age

As shown in the Table 3-4, there are 24 interlocutors of the age group in their teens (11%), 158 interlocutors in their 20s and 30s (72%), and 37 interlocutors in the over-40 age group (17%). The majority of the participants were in their 20s or 30s, who were mostly students. Table 3-4 is depicted visually in Figure 3-3.

Table 3-4 Distribution of Age

Age	Number	Percentage
Teens	24	11%
20s-30s	158	72%
Over 40	37	17%
Total	219	100%

Figure 3-3 Distribution of Age

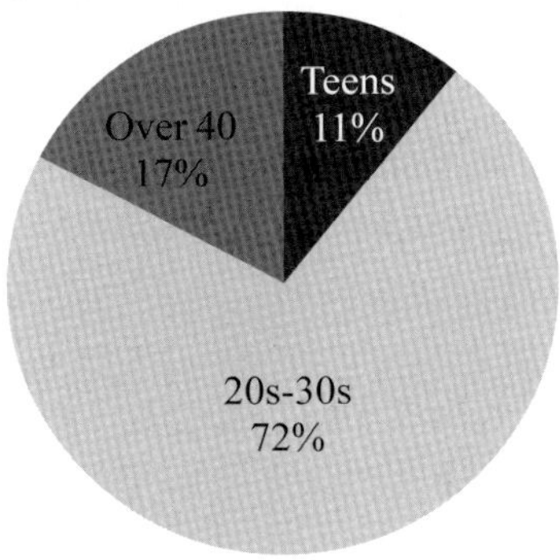

Age is considered one of the major sociolinguistic factors that influence the choice of language. Some young people adopt informal forms to show solidarity or intimacy with peer group members. Such forms are regarded as youth language and are used often to express solidarity.

The frequent use of hedges may play an important role in facilitating their solidarity.

3.2.4 Distribution of region

As shown in Table 3-5, there were 122 interlocutors from metropolitan areas such as *Seoul* city and cities in *Kyengki* Province (56%) while there were 97 interlocutors from non-metropolitan areas including several different Korean provinces such as *Kangwen, Cenla, Kyengsang, Chwungcheng*, and so on (44%). Figure 3-4 visually represents Table 3-5.

Table 3-5 Distribution of Region

Region	Number	Percentage
Metropolitan areas	122	56%
Non-metropolitan areas	97	44%
Total	219	100%

Figure 3-4 Distribution of Region

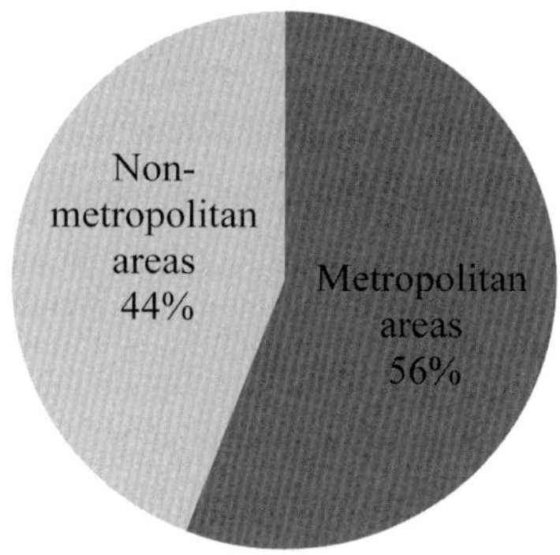

3.2.5 Distribution of occupation

Table 3-6 Distribution of Occupation

Occupation	Number	Percentage
Student	172	78%
Office Worker	30	14%
Housewife	17	8%
Total	219	100%

Figure 3-5 Distribution of Occupation

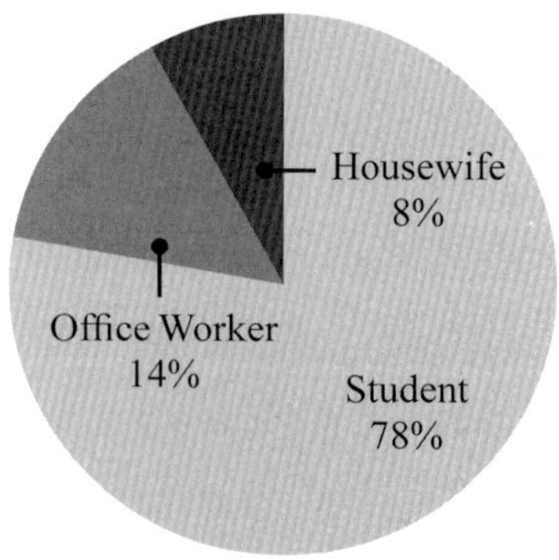

As shown in Table 3-6, there were 172 students (79%), 30 office workers (14%), and 17 housewives (8%). Figure 3-5 is a visual representation of Table 3-6.

3.2.6 Distribution of power relations (social status)

As shown in the Table 3-7, there were 61 sets of conversation with power relations between interlocutors (61 %), while there were 39 sets of conversation without power relations between interlocutors (39%). Figure 3-6 is the visual representation of Table 3-7.

Table 3-7 Distribution of Power Relations

Power	Number	Percentage
+P	61	61%
- P	39	39%
Total	100	100%

Figure 3-6
Distribution of Power Relations

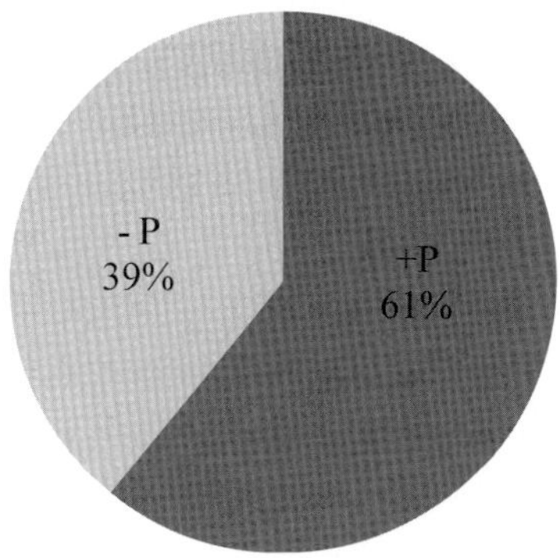

The concept of power is related to vertical and non-reciprocal control and submission hierarchy. Power variables such as age, kinship, and social status function as sociocultural constraints that may be manipulated as a speaker's communicative strategies. Sohn (1986) mentions that strong hierarchism still remains in age, kinship, and achieved social status in Korean society, and thus this shows the importance of power in the Korean language. Therefore, power relations in conversation between interlocutors result from differences in power variables such as kinship, age and social status. In this study, I define that [+power] relations in conversations include parent-child, older brother/sister – younger brother/sister, boss-employer at workplace, teacher-student, senior-junior relations in university setting or workplace, and so on.

On the other hand, [-power] relations in conversations include friend-friend, coworker-coworker in workplace relations, and so on.

3.2.7 Distribution of distance relations (Social solidarity)

As shown in Table 3-8, there were 31 sets of conversations without distance relations between interlocutors (31%), while there were 69 sets of conversations with distance relations between interlocutors (69%). Figure 3-7 is the visual representation of Table 3-8.

Table 3-8
Distribution of Distance Relations

Distance	Number	Percentage
+D	31	31%
-D	69	69%
Total	100	100%

Figure 3-7
Distribution of Distance Relation

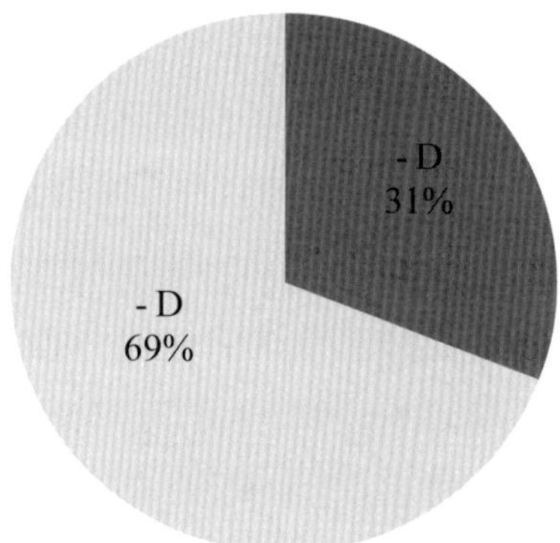

The concept of solidarity is related to horizontal and reciprocal closeness and distance. Solidarity variables such as intimacy/distance, in/out-groupness may be manipulated as a speaker's communicative strategies. Therefore, distance relations in conversation between interlocutors result from differences in solidarity variables such as in/out groupness, etc. In this study, I define that [+distance] relations in conversations include out-groupness or distance between interlocutors such as distant co-workers, distant classmate, clerk and customer and so on. On the other hand, [-distance] relations in conversations include in-groupness and intimacy such as family members, close friends, close coworkers, neighbors, and so on.

Sociolinguistic competence is the knowledge which underlies people's ability to use language appropriately (Holmes 2001, p. 367). In other words, it is the ability to interpret the social meaning of the choice of linguistic varieties and to use language with the appropriate social meaning for the communication setting, the topic, and the relationships among the people communicating. Thus, when people communicate they should consider the social and contextual factors such as the relationship between the participants in terms of power and solidarity, and the purpose of interaction. According to Cohen (1999), sociolinguistic competence refers to the respondents' skill at selecting appropriate linguistic forms in order to express the particular strategy used to realize the speech act (e.g., expression of regret in an apology, registration of a grievance in a complaint, specification of the objective of a request, or refusal of an invitation). People say the same thing in different forms and strategies, as the ways of speaking reflect different social functions. Let us assume that a person arriving late for a meeting might offer a more intensified apology when the addressee is the boss, rather than a friend. Other factors such as age, social distance or situation might play a significant role in selecting strategies, too. A person should use *coysong-hapnita* 'I 'm sorry' in a formal setting, but usually does not say it when talking to a friend or family members. The process of selecting the sociolinguistically appropriate forms or strategies in Korean is complex since it is conditioned by social, cultural, situational, and personal factors.

3.3 Summary

First, this chapter introduced the methodology and procedure of data collection for this study. The data is named Yoon's corpus. The data collected for this study were unplanned, spontaneous, and face-to-face naturally-occurring conversations in Korean. 219 native Korean who speak either the standard Korean or a dialect of Korean participated in this study. The entire dataset is comprised of one hundred sets of recordings of about 10 minutes in length. Second, I explained how to change the recorded data to text data. One hundred files of recording were transcribed to one hundred files of texts without editing. Hedge tokens were searched using the search engine of Seycong Corpus called *hanmalwu*. Third, the classification of Korean hedges was presented. Korean hedges are divided into lexical hedges and syntactic hedges. Lexical hedges include discourse markers (DM), interactive sentence enders (ISEs), auxiliary verbs (AVs), particles (P), filler (F), Adverbs (Ab), suffixes (Sf), and Phrases (Ph), while syntactic hedges include main clause omission, conditionals, tag questions, and impersonalization. Fourth, the statistical methods for the qualitative analysis were briefly introduced. Fifth, the overview of Yoon's data was introduced. The frequency and percentage of gender (female, male), gender composition (female-female, male-male, female-male, and multiple), age (teens, 20s-30s, over 40s), region (metropolitan area, non-metropolitan area), occupation (student, housewife, and office worker), social power relations between interlocutors, and social distance relations between interlocutors were shown.

CHAPTER 4

THE CLASSIFICATION AND FREQUENCY OF KOREAN HEDGES IN SPOKEN DISCOURSE

This chapter will explore the classification and frequency of Korean hedges in my corpus, which are unplanned, naturally-occurring spoken discourse. The hedges in my corpus are classified based on the classification presented in Chapter 3. The classification will include only lexical hedges and syntactic hedges since other hedges such as morphological, phonological, prosodic, and rhetorical hedges are beyond the scope of the current study.

4.1 Classification of Korean Hedges in Spoken Discourse

Table 4-1 shows the classification and its inventory of Korean hedges in spoken discourse based on my corpus. Hence, there might be more hedge items that are not found in my data. Let me describe briefly the Korean lexical hedges and syntactic hedges listed in Table 4-1.

Table 4-1 Classification and Inventory of Korean Hedges in Spoken Discourse

Classification		Inventory
Lexical Hedges	(1) Discourse marker (DM)	1. *com/ccom* 2. *mwe/mo/me; way* 3. *ani* 4. *isscanh-a(yo); iss-ci; iss-cyo* 5. *ce/ceki* 6. *icey/ incey* 7. *mak* 8. *cham* 9. *kunyang* 10. *kuntey* 11. *kulenikka/ kunikka(n)/ ku(n)kka* 12. *kulaykaciko/kulaykacko*
	(2) Interactive sentence ender (ISE)	1. *-canha(yo)* 2. *-nuntey(yo)* 3. *-ketun(yo)* 4. *-telako(yo)* 5. *-ci(yo)* 6. *-ney(yo)* 7. *-tay(yo)*

Lexical Hedges	(3) Auxiliary verb (AV)	1. *-kes kath-* 2. *-ci molu-* 3. *-tus ha-* 4. *-na po-* 5. *-e/ato toy-* 6. *-e/a cwu-* 7. *-e/a po-*
	(4) Particle (P)	1. *-(i)latunci* 2.- *yo* (floater)
	(5) Filler (F)	*e, a, um, hum, ca, he, i, ku*
	(6) Adverb (Ab)	*amato , yakkan , hoksi , pyello , taycheylo*
	(7) Suffix (Sf)	*-keyss-*
	(8) Phrase (Ph)	1. *-e/a kaciko/kwu* 2. *-e/a kacko/kwu*
Syntactic Hedges	(1) Main Clause Omission	*-e/ase(yo); -ko/kwu(yo)*
	(2) Conditional	*-myen*
	(3) Tag Question	*-ci anha(yo)? ; -ci anh-ullay(yo)?; -ci anhulkka(yo)?*
	(4) Impersonalization	*ta-tul, wuli* (plural expression)

*Allomorphs are divided by a slash (/).

4.1.1 Lexical hedges

(1) Discourse markers

In general, discourse markers (henceforth, DMs) are defined as a class of syntactically-optional, non-truth-conditional connective expressions (Schourup, 1999). Schiffrin (1987, p. 31) defines DMs as "sequentially-dependent elements that brackets units of talk." In Korean DMs research, Cheon (2002) identified DMs as expressions that have acquired new functions and have been studied under various terms such as expletives, hesitation markers, exclamation markers, discourse substitute markers, etc. However, Cheon (2002) states that DMs should be focused on at the discourse level rather than in their original grammatical class. Also, she argued that DMs do not conjugate and cannot take particles, except for a few limited instances, whereby a partial conjugation does not affect the meaning or function of the DM. Let me explain briefly about DMs in my inventory of the lexical hedges.

com: Diminutive *com* derived from *cokem* 'a little' is interpreted as a DM 'please' or hesitation as in (b) & (c).

(a) *mas-i* **com** *pyenhan-kes kath-untey?*(diminutive 'a little')
taste-NM a little change-seems to be-ENDER
'It seems that the taste has changed a little.'

(b) *mwun* **com** *yel-e* *cwu-si-keyss-eyo?* (DM 'please')
door DM open-INF give-SH-may-POL
'Could you open the door, please?'

(c) *cey-ka* *yocum* **com** *saceng-i*
I (humble)-NM recently DM situation-NM
an coh-untey-yo.(Hesitation)
not-good-ENDER- POL
'My (economic) situation isn't that good these days.'

mwe, way : The discourse markers *mwe* and *way* are evolved from wh-interrogative word *mwe* 'what' and *way* 'why' through the process of grammaticalization (Koo, 2000). The discourse maker *mwe* is primarily used as an interrogative and an indefinite pronoun in spoken discourse as in (a) and (b). On the other hand, *mwe* is also used as a DM in example (c). Moreover, *mwe* + question enders (e.g., *mwe-ci*? 'umm' *mwe-nya* 'what is it? *mwe-lalkka* 'how should I put it?') are used when seeking for the best word or expression, or recalling. The discourse marker w*ay*[12] is primarily used as an interrogative 'why' in spoken discourse as in (d). On the other hand, *way* is also used as a DM in example (e).

(a) *cikum* **mwe** *nokum* *ha-ko* *iss-nun* *ke-ni*? (interrogative)
now what record do-and exist-RL thing-PLN
'What are you recording now?'

(b) ***mwe****-ka* *issta-ko* *palapo-ko* *iss-ni?* (indefinite pronoun)
what-NM exist-and look-and exist-PLN
'Is there anything which makes you look like that?'

(c) *icey kuman* *kaci* **mwe**. (DM)
now to that extent go DM
'Now, let's get going, well'

12 Unlike other interrogative, *way* is not used as an indefinite pronoun (Kim, 2006).

(d) ***way*** *ecey* *swuep- ey* *an* *wass-eyo*? (interrogative)
why yesterday class-at not went-POL
'Why didn't you come to class yesterday?

(e) *kule-n ke* *isscanha* ***way*** *nwun o-l* *ttay* *ha-nun ke.* (DM)
that-RLthing DM DM snow come-RL time do-RL thing
'You know something like that, what you usually do when it snows.'

ani: The adverb *ani*, which is originally used as a sentential adverb in the sense of 'no' in response to a question as in (a), is considered to be evolved into a discourse marker through the process of grammaticalization indicating hesitation or an attention-getter in spoken discourse as in (b).

(a) A: *pay* *an kophu-ni?*
stomach not hungry-PLN
'Aren't you hungry?"

B: ***ani****-yo*.(Adverb)
No-POL
'No (I am not hungry)'

(b) ***ani*** *ku-key* *nay-ka* *ecey* *pappa-se*
DM that thing I-NM yesterday busy-because
mos *kass-ci.*(DM)
cannot go-PST-ENDER
'Well, I couldn't go because I was busy yesterday.'

isscanh-a(yo): Discourse marker *isscanh-a(yo)* 'well, you know' as an attention-getter in (a) is derived from *iss-ci ani hay-yo* 'isn't there something.'

(a) ***isscanha***, *cakyekcung* *sincheng* *hanun ke*
DM certificate apply do-RL thing
towa-cwu-llay? (DM)
help-give-will-ENDER
'You know (Well), can you help me apply the certificate?

ce/ceki : Demonstrative *ceki* 'over there' is considered to be evolved into a discourse marker through the process of grammaticalization indicating 'Excuse me' as in (a). In social interactions which inherently contain a potential threat to an interlocutor's face, as in speech settings of request, apology, disagreement/argument, and in turn taking, the employment of the discourse marker ce/*ceki* and its compositional forms preserves and promotes social relationships by softening the potential face-threatening acts (Park, 2001).

(a) ***ceki*** *cikum myech si-yey-yo?* (DM)
DM now what time-be-POL
'Excuse me, what time is it now?'

icey/incey: A deitic temporal adverb *icey/incey* 'now' in (a) is considered to be evolved into a discourse marker through the process of grammaticalization indicating the speaker's stance on the utterance in (b).

(a) *cal ka, ne* ***icey*** *ka-nun ke-ni*? (Temporal adverb)
well go you now go-RL thing-PLN
'Good-bye, are you going now?'
(b) *ay- tul-un* ***incey*** *sensayng-nim phingkyey*
child-PL-NM DM teacher-HT excuse
tay-nun ke-ci mwe. (DM)
make-RL thing-ENDER DM
'Children (Students) are blaming their teacher.'

mak : An informal variant of the adverb *maku* 'very, severely' is used as a DM when the speaker's feeling precedes the utterance indicating an emotion connection between the speaker and the listener as in (a).

(a) *yocum mayil* ***mak*** *suthuleysu emcheng pat-ass-ketun.*
recently everyday DM stress terrible receive-PST-ENDER
'I've been extremely stressed these days."

cham : A degree adverb 'very, truly' becomes a discourse marker *cham* denoting a speaker's realization or an attention-getter in order to inform the listener of a topic change for a smooth interaction in a discoursal context.

kunyang : An adverb *kunyang* 'just, as it is' becomes the discourse marker *kunyang* denoting a less significant or less accurate utterance in order to achieve a smooth interaction in discoursal context.

kuntey : The contrastive connector *kulentey* 'but' becomes the discourse marker *kuntey* denoting hesitation or a topic change in discourse context.

kulenikka/ kunikka(n)/kukka/ kunkka: The causal connective *-nikka* becomes the discourse marker *kulenikka* denoting strong subjectivity/intersubjectivity. *Kulenikka* delivers agreement or disagreement in social interactions.

kulaykaciko/ kulaykacko : The discourse marker *kulaykaciko* adopts the previous utterance as a cause or a reason. It functions as returning to the original topic or the succession of the topic.

(2) Interactive Sentence Enders (ISEs)

Mitigating strategies are widely employed in Korean daily conversation in a variety of speech act situations (e.g., request, refusal, apology, etc.) in order to soften a face-threatening act. In Korean, there are many illocution-mitigating devices, such as hedges, indirect speech acts, and intonation contours in order to weaken the illocutionary force. One of the conventionalized illocution-mitigating devices in Korean is related to the interactive sentence enders (ISE)[13]. Korean is an SOV (subject-object-predicate) language, which is a predicate-final language. In Korean, a predicate without a sentence ender would be incomplete and interactive sentence enders (ISEs) in particular convey a speaker's attitude and feelings toward a proposition or an addressee. It is said that Korean sentence enders denote a speaker's attitudes and judgment.

---

13 The ISEs reflect the speaker's social and psychological empathy toward the participants (cf. Delancy, 1986; Yuen, 2001).

Especially, Korean interactive sentence enders (ISEs) function as markers of discourse modality in conversational contexts. According to Marynard (1993, p.38) *discourse modality* conveys the speaker's subjective emotional, mental, or psychological attitude toward the message content of the speech act itself or toward his or her interlocutor in discourse. Discourse modality operates to define and to foreground certain ways of interpreting the propositional content in discourse; it directly expresses the speaker's personal voice on the basis of which the utterance is intended to be meaningfully interpreted.

As Sohn (2007) asserted, a series of newly innovated sentence enders such as *-canha(yo)*, *-nuntey(yo), -ketun(yo), -telako(yo)* and so on are used productively in daily conversation in Korean, more frequently than the canonical sentence-type enders that are associated with the six speech levels[14] in Korean. Additionally, those sentence enders are used to tone down a speaker's assertiveness in contemporary Korean. When used at the end of an utterance, newly innovated sentence enders in Korean serve to indicate interactive communication such as hedging, surprise, etc. Therefore, interactive sentence enders (ISEs) as lexical hedges are employed to mitigate or weaken the illocutionary force in order to smooth interaction. Interestingly, these newly innovated sentence enders occur in only two speech levels, polite (marked) and intimate (unmarked) and take only one sentence type[15], declarative or interrogative[16]. Furthermore, these interactive sentence enders (ISEs) are claimed to have a special pragmatic function: conventionalized illocution-mitigating devices in Korean. Many of these enders have been grammaticalized from phrasal or clausal constructions, deletion of a main clause, or deletion of the quotative phrase *ko ha* 'say that…'. (H. Sohn 1999, p. 357). Newly innovated sentence enders have been developed by contracting various complex constructions. Let me sum-

14 There are six speech levels in Korean: plain, intimate, familiar, blunt, polite, deferential (Cf. H.Sohn, 1999, p. 355)

15 There are four sentence types in Korean: declarative, interrogative, imperative, propositive (Cf. H. Sohn, 1999, p. 355).

16 Note that *-ci(yo)* takes declarative and interrogative.

marize the seven ISEs in lexical hedges.

-canha(yo) : In contemporary Korean, *-canha(yo)* 'as you know, you know that' is often used as one of the numerous sentence enders in spoken discourse. The sentence ender *-canha(yo)* 'you see!, as you know' is evolved from *-ci anha(yo)* , which is the long-form negation in Korean. Moreover, the long-form negation *-ci anha(yo)* is originally from *-ci ani*[17] *hay-yo* (NOM[18] not do/be-POL) 'Isn't it the case that⋯.' (Sohn H., 1999b). The long-form negation *-ci anha(yo)* in contemporary Korean occurs in pure negative context; on the other hand, the reduced form *-canha(yo)* is used as a hedge to enhance interpersonal rapport, establish solidarity, or seek agreement, etc. Moreover, it is said that ISE *-canha(yo)* functions as an information-state checker (propositional function of hedges) and an interactive marker (interpersonal function of hedges) like *y'know* in English. ISE *-canha(yo)* can also be used to ascertain meta-knowledge of generally shared knowledge.[19]

From my data, *-canha(yo)* is used for interactive alignment such as seeking agreement and confirmation while it is used for mitigation when complaining, telling a problem or expressing opposition. In short, the hedge functions of *-canha(yo)* are to confirm shared knowledge between interlocutors, to elicit the listener's agreement or confirmation, to soften the force of a criticism, to enhance interpersonal rapport, establish solidarity, and so forth. ISE *-canha(yo)* tend to be used more in informal,

17 The negation marker *an* in *anh-ayo* has its origin in *ani-hay-yo* which was used in early Modern Korean (17C-18C) and started being replaced with *an* in the late 19th century (Lee, 1993).

18 The suffix *-ci* is called an aspectual marker, nominalizer, complementizer, or committal suffix depending on the author. Following H. Sohn (1999, p. 262), this is glossed as NOM (nominalizer) in this paper.

19 The meta-knowledge of speaker-hearer shared knowledge are (a) the hearer knows the background information and the speaker knows that, (b) the hearer knows the background information and the speaker does not know that, (c) the hearer does not know the background information and the speaker knows that, and (d) the hearer does not know the background information and the speaker does not know the background information. If the information in situation (b), (c), or (d), *y'know* could be used to check out the information state, and transit from situations (b), (c), or (d) to situation (a).

personal interactions to express solidarity or facilitate interactions and to manage conversation effectively.

-nuntey(yo): *-nuntey*[20] 'and, but, while, given that' is mainly known as a conjunctive suffix, linking a subordinate *-nuntey-* clause, providing background circumstance, contrasting two situations (H.S.Lee, 1999; Y. Park, 1999). *-nuntey* consists of the indicative relative clause ender *-n-un* (IN-RL) and a defective noun *tey* 'place, circumstance' (H. Sohn, 1999). However, in spoken discourse *-nuntey* occurs in sentence-final position without *a* main clause. One motivation for the omission of a main clause is to mitigate the assertiveness of various speech acts in terms of pragmalinguistics. By omitting main clauses the speaker can give the addressee the option of making the final decision on the basis of the background information expressed in the unomitted clause (Sohn 1999, p. 418). As Y. Park (1997, 1999) summarized in her study, *-nuntey(yo)* in the utterance-final position has various interactive functions. First, *-nuntey(yo)* signaling incompatibility or discrepancy is utilized commonly in the contexts of dispreferred responses such as rejection of a request, declining an offer, denial of accusation or blame, and disagreement with the assessment or suggestion made by the other interlocutors. Second, it is utilized to solicit the other interlocutor's involvement in the contexts of requesting the addressee's confirmation or clarification, and expressing one's wish or intention in a request.

-ketun(yo): In contemporary Korean, ISE *-ketun(yo)* 'you see', like *-canha(yo)* 'you know' is often used as one of the interactive sentence enders (ISEs) in spoken discourse. ISE *-keten(yo)*, which was originally a subordinate clausal ender, became a sentence ender via grammaticalization with the omission of the main clause. Note that the motivation of the main clause omission is to express strategic politeness[21] toward

20 *-nuntey* is used for verbs, *-(u)ntey* for adjectives in the present tense. With the anterior suffix *-ess/ass*, it is invariably *-nuntey* regardless of verbs or adjectives (H.S. Lee, 1999).

21 There are two types of 'linguistic politeness': one is 'normative' politeness

the hearer or to avoid directness by mitigating the illocutionary force of speech acts.

Y. Park (1998) argues that the sentence ender *-ketun* can be used for various interactive functions such as justification, clarification, or tightening up an argument better. She shows various interactive and pragmatic functions of *-ketun*: (a) justifications, clarifications, elaborations, or tightening up an argument, (b) dispreferred responses such as disagreements or refusals, (c) initiating problem-telling and requests. She also elucidates that *-ketun* has undergone the grammaticalization process from conditional marker to connective providing a reason to sentence-final particle marking the speaker's stance regarding information status.

M. Park & S.Sohn (2002) argue that the diachronic function of *-ketun* is the result of the interplay of grammar and discourse by strategic interactions and intonational contours encoded in *-ketun*. Their data reveal that a majority of *-ketun* at the sentence-final position takes a high boundary tone (H%), which manifests the speaker's stance and intensifies the meaning of the utterance as well as ratifies the particular stance of the interactive relationship between the speaker and the interlocutor(s). Especially, the *-ketun* functions to mitigate the illocutionary force of making a direct request. That is, the speaker gives the hearer the option of making the final decision (cf. Park & S. Sohn 2002, p. 314).

Yuen (2001) analyzes the sentence ender *-ketun* from the perspective of politeness strategies in a variety of social contexts and proposes seven discourse pragmatic functions of *-keten*: (a) to mitigate the force of urgency and for efficiency in communicating a problem, leading to a request (with a falling tone), (b) to soften illocutionary force in order to persuade the listener (with a falling tone), (c) to soften the force of a reply to a question (with a two-level falling tone), (d) to avoid responsibility for an utterance and to soften the force of assertion in respect to

---

expressed by grammatical and lexical means such as honorifics while the other is 'strategic' politeness expressed by illocutionary force-modifying devices such as indirect speech acts, hedges and so on. (Cho 1982; Blum-Kulka 1987; H. Sohn 1987; Ide 1989).

the validity of the speaker's assumption (with a two-level rising tone), (e) to mitigate the force of justification to request and seek agreement based on that justification (with a two-level falling intonation contour), (f) to soften the force of an attempt to clarify misunderstanding (with two-level falling tone), (g) to mitigate the force of an attempt to persuade the addressee (with a falling tone).

-telako(yo): The newly innovated sentence ender *-telako(yo)* is a Korean experiential evidential marking, which indicates the information acquired through the speaker's perceptual experience[22] in the past (Lee, 1999). As Yuen's (2001) study shows, *-telako(yo)*[23] is the sentence ender frequently used by all age groups in daily Korean conversation. The speaker makes a strategic choice of employing the experiential evidential marking *-telako(yo)* to mitigate illocutionary force as well as achieve detachment in carrying out interactively delicate actions, such as refusals, disagreements, or challenges to other interlocutors (M.S.Kim, 2005). That is, the speaker makes these delicate actions in an indirect manner by reporting what s(he) has observed/experienced without explicitly stating his/her intention.

The *-telako(yo)* (RT-INTROS-QT- POL) 'I saw/experienced/felt that···, indeed' is a sentence ender which consists of four suffixes: the retrospective suffix *te* which denotes an act or state as the speaker's past observation or experience, the introspective suffix *la* which expresses the speaker's introspection, the quotative particle *ko* which serves as a complementizer connecting the quoted speech and the predicate (say verb), and the polite ender *yo*. H. Sohn (1990) argues that the sentence ender *-telako(yo)* has been grammaticalized from a quotative construction that formally required a quoted complement clause followed by a main clause, as indicated in example (a) and (b).

22 The speaker's perceptual experience includes visual, auditory, and sensory experience.

23 Allomorphic variant *-telakwu-* is commonly used in daily conversation since *-kwu* is a phonetic lenition of *-ko* that sounds more polite and weaker. (Yuen, 2001).

(a) [*yenghwa-ka coh-**te-la-ko***] [*Mia ka malhay-ss-e.yo*].
Movie-NM good-RT-INTROS-QT Mia-NM say-PST-POL
'Mia (who saw the movie) said that the movie was good.'

(b) *yenghwa-ka coh-**te-la-ko-yo***.
Movie-NM good-**TELAKO**-POL
'(**I noticed/perceived**) that the movie was good.'

As seen in the above examples, *-telako* was originally part of a subordinate clause in a quotative construction and became a sentence ender through a process of main clause omission (H. Sohn, 1999). That is, the subordinate clause has become a complete sentence through a series of grammaticalization processes in that the formerly subordinate clause-final elements have been functionally transferred into a sentence-final ender. Also, the quotative particle *ko* is grammaticalized from the conjunctive construction *ha-ko* 'say…and' through meaning shift, grammatical reanalysis, and phonological contraction. As a result, *-telako(yo)* has come to express the speaker's modal attitude toward the propositional content or the addressee due to main clause omission.

With the unrecoverable main clause omission and subsequent grammaticalization *te-la-ko* closely agglutinates together to be restructured as an innovated sentence ender, obtaining an independent modal category (Sohn, 1999a). The derived grammatical meaning in (b) involves only the speaker as the reporter[24] while only the third person subject is allowed in the undeleted construction in (a). Furthermore, the derived grammatical meaning becomes the speaker's own report of the propositional content (subjectification). The *-telako(yo)* retains the basic meaning of "mildly and casually inform you that I observed···" (H.

24 According to Sohn (1986), the basic syntactic structure which underlines the retrospective suffix *te* is that of a transitive sentence of 'Agent + Complement Sentence + Time + Predicate'. Sohn notes that *te* requires an agent argument, the REPORTER (the speaker) who PERCEIVES an event or situation, and a complement sentence as another argument which describes the event or situation. Although the agent of the predicate is not verbally identified in the *–telako* construction, understanding that the agent of the predicate is the speaker of the moment who reports his perception is crucial. The suffix *-te* has some inherent grammatical constraints so called 'non-equi subject constraint'(Sohn 1986).

Sohn, 1999, p. 171). The non-recoverable main clause deletion results from the speaker's strategy to mitigate illocutionary force.[25]

S. Yeun (2001) argues that ISE *-telako(yo)* is a speaker-oriented device employed to save the speaker's own face and maintain smooth and polite interaction with the addressee. On the other hand, M.S. Kim (2005) argues that *-telako* is used for achieving various social interactive meanings such as entitlement, objectivity, and detachment in terms of social interaction.

-ci(yo) : The sentence ender *-ci* has been defined as an epistemic modality (H. Lee, 1999; S. Choi, 1995). K. Lee (1993) pointed out that *-ci* is used when a speaker seeks a listener's conformation or agreement in an interrogative context since the listener has some knowledge of the information provided by the speaker. H. Sohn (1999) claimed that *-ci* should be considered to be a suppositive suffix in the mood category that denotes a speaker's supposition or makes a casual suggestion. H. S. Lee (1999) claimed that *-ci* is used when a speaker commits to a proposition with varying degrees of certainty from supposition to conjecture, conviction or assurance, depending on the various contextual factors. He also claims that committal *-ci* emphasizes the speaker's belief about the conveyed message. J. Kim (2000) argued that *-ci* is used to denote the information that is unknown to the speaker although it is also used to denote already known information. M. Park (2003) in her study of the meaning of Korean prosodic boundary tones, mentioned that the suffix *-ci* is often accompanied with modal suffixes which convey a speaker's low certainty such as *-na po-* and*-keyss-*.

-ney(yo) : According to H. Sohn (1999), in a so-called apperceptive

25 Mitigation is a set of strategies by which people try to make their speech act more effective. The notion of mitigation is used in pragmatics (Fraser, 1980) and it is opposed and complementary to the notion of 'reinforcement'. Generally, it reduces participants obligations, to which the felicity conditions of a speech act belong, thereby furthering the achievement of interactive goals. Thus, mitigation is functional to smooth interactive management in that it reduces risks for participants at various levels, e.g. risks of request, refusal, conflict, and so forth.

sentence *-ney* denotes 'counter-expectation' as in *pi-ka o-**ney*** 'while *-kwun* denotes 'discovery and confirmation' as in *pi ka o-nun-kwun* 'Oh, it's raining.' The suffix *-ney* is used as a familiar declarative sentence ender by the older generation while it is often used in lieu of the polite declarative *-e/a-yo* form as in *onul com papp-ayo* ' I am kind of busy today' vs. *pappu-**ney**-yo.*

H.S. Lee (1993) mentions that the *-ney* "factual realization" marker is a non-informative expression and conveys information that is more factual and definite contrary to background expectations and which is immediately surprising in the moment.

M. Park (2003) highlights the pragmatic difference between two apperceptive suffixes *-ney* and *-kwun* in terms of boundary tones. She argues that L% (a falling boundary tone) focuses attention on the speaker's belief, while H% (a rising boundary tone) relates to the speaker's sense of surprise. Thus, *-ney* occurs with LH%, which highlights the disjunction between the speaker's previous belief and the current surprise, and H%, which points more to the speaker's immediate surprise. On the other hand, *-kwun* occurs with HL%, which represents surprise followed by realization, and L%, which highlights the speaker's realization of newly perceived information.

-tay (yo) : The newly innovated sentence ender *-tay* is an indirect reported evidential marker which indicates the speaker's information as hearsay (H.S. Lee, 1991). It is the short form of an indirect quotation which resulted from the long form indirect quotation construction, *-ta(ko) ha-*, consisting of declarative sentence ender *ta*, quotative marker *ko*, and the main verb *ha-* or *kule-* (S. Sohn & M. Park, 2003), as in examples (a) & (b).

(a) *Ciswu-ka* *nayil* *sewul-ey* *o-n-**ta-(ko)***
Ciswu-NOM tomorrow Seoul-to come-IMPFV-DC-QT
***kulay**-ss-e-yo.*
say-PST-IE-POL
'Ciswu said that she was coming to Seoul tomorrow.'

(b) *Ciswu-ka* *nayil* *sewul-ey o-n-**tay**-yo.*
Ciswu-NOM tomorrow Seoul-to come-IMPFV-HEARSAY-POL
'I hear (they say) that Ciswu is coming to Seoul tomorrow.'

The hearsay marker *-tay* conveys the propositional content of the quoted message without referring to the actual event. S. Sohn & M. Park (2003) claim that the indirect quotation *-tay* functions to anchor an utterance to participants who are not present at the speech event and conveys the speaker's personal stance with regard to a reported message. Furthermore, the speaker employs the hearsay marker *-tay* as an interactive resource for displaying or modifying the speaker's stance (M. S. Kim, 2006). The hedge functions of *-tay(yo)* are to negotiate and establish one's stance in different ways, such as mitigating the speaker's opposing stance toward the addressee, displaying the speaker's stance as a shared stance, setting up or undercutting an alignment between the speaker and the addressee, and so on.

(3) Auxiliary Verbs (AVs):
-kes kath-: One of the epistemic modality[26] grams in Korean, *-n(un)/ul kes kath-ayo,* roughly means 'it seems that…/it is likely that…', which is evolved from *-n(un)/ul kes kwa kath-ayo* 'to be the same as…'. The original construction *-n(un)/ul kes kwa kath-ayo* (RL thing with to be same-POL) contains a relativizer[27], a defective noun[28] *kes* 'thing', a commitative particle *kwa* 'with' and adjective *kath-*, which has the lexical meaning of 'to be the same' with the polite sentence suffix *yo*,

26 As Oh (1998) summarizes, there are several epistemic modality *grams* (grammatical morphemes) in Korean; for example *-ci molu-* 'may, might' (weak possibility), *-kes kath-* 'be likely' (strong/subjective possibility), *-tus ha-* 'seem/look like' (strong/objective possibility), and *-na po-* (inference).

27 Korean RL (relativizer) suffixes are summarized as follows.

	Predicate	*Indicative*	*Retrospective*	*Prospective*
Verb	non-past:	*-nun*	*-ten*	*-(u)l*
	past:	*-(u)n*	*-e/ass-ten*	*-e/ass-ul*
Adjective	non-past:	*-(u)n*	*-ten*	*-(u)l*
	past:	Ø	*-e/ass-ten*	*-e/ass-ul*

28 A defective noun *kes* always occurs with a modifier and never stands alone.

as in (a) excerpted from Oh (1998). On the other hand, the evolved form *-n(un)/ul kes kath-ayo* contains a defective noun, *kes*, modified by a preceding relativizer with *kath-* as in (b). In these constructions, a commitative particle *kwa* 'with' cannot occur after *kes*.

(a) *ku* *kes-un* *san-eyse* *mwulkoki-lul chac-**nun*** ***kes*** ***kwa***
that thing-TC mountain-at fish-ACC seek-RL thing with
kath-ayo.
to be same-POL
'It is the same as asking for fish in the mountain.'
(It is an impossible thing to do.)

(b) *Mia-ka* *o-**l-kes*** ***kath-ayo***.
Mia-NM come-RL-thing seem-POL
'It seems/is likely that Mia will come.'

Notice that through reanalysis the main predicate *kath-* becomes a sentential modal ending, which marks the speaker's modal attitude toward the proposition. That is, the composition of *kes* and *kath-* has grammaticalized into a modality[29] of conjecture or possibility through the structural reanalysis of the two morphemes into a single grammatical morpheme. One function of *-n(un)/ul kes kath-ayo* is conjecture as in (b) ; however, the other function of *-n(un)/ul kes kath-ayo* is generally known as a phrasal hedge[30] and is preferably used when the speaker wishes to express his/her feelings or thoughts in an indirect way through semantic transfer as in (c) & (d). *-n(un)/ul kes katha-yo* has the importance of pragmatic motivation in that the use of this expression is useful to mitigate/soften the speakers' assertion via grammaticalization which has been recognized as a process of language change with pragmatic aspects. Let us consider the examples from spoken discourse data:

29 Korean expresses modality through sentence enders. Modality is defined as a facet of illocutionary force, signaled by grammatical devices (moods, modals, etc.), that expresses: (i) the illocutionary point or general intent of a speaker, or (ii) a speaker's degree of commitment to the expressed proposition's believability, obligatoriness, desirability, or reality (Givon 1984; Bybee 1985; Park, 2003).

30 According to Hwang (1990) Korean hedges are identified as lexical hedges, phrasal hedges and structural hedges.

(a) A: *chayk com pilly-e cwu-si-keyss-eyo*?
book just lend-INF give-SH-PRS-POL
'May I borrow your book?'
B: *kulsse-yo na-to nayil sihem-i iss-ese*
well-POL, I-also tomorrow exam- NM have-because
an toy-l ***kes katha-yo.***
not become-RL seem-POL
'Well, it seems that I can't lend my book because I also have an exam tomorrow.'

(b) A: *i os ettay*?
this cloth how
'How do I look on this dress?'
B: *kulssey, ne-hanthey an ewulli-**nun kes kath**-a.*
well you-to not fit-RL seem-INT
'It doesn't seem to look good on you.'

Let us assume that the speaker B in (c) refuses with the direct expression, *an toy-yo* (not become-POL) 'I can't' instead of *an toyl* ***kes katha-yo*** (not become thing seem-POL) 'It seems that I can't'; or the speaker B in (d) comments on A's question with the direct expression, *an ewully-e* 'it doesn't look good on you' instead of *an ewulli-nun kes kath-a* 'It doesn't seem to look good'. Those replies are too direct, and would threaten the hearer's *face* in Korean. Hence, the illocution-mitigating devices such as the epistemic modality *-n(un)/ul kes kath-ayo* is used in terms of politeness. Grice's second cooperative maxim of manner is "avoid ambiguity," and it is an intuitive statement that the avoidance of ambiguity is a pragmatic factor that influences the language choices of speakers and writers. But the mechanisms through which ambiguity avoidance shapes the process of grammaticalization should be more systematically studied. The ways in which we "avoid ambiguity" are varied and subtle. Purposeful ambiguity is a rhetorical and stylistic tool which is certainly part of effective communication.

-ci molu-: *-ci molu-* (DN + 'don't know') 'It seems like~' denoting weak possibility is one of the epistemic modality grams in Korean.

-tus ha- : *-tus ha-* (DN + 'do') 'It seems like~' denoting strong possibility is one of the epistemic modality grams in Korean.

-na po- : *-na po-* (DN + 'see') 'It looks like~' denoting inference is one of the epistemic modality grams in Korean.

-e/a-to toy- : *--e/a-to toy-* 'may' (INF CONC become) denoting permission is the agent-oriented modality grams in Korean.

-e/a cwu- : *-cwuta* 'give' becomes the benefactive auxiliary verb 'do for' with the infinitive -e/a. Commands are often turned into requests with the help of *-e/a/ cwuta* which is used to indicate that compliance with the request would be of benefit to the speaker. Turning a command into a request for a favor has a dramatic softening effect (Choo & Kwak, 2008).

-e/a po- : *-pota* 'try, look at' becomes the experiential, attemptive auxiliary verb 'to try' with the infinitive *-e/a*. The auxiliary verb *-e/a pota* is widely used to soften the speaker's assertion by making it less direct and by reducing his/her commitment to the statement. Especially, commands become milder and less direct, creating the impression that the speaker is leaving some room for the other person to make a choice by saying 'Try it (if you'd like).'(Choo & Kwak, 2008).

(1) **Particles (P)**

-(i)latunci : The particle *-(i)latunci* 'or something' was not counted in my data.

-yo : The particle *-yo* can be attached as a floater to particles or conjunctive enders.

cey-ka-yo	*hakkyo-e-lul-yo*	*pappase-yo*	*ppaci-ess-eyo.*
I(humble)-NM-YO	school-to-AC-YO	busy-YO	skip-PST-POL

(2) **Fillers (F):**

Korean hesitation fillers such as *e, a, um, hum, ca, he, i, ku* occur to soften the statement in interaction or search the word without any meaning.

(3) **Adverbs (Ab):**
amato 'perhaps', *yakkan* 'a little', *hoksi* 'by any chance', *pyello* ' particularly', *taycheylo* 'generally, mostly' are used for hedge functions to lower effect on the force of the modified verb (Quirk et al. 1972, p. 452).

(4) **Suffixes (Sf):**
The modal suffix *-keyss* which denotes a conjecture can be used as a politeness marker. For example,

*mwun com yele-cwu-si-**keyss**-eyo?*
door please open-give-SH-SF-POL
'Would you please open the window?'

(5) **Phrases (Ph):**
Phrasal hedges *-e/a/ kaciko/kwu, -e/a kacko(kwu)* are used to soften or mitigate the utterances instead of *-e/ase* 'because, since.'

4.1.2 Syntactic hedges

(1) **Main Clause Omissions**: One motivation for the omission of a main clause is to mitigate the assertiveness of various speech acts in terms of pragmalinguistics. The speaker can give the addressee the option of making the final decision on the basis of the background information expressed in the unomitted clause (Sohn 1999, p. 418). The option of making the final decision on the basis of the background information expressed in the unomitted clause (Sohn, 1999).

(2) **Conditionals:** Conditional constructions indicate that the speaker is not trying to impose anything on the listener. For example, the conditional hedge *-myen* 'if' shows that a speaker respects a listener's feelings and circumstances.

(3) **Tag Question:** Tag questions are a useful resource for speakers trying to protect their and their addressee's face, since asking a question can be less face-threatening than making an assertion (Coates, 1996). For example as in (a) & (b),

(a) *mas iss-ci anh-a?*
taste exist-NOM not-INT
'Is it delicious, isn't it?'

(b) *ce key te nas-ci anhulkka-yo?*
that thing much better-NOM not-RL-POL
'Is it much better, isn't it?'

(4) **Impersonalizations**: Plural expressions *ta-tul* 'everyone', *wuli* 'we' or 'our' are used as hedges.

4.2 Frequency of Korean Hedges in Spoken Discourse

Table 4-2 summarizes the frequency of Korean hedges including all the inventories from my corpus. All the tokens of hedges in my data were classified based on Table 3-1 presented in Chapter 3. First, I divided Korean hedges into lexical hedges and syntactic hedges. Second, both lexical hedges and syntactic hedges were subcategorized into subtypes. The frequency of hedges in my data was investigated by the search engine *hanmalwu* of the *Seycong* corpus.

As shown in Table 4-2, 9,139 lexical hedges and 823 syntactic hedges were counted.

First, among lexical hedges, a total of 3,216 discourse markers (henceforth, DM) were counted. According to the inventory of DMs, there were 658 *kuntey*, 589 *mwe* type, 424 *com*, 379 *kunyang*, 339 *kulenikka* type, 300 *mak*, 266 *icey* type, 76 *kulaykaciko* type, 62 *ani*, 57 *cham*, 42 *isscanh-a* type, and 27 *ce*. Second, among lexical hedges, a total number of 3,445 interactive sentence enders (henceforth, ISEs) were counted. According to the inventory of ISEs, there were 792 *-canha(yo)*, 936 *-nuntey(yo)*, 190 *-ketun(yo)*, 58 *-telako(yo)*, 1030 *-ci(yo)*, 217 *-ney(yo)*, and 222 *-tay(yo)*. Third, among lexical hedges, a total number of 575 auxiliary verbs (henceforth, AV) were counted. According to the inventory of AVs, there were 380 *-kes kath-*, 27 *-ci molu-*, 2 *-tus ha-*, 61 *-na po-*, 7 *-e/ato toy-*, 17 *-e/a cwu-*, and 81 *-e/a po-*. Fourth, among lexical hedges, a total of 44 particles (henceforth, P) were counted. According to the inventory of Ps, there were 44 *-yo,* 0 *-(i)latunci*. Fifth, among lexical hedges, a total of 1,509 filler items (henceforth, F) were counted. According to the inventory of Fs, there were 762 *a*, 307 *ku*, 202 *e,* 148 *um*, 52 *i*, 14 *ca,* 13 *hum*, and 4 *he*. Sixth, among lexical hedges, a total of 108 adverbs (henceforth, Ab) were counted. According to the inventory of Ab, there were 66 *pyello,* 34

Table 4-2 Frequency of Korean Hedges

Classification		Code	Inventory	Frequency (Row Score)
Lexical Hedges	(1) Discourse Marker (DM)	1	*com/ccom*	424
		2	*mwe/mo/me/mwe-nya/ mwe-ci/way*	589
		3	*ani*	62
		4	*isscanh-a/ iss-ci/ iss-cyo*	42
		5	*ce/ceki*	27
		6	*icey/ incey*	266
		7	*mak*	300
		8	*cham*	57
		9	*kunyang*	376
		10	*kuntey*	658
		11	*kulenikka/ kunikka(n)/ kukka/ kunkka*	339
		12	*kulaykaciko/kulaykacko*	76
			Total	**3,216**
	(2) Interactive Sentence Ender (ISE)	1	*-canha(yo)*	792
		2	*-nuntey(yo)*	936
		3	*-ketun(yo)*	190
		4	*-telako(yo)*	58
		5	*-ci(yo)*	1030
		6	*-ney(yo)*	217
		7	*-tay(yo)*	222
			Total	**3,445**
	(3) Auxiliary Verb (AV)	1	*-kes kath-*	380
		2	*-ci molu-*	27
		3	*-tus ha-*	2
		4	*-na po-*	61
		5	*-e/a-to toy-*	7
		6	*-e/a cwu-*	17
	(3) Auxiliary Verb (AV)	7	*-e/a po-*	81
			Total	**575**
	(4) Particles (P)	1	*-(i)latunci*	0
		2	*-yo*	44
			Total	**44**

Lexical Hedges	(5) Filler (F)	1	*e*	202
		2	*a*	762
		3	*um*	148
		4	*hum*	13
		5	*ca*	14
		6	*he*	4
		7	*i*	52
		8	ku	307
			Total	**1,509**
	(6) Adverb (Ab)	1	*amato*	2
		2	*yakkan*	34
		3	*hoksi*	6
		4	*pyello*	66
		5	*taycheylo*	0
			Total	**108**
	(7) Suffix (Sf)	1	*-keyss-*	237
	(8) Phrase (Ph)	1	*-e/a/ kaciko/kwu*	4
		2	*-e/a kacko(kwu)*	1
			Total	**5**
			Total	***9,139***
Syntactic Hedges	(1) Main Clause Omission	1	*-e/ase(yo)/ -ko/kwu(yo)*	645
			Total	**645**
	(2) Conditional	1	*-myen*	23
	(3) Tag Question	1-1	*-ci anh-ullay(yo)?*	0
		1-2	-c*i a*nha(yo)?	19
		1-3	*-ci anhulkka(yo)?*	2
			Total	**21**
	(4) Impersonalization	1	ta*tul*/wuli	134
			Total	**134**
			Total	***823***

*Allomorphs are divided by slash (/).

yakkan, 6 *hoksi,* 2 *amato*, 0 *taycheylo*. Seventh, among lexical hedges, a total of 237 suffixes (Sf) were counted. According to the inventory of Sf, there were 237 *-keyss*. Eighth, among lexical hedges, a total of 5 phrases (Ph) were counted. According to the inventory of phrases, there were 4 *-e/a/ kaciko* type and 1 *-e/a kacko(kwu)*.

Next, as shown in Table 4-2, the frequency of syntactic hedges are as follows. Among syntactic hedges, there were 645 main clause omissions including *-e/ase(yo)/-ko/kwu(yo)/ -nikka(n)(yo),* 23 conditionals including *-myen*, 21 tag questions including 19 *-ci anha(yo)?*, 2 *-ci anhulkka(yo)?*, and 134 impersonalizations including *tatul/wuli*.

Table 4-3 summarizes the frequency and percentage of all hedges which appeared in my corpus. They are primarily divided into lexical hedges (including discourse markers, interactive sentence enders, auxiliary verbs, particles, fillers, adverbs, suffixes, and phrases) as well as syntactic hedges (including main clause omission, conditionals, tag questions, impersonalizations). There were 9,139 lexical hedges (91.8%) and 823 syntactic hedges (8.2%). In short, lexical hedges are

Table 4-3 Frequency & Percentage of All Hedges

Classification		Frequency	Percentage
Lexical Hedges	① Discourse Marker (DM)	3,216	32.3%
	② Interactive Sentence Ender (ISE)	3.,445	34.6%
	③ Auxiliary Verb(AV)	575	5.8%
	④ Particle (P)	44	0.4%
	⑤ Filler(F)	1,509	15.1%
	⑥ Adverb(Ab)	108	1.1%
	⑦ Suffix(Sf)	237	2.4%
	⑧ Phrase(PH)	5	0.1%
	Total	**9,139**	**91.8%**
Syntactic Hedges	⑨ Main Clause Omission	623	6.5%
	⑩ Conditional	21	0.2%
	⑪ Tag Question	21	0.2%
	⑫ Impersonalization	134	1.3%
	Total	**823**	**8.2%**
Total		**9,962**	**100.0%**

the dominant hedges in my corpus. Figure 4-1shows the percentage of all hedges in my corpus, which is spoken discourse in contemporary Korean.

Figure 4-1 Percentage of All Hedges

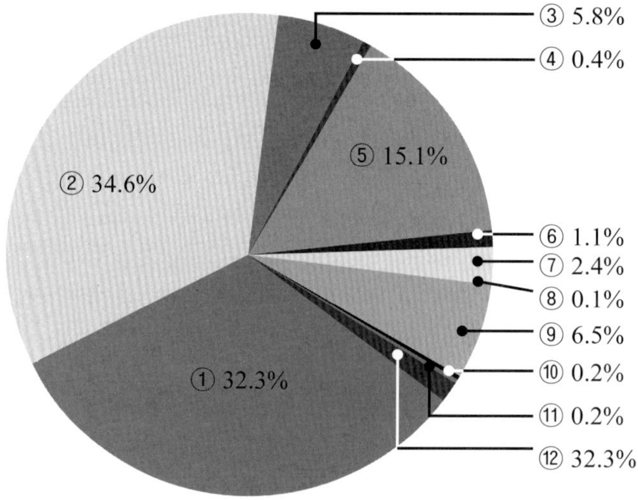

Table 4-4 summarizes the frequency and percentage of lexical hedges. Lexical hedges are subcategorized into discourse marker (DM), interactive sentence ender (ISE), auxiliary verb (AV), particle (P), filler (F), adverb (Ab), suffix (Sf), and phrase (Ph). In order to investigate the frequency of lexical hedges the search engine *hanmalwu* of *Seycong* Corpus was used. As shown in Table 4-4, there were 3,216 discourse markers (35.2%), 3,445 interactive sentence enders (37.7%), 575 auxiliary verbs (6.3%), 44 particles (0.5%), 1,509 fillers (16.5%), 108 adverbs (1.2%), 237 suffixes (2.6%), and 5 phrases (0.1%). In my corpus, the most frequently counted hedge among lexical hedges is interactive sentence enders (37.7%) followed by discourse markers (35.2%) and fillers (15.1%) (ISE > DM > F). The results prove that the Korean sentence enders such as interactive sentence enders (ISEs) encode hedging through discourse modality of interactive sentence enders. Figure 4-2 shows the percentage of each lexical hedge.

Table 4-4 Freq. & Perc. of Lexical Hedges

Lexical Hedges	Frequency	Percentage
① Discourse marker (DM)	3,216	35.2%
② Interactive sentence ender (ISE)	3,445	37.7%
③ Auxiliary verb (AV)	575	6.3%
④ Particle (P)	44	0.5%
⑤ Filler (F)	1,509	16.5%
⑥ Adverb (Ab)	108	1.2%
⑦ Suffix (Sf)	237	2.6%
⑧ Phrase (Ph)	5	0.1%
Total	**9,139**	**100%**

Figure 4-2 Percentage of Lexical Hedges

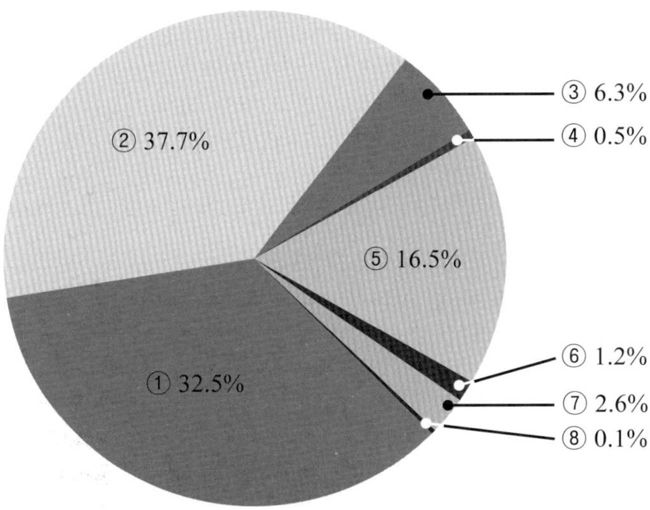

Table 4-5 summarizes the frequency and percentage of syntactic hedges. Syntactic hedges are subcategorized into main clause omission, conditional, rhetoric question, tag question, passive construction, and impersonalization. In order to investigate the frequency of syntactic hedges the search engine *hanmalwu* of *Seycong* Corpus was used. As

Table 4-5
Freq. & Perc. of Syntactic Hedges

Syntactic Hedges	Frequency	Percentage
① Main Clause Omission	645	79%
② Conditional	23	3%
③ Tag Question	21	2%
④ Impersonal-ization	134	16%
Total	**823**	**100%**

Figure 4-3
Perc. of Syntactic Hedges

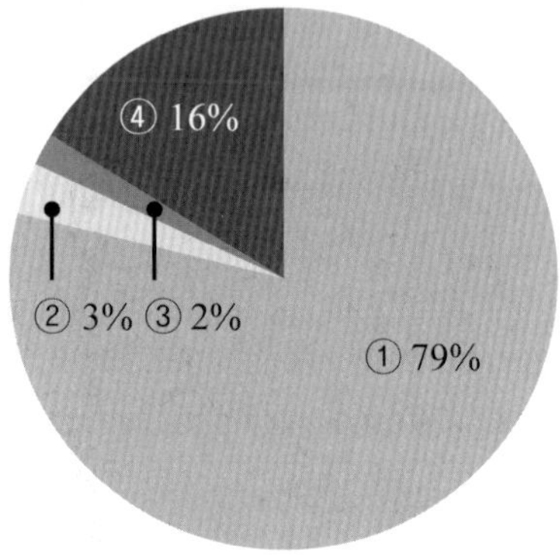

Table 4-6 Freq. & Perc. of Discourse Markers

DM	Frequency	Percentage
① *com / ccom*	424	13%
② *mwe / mo /me*	442	14%
③ *mwe-nya / mwe-ci*	94	3%
④ *way*	53	2%
⑤ *ani*	62	2%
⑥ *isscanh-a / iss-ci / iss-cyo*	42	1%
⑦ *ce / ceki*	27	1%
⑧ *icey / incey*	266	8%
⑨ *mak*	300	9%
⑩ *cham*	57	2%
⑪ *kunyang*	376	12%
⑫ *kuntey*	658	20%
⑬ *kulenikka / kunikka(n)/*	335	10%
⑭ *kukka / kunkka*	4	0%
⑮ *kulaykaciko/kwu*	66	2%
⑯ *Kulaykacko / kwu*	10	0%
Total	**3,216**	**100%**

Figure 4-4 Percentage of Discourse Markers

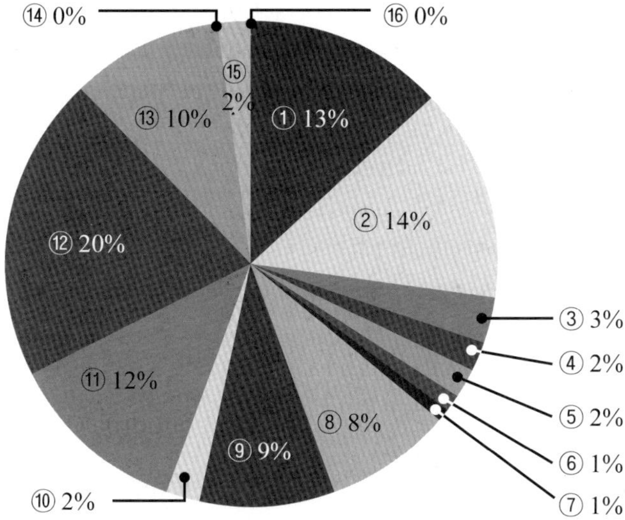

shown in Table 4-5, there were 645 main clause omissions (79%), 23 conditional (3%), 21 tag questions (2%), 134 impersonalizations (16%). In my corpus, the most frequently counted hedge among syntactic hedges is main clause omission (79%) followed by impersonalization (16%). One motivation of a main clause omission is to mitigate the assertiveness of various speech acts in terms of an indirect speech act ,since the main clause usually carries the speaker's assertion. Hence, by omitting a main clause, the speaker can give the addressee the option of making the final decision on the basis of the background information expressed in the unomitted clause. Thus, main clause omission functions as a hedge to mitigate illocutionary force. Figure 4-3 shows the percentage of each syntactic hedge.

The following six tables and six charts show the frequency and percentage of each lexical hedge item.

First, Table 4-6 summarizes the frequency and percentage of each discourse marker (henceforth, DM). The frequency of each DM was investigated by the search engine *hanmalwu* of *Seycong* corpus. As shown in Table 4-6, there were 424 *com/ccom* (13%), 442 *mwe/mo/me* (14%), 94 *mwe-nya/ mwe-ci*(3%), 53 *way* (2%), 62 *ani* (2%), 42 *isscanh-a/ iss-ci/ iss-cyo* (1%), 27 *ce* (1%), 266 *icey/ incey* (8%), 300 *mak* (9%), 57 *cham* (2%), 376 *kunyang* (12%), *658 kuntey* (20%), 335 *kulenikka/ kunikka(n)* (10%), 4 *kukka/ kunkka* (0%), 66 *kulaykaciko/kwu* (2%), 10 *kulaykacko* (0%). In my corpus, the most frequently counted hedge among discourse makers is *kuntey* (20%) followed by *mwe/mo/ me* (14%), *com/ccom*(13%), and *kunyang* (12%). Figure 4-4 shows the percentage of each discourse marker item.

Second, Table 4-7 summarizes the frequency and percentage of interactive sentence enders (henceforth, ISEs). The frequency of each ISE was investigated by the search engine *hanmalwu* of *Seycong* Corpus. As shown in Table 4-7, there were 792 *-canha(yo)* (23%), 936 *-nuntey(yo)* (27%), 190 *-ketun(yo)*(6%), 58 *-telako(yo)*(2%), 1,030 *-ci(yo)*(30%), 217 *-ney(yo)*(6%), 222 *-tay(yo)*(6%). In my corpus, the most frequently counted hedge among interactive sentence enders is *-ci(yo)*(30%) followed by *-nuntey(yo)* (27%), and *-canha(yo)* (16%). Figure 4-5 shows the percentage of each item.

Table 4-7 Freq. & Perc. of ISEs

ISE	Frequency	Percentage
① *-canha(yo)*	792	23%
② *-nuntey(yo)*	936	27%
③ *-ketun(yo)*	190	6%
④ *-telako(yo)*	58	2%
⑤ *-ci(yo)* / *-cyo*	1,030	30%
⑥ *-ney(yo)*	217	6%
⑦ *-tay / cay/ lay(yo)*	222	6%
Total	**3,445**	**100%**

Figure 4-5 Percentage of ISEs

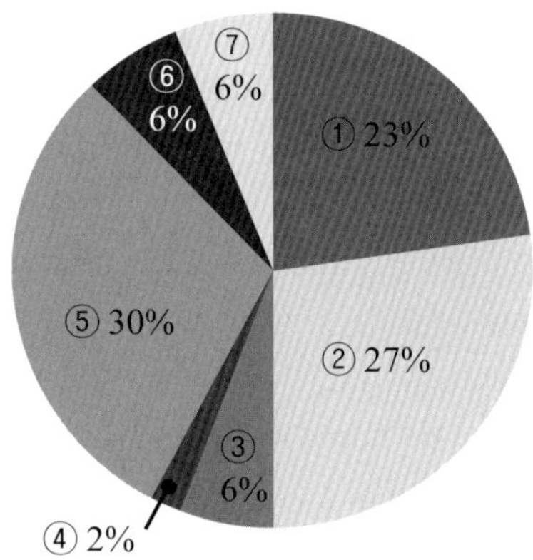

Third, Table 4-8 summarizes the frequency and percentage of auxiliary verbs (AV). The frequency of each AV was investigated by the search engine *hanmalwu* of *Seycong* Corpus. As shown in Table 4-8, there were 380 *-kes kath-* (66%), 27 *-ci molu* (5%), 2 *-tus ha* (0%), 61

-na po-(11%), 7 *-e/a-to toy-* (1%), 17 *-e/a cwu-* (3%), 81 *-e/a po-*(14%). In my corpus, the most frequently counted hedge among auxiliary verbs is *-kes kath-* (66%) followed by *-e/a po-*(14%). Figure 4-6 shows the percentage of each AV item.

Table 4-8 Freq. & Per. of Auxiliary Verbs

AV	Frequency	Percentage
① *-kes kath-*	380	66%
② *-ci molu-*	27	5%
③ *-tus ha-*	2	0%
④ *-na po-*	61	11%
⑤ *-e / a-to oy-*	7	1%
⑥ *-e / a cwu-*	17	3%
⑦ *-e / a po-*	81	14%
total	**575**	**100%**

Figure 4-6
Percentage of Auxiliary Verbs

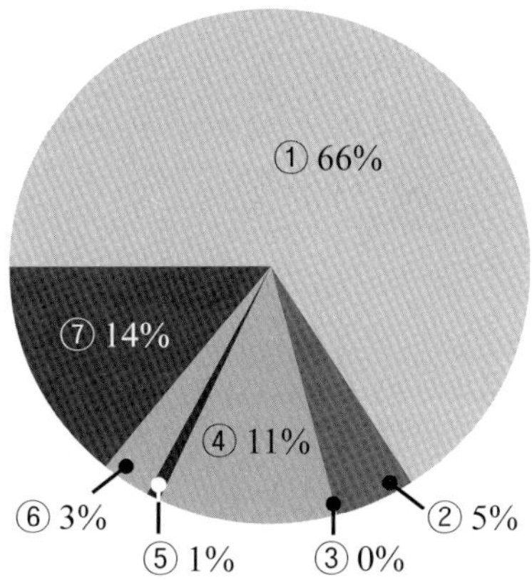

Fourth, Table 4-9 summarizes the frequency and percentage of each particle (P). The frequency of each particle was investigated by the search engine *hanmalwu* of *Seycong* Corpus. As shown in Table 4-9, there were 0 *-(i)latunci* (0%) and 44 *-yo*(16%) as particles. In my corpus, only the particle *-yo* appeared among particles. Figure 4-7 shows the percentage of each particle item.

Table 4-9 Freq. & Per. of Particles

Particles	Frequency	Percentage
-(i)latunci	0	0%
-yo	44	100%
total	**44**	**100%**

Figure 4-7 Frequency of Particles

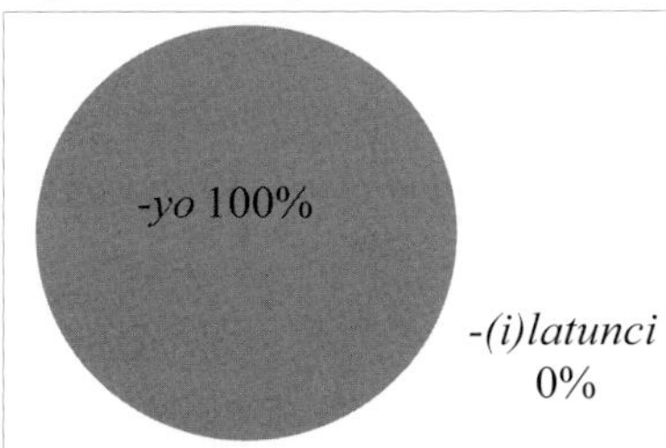

Fifth, Table 4-10 summarizes the frequency and percentage of filler items (F). The frequency of individual filler was investigated by the search engine *hanmalwu* of *Seycong* Corpus. As shown in Table 4-10, there were 207 *e* (13%), 762 *a* (50%), 148 *um* (10%), 15 *hum* (1%), 14 *ca* (1%), 2 *heye* (0%), 52 *i* (3%), 307 *ku* (20%). In my corpus, the most frequently counted hedge among fillers is *a* (50%) followed by *ku* (20%) and *e* (13%). Figure 4-8 shows the percentage of each filler item.

Table 4-10 Freq. & Per. of Fillers

Filler	Frequency	Percentage
e	207	13%
a	762	50%
um	148	10%
hum	15	1%
ca	14	1%
he	4	0%
i	52	3%
ku	307	20%
total	**1,509**	**100%**

Figure 4-8 Percentage of Fillers

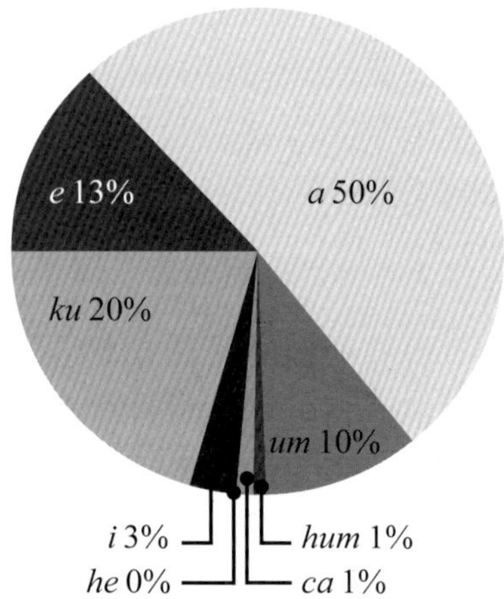

Table 4-11 Freq. & Perc. of Adverbs

Adverb	Frequency	Percentage
amato	2	2%
yakkan	34	31%
hoksi	6	6%
pyello	66	61%
taycheylo	0	0%
total	**108**	**100%**

Figure 4-9 Percentage of Adverbs

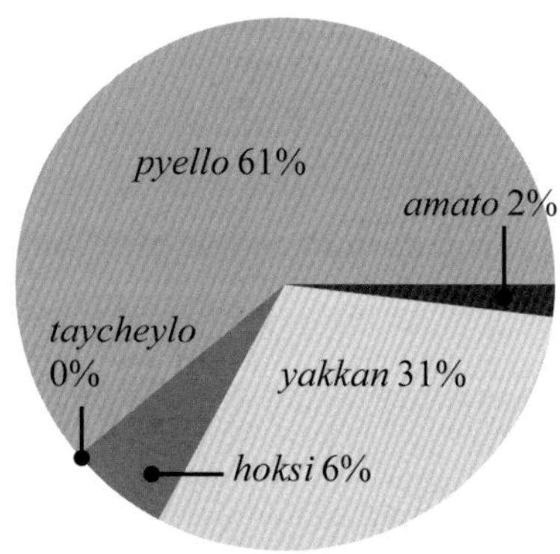

Sixth, Table 4-11 summarizes the frequency and percentage of adverbs (Ab). The frequency of each adverb was investigated by the search engine *hanmalwu* of *Seycong* Corpus. As shown in Table 4-11, there were 2 *amato* (2%), 34 *yakkan* (31%), 6 *hoksi* (6%), 66 *pyello* (61%), 0 *taycheylo* (0%). In my corpus, the most frequently counted hedge among adverbs is *pyello* (61%) followed by *yakkan* (31%). Figure 4-9 shows the percentage of each adverb item.

4.3 Summary

This chapter illustrates the frequency of eight lexical hedges (discourse marker, interactive sentence ender, auxiliary verb, particle, filler, adverb, suffix, and phrase) and syntactic hedges (main clause omission, conditional, tag question, and impersonalization) based on the classification of hedges in Korean spoken discourse. A total of 9,139 hedges in my corpus were analyzed. The import of this chapter is that this is the first attempt to classify Korean hedges in spoken discourse and investigate the frequency of Korean hedges empirically. The search engine *hanmalwu* of *Seycong* Corpus was used in order to analyze the frequency of each hedge item. The search engine searched all the hedge items including allomorphs and then I checked each item manually as well as excluded data which were not appropriate for hedges based on the classification. Therefore, the validity of the data is reliable.

CHAPTER 5

SOCIOPRAMATIC ANALYSIS OF INTERACTIVE SENTENCE ENDERS (ISEs)

In this chapter I will analyze the frequency of selected lexical hedges (seven interactive sentence enders, ISEs) in Korean spoken discourse in terms of sociopragmatics. The seven interactive sentence enders are *-canha(yo)*, *-nuntey(yo)*, *-ketun(yo)*, *-telako(yo)*, *-ci(yo)*, *-ney(yo)*, *-tay(yo)*. In order to analyze the meaning of hedge use in relation to sociopragmatic variables empirically, the statistical methods such as *t*-test, ANOVA, and post-hoc comparison were employed. In Section 5.1, the sociopragmatic variables are divided into social structural factors and social situational factors based on the social factors and language use in Table 5-1.

Table 5-1 Social Factors and Language Use

Social Structural Factors	Social Situational Factors
Gender	Formality of situation
Age	Solidarity/distance between interlocutors
Social class (education/ occupation)	Power relations between interlocutors
Region	Function/ends of utterances
Ethnicity/ nationality	Topic/context of conversation

For this study the social structural factors include five variables such as gender (female vs. male), gender composition of conversations (same-gender vs. mixed-gender), age (teens, 20s-30s, over 40s), occupation (housewife, office worker, student), and region (metropolitan area vs. non-metropolitan area). On the other hand, social situational factors include four variables such as the number of speakers in conversation (two-party conversations vs. multiple-party conversations), topic of conversation (personal topics vs. impersonal topics), social power relations between interlocutors, and social distance relations between interlocutors. In Section 5.2, the results and findings of the sociopragmatic analysis of seven hedge items in Section 5.1 will be summarized. In Section 5.3, I will re-examine two major findings of Section 5.2 with the results of the sociopragmatic analysis of seven auxiliary verbs (AVs), which are *-kes kath-, -ci molu-, -tus ha-, -na po-, -e/a-to toy-, -e/a cwu-,-e/a po-.*

5.1. Sociopragmatic Factor Analysis

5.1. 1. *-canha(yo)*

Table 5-2 Statistical Verification of -canha(yo) (t-test and ANOVA)

<table>
<tr><th colspan="2">Factors</th><th>Group</th><th>N</th><th>Mean</th><th>Fre-quency</th><th>Std. (Error) Deviation</th><th>t (F)-Value</th><th>P-Value</th></tr>
<tr><td rowspan="13">Social Structural Factors</td><td rowspan="2">Gender</td><td>F</td><td>112</td><td>3.92</td><td>439</td><td>3.542</td><td rowspan="2">(t) 1.348</td><td rowspan="2">0.179</td></tr>
<tr><td>M</td><td>107</td><td>3.30</td><td>353</td><td>3.257</td></tr>
<tr><td rowspan="3">Gender Composi-tion</td><td>FF</td><td>58</td><td>4.33</td><td>251</td><td>3.526</td><td rowspan="3">(F) 0.780</td><td rowspan="3">0.460</td></tr>
<tr><td>MF</td><td>58</td><td>3.79</td><td>220</td><td>3.365</td></tr>
<tr><td>MM</td><td>58</td><td>3.57</td><td>207</td><td>3.179</td></tr>
<tr><td rowspan="3">Age</td><td>Teens</td><td>24</td><td>3.54</td><td>85</td><td>3.217</td><td rowspan="3">(F) 0.031</td><td rowspan="3">0.970</td></tr>
<tr><td>20s-30s</td><td>158</td><td>3.65</td><td>577</td><td>3.198</td></tr>
<tr><td>Over 40s</td><td>37</td><td>3.51</td><td>130</td><td>4.388</td></tr>
<tr><td rowspan="3">Occupation</td><td>House-wife</td><td>17</td><td>4.18</td><td>71</td><td>4.433</td><td rowspan="3">(F) 0.254</td><td rowspan="3">0.776</td></tr>
<tr><td>Office worker</td><td>30</td><td>3.50</td><td>105</td><td>4.092</td></tr>
<tr><td>Student</td><td>172</td><td>3.58</td><td>616</td><td>3.182</td></tr>
<tr><td rowspan="2">Region</td><td>Metro-politan</td><td>122</td><td>3.94</td><td>481</td><td>3.635</td><td rowspan="2">(t) 1.623</td><td rowspan="2">0.106</td></tr>
<tr><td>Non-metro</td><td>97</td><td>3.21</td><td>311</td><td>3.079</td></tr>
</table>

Social Situational Factors	Number of Speakers	1:1	174	3.90	678	3.356	(t) 2.415	**<u>0.017</u>**
		Multi.	45	2.53	114	3.448		
	Topic	Imper-sonal	219	0.12	27	0.823	(t) -14.173	**<u>0.000</u>**
		Personal		3.49	765	3.367		
	Social Power	-	79	3.92	310	3.226	(t) 1.002	**0.317**
		+	140	3.44	482	3.512		
	Social Distance	-	174	3.66	636	3.216	(t) -0.330	**0.742**
		+	45	3.47	156	4.121		

<u>**Gender**</u>

Table 5-2 summarizes the results of the analysis of sociopragmatic variables of interactive sentence ender *-canha(yo)*, 'you know'. First, I analyzed the social structural variable of gender. A total frequency of 792 *-canha(yo)* hedges were counted from my data via the search engine, '*hanmalwu*' of *Seycong* corpus. In addition, 439 uses of *-canha(yo)* by 112 females (i.e., 3.92 uses/ female) and 353 uses of *-canha(yo)* by 107 males (i.e., 3.30 uses/male) were counted through investigating the gender of all the interlocutors, for a total of 792 uses of *-canha(yo).* I subsequently investigated the frequency of *-canha(yo)* uses by individual interlocutors followed by an independent *t*-test statistical analysis in order to investigate difference in usage by gender. As shown in table 5-2, the standard deviation of females is 3.542 while that of males is 3.257. In addition, the *t*-value is 1.348 and the P-value is 0.179. According to the *t*-test analysis, there is no significant difference between two groups if the P-value is greater than 0.05. Hence, my data shows that there is no statistical difference between females and males in terms of the frequency of using the ISE (interactive sentence ender) *-canha(yo).*

<u>**Gender composition**</u>

Second, an analysis of gender composition was conducted. According to the results of the search engine *hanmalwu* , there were 678 tokens of *-canha(yo)* counted in two-party conversations (two participants) while there were 114 tokens of *-canha(yo)* counted in multiple-party conversations (involving more than two participants) among the total number of 792 tokens of *canha(yo)*. Moreover, among two-party conversations there were 251 tokens used by 58 females (i.e., 4.33 tokens/person) in female-female (FF) gender composition, 220 tokens used by 58 males and females (i.e., 3.79 tokens/ person) in male-female (MF) gender composition, and 207 tokens used by 58 males (i.e., 3.57 tokens/person) in male-male (MM) gender composition. ANOVA was used in order to investigate the differences of gender composition. As shown in Table 5-2, the standard error deviation of female-female (FF) gender composition is 3.526, that of male-female (MF) gender composition is 3.365, and that of male-male (MM) gender composition is 3.179. In addition, the F-value is 0.780 and the P-value is 0.460. According to the ANOVA analysis, there is no significant difference among groups if the P-value is greater than 0.05. Hence, my data shows that there is no statistical difference among gender compositions (i.e., FF, MF, MM) in terms of the frequency of using ISE *-canha(yo)*.

Age

Third, the age variable was analyzed. According to the results of the search engine *hanmalwu*, among 792 tokens in my data, there were 85 tokens used by 24 interlocutors of the age group in their teens (i.e., 3.54 tokens/person), 577 tokens used by 158 interlocutors in their 20s-30s (i.e., 3.65 tokens/person), and 130 tokens used by 37 interlocutors in the over 40 age group (i.e., 3.51 tokens/ person). ANOVA was used in order to investigate the difference of each age group. As shown in Table 5-2, the standard error deviation of the teenage group is 3.271, that of those in their 20s-30s is 3.198, and that of those over the age of 40 is 4.388. In addition, the F-value is 0.031 and the P-value is 0.970. According to the analysis of ANOVA, there is no significant difference between groups if the P-value is greater than 0.05. Hence, my data shows that there is no statistical difference among age groups (i.e., teens, 20s-30s, and over 40s) in terms of the frequency of using the ISE *-canha(yo)*.

Occupation

Fourth, usage by occupational background was analyzed. According to the results of the search engine *hanmalwu*, among 792 tokens in my data, there were 71 tokens used by 17 housewives (i.e., 4.18 tokens/person), 105 tokens used by 30 office workers (i.e., 3.50 tokens/person), and 616 tokens used by 172 students (i.e., 3.58 tokens/person). ANOVA was used in order to investigate the differences by occupation. As shown in Table 5-2, the standard error deviation of housewives is 4.433, that of office workers is 4.092, and that of students is 3.182. In addition, the F-value is 0.254 and the P-value is 0.776. According to the analysis of ANOVA, there is no significant difference between groups if the P-value is greater than 0.05. Hence, my data shows that there is no statistical difference by occupation (housewives, office workers, or students) in terms of the frequency of using the ISE *-canha(yo)*.

Region

Fifth, usage by the region was analyzed. According to the results of the search engine *hanmalwu*, among 792 tokens in my data, there were 481 tokens used by 122 interlocutors (i.e., 3.94 tokens/person) from metropolitan areas such as *Seoul* city and cities in *Kyengki* Province while there were 311 tokens used by 97 interlocutors (i.e., 3.21 tokens/person) from non-metropolitan areas such as several different Korean provinces such as *Kangwen, Cenla, Kyengsang, Chwungcheng*, and so on. The independent *t*-test was used in order to investigate the differences by region (metropolitan areas vs. non-metropolitan areas). As shown in Table 5-2, the standard deviation of metropolitan areas is 3.635 while that of non-metropolitan areas is 3.079. In addition, the *t*-value is 1.623 and the P-value is 0.106. According to the analysis of the *t*-test, there is no significant difference between groups if the P-value is greater than 0.05. Hence, my data shows that there is no statistical difference by region (metropolitan vs. non-metropolitan area) in terms of the frequency of using the ISE *-canha(yo)*.

Number of Speakers

Sixth, usage by the number of speakers was analyzed. According to the results of the search engine *hanmalwu*, there were 678 tokens of *-canha(yo)* used by 174 interlocutors (i.e., 3.90 tokens/person) in two-party conversations (two participants) while there were 114 tokens of *-canha(yo*) used by 45 interlocutors (i.e., 2.53 token/person) in multiple-party conversations (more than two participants) among the total number of 792 tokens of *-canha(yo)*. The *t*-test was used in order to investigate the difference between two-party conversations (two participants) and multiple-party conversations (involving more than two participants). As shown in Table 5-2, the standard deviation of two-party conversations is 3.356 while that of multiple-party conversations is 3.448. In addition, the *t*-value is 2.415 and the P-value is 0.017. According to the *t*-test analysis, there is a significant difference between two groups if the P-value is smaller than 0.05. Hence, my data shows that there is a significant difference between two-party conversations and multiple-party conversations in terms of the frequency of using the ISE *-canha(yo)*. Since the *t*-value is a positive number (2.724) the result can be analyzed as showing that *-canha(yo)* is used more in two-party conversations than in multiple-party conversations.

Topic

Seventh, the topic (personal topics vs. impersonal topics) of conversation was analyzed. I distinguished personal topics (i.e., individual/ private topics such as boyfriend/girlfriend, grades, appearances, etc.) and impersonal topics (i.e., social issues, political issues such as the suicide by the former president, a college entrance exam, the free trade agreement, Korea's unification, etc.). According to the results of the search engine *hanmalwu*, among the total number of 792 tokens of *-canha(yo)* in my data, there were 27 tokens used by 219 interlocutors (0.12 tokens/ person) in conversations with impersonal topics while there 765 tokens used by 219 interlocutors (i.e., 3.49 tokens/person) in conversations with personal topics. The paired *t*-test[31] was used in order to investigate the difference between conversations with impersonal topics and conversations with personal topics. As shown in Table 5-2, the standard deviation of conversations with impersonal topics is 0.823 while that of conversations with personal topics is 3.367. In addition, the *t*-value is -14.173 and the P-value is 0.000. According to the *t*-test analysis, there is a significant difference between two groups if the P-value is smaller than 0.05. Hence, my data shows that there is a significant difference between conversations with impersonal topics and conversations with personal topics in terms of the frequency of using the ISE *-canha(yo)*. Since the *t*-value is a negative number (-14.173) the result can be analyzed as showing that *-canha(yo)* is used more in conversations with personal topics than in conversations with impersonal topics.

Power

Eighth, power relations between interlocutors were analyzed. According to the results of the search engine *hanmalwu*, among 792 tokens in my data, there were 310 tokens used by 79 interlocutors (i.e., 3.92 tokens/person) in conversations without power relations between interlocutors, while there were 482 tokens used by 140 interlocutors (i.e., 3.44 tokens/person) in conversations with power relations between interlocutors. The independent *t*-test was used in order to investigate the difference between conversations without power relations among interlocutors and conversations with power relations. As shown in Table 5-2, the standard deviation of conversations without power relations among interlocutors is 3.226 while that of conversation with power relations among interlocutors is 3.512. In addition, the *t*-value is 1.002 and P-value is 0.317. According to the *t*-test analysis, there is no significant difference between two groups if the P-value is greater than 0.05. Hence, my data shows that there is no statistical difference between conversations without power relations among interlocutors and conversations with power relations among interlocutors in terms of the frequency of using the ISE *-canha(yo)*.

---

31 The paired t-test is used when there is one measurement variable and two nominal variables.

Distance

Ninth, distance relations between interlocutors were analyzed. According to the results of the search engine *hanmalwu*, among 792 tokens in my data, there were 636 tokens used by 174 interlocutors (i.e., 3.66 tokens/person) in conversations without distance relations between interlocutors while there were 156 tokens used by 45 interlocutors (i.e., 3.47 tokens/person) in conversations with distance relations between interlocutors. The independent *t*-test was used in order to investigate the difference between conversations without distance relations and conversations with distance relations among interlocutors. As shown in Table 5-2, the standard deviation of conversations without distance relations among interlocutors is 3.216 while that of conversations with distance relations among interlocutors is 4.121. In addition, the *t*-value is 0.330 and the P-value is 0.742. According to the t-test analysis, there is no significant difference between two groups if the P-value is greater than 0.05. Hence, my data shows that there is no statistical difference between conversations without distance relations among interlocutors and conversations with distance relations among interlocutors in terms of the frequency of using the ISE *-canha(yo)*.

5.1.2 *-nuntey(yo)*

Table 5-3 Statistical Verification of *-nuntey(yo)* (t-test and ANOVA)

<table>
<tr><th colspan="2">Factors</th><th>Group</th><th>N</th><th>Mean</th><th>Frequency</th><th>Std. (Error) Deviation</th><th>t (F)-Value</th><th>P-Value</th></tr>
<tr><td rowspan="8">Social Structural Factors</td><td rowspan="2">Gender</td><td>F</td><td>112</td><td>4.31</td><td>483</td><td>3.227</td><td rowspan="2">(t) 0.174</td><td rowspan="2">0.862</td></tr>
<tr><td>M</td><td>107</td><td>4.23</td><td>453</td><td>3.487</td></tr>
<tr><td rowspan="3">Gender Composition</td><td>FF</td><td>58</td><td>5.24</td><td>304</td><td>3.624</td><td rowspan="3">(F) 3.020</td><td rowspan="3">0.051</td></tr>
<tr><td>MF</td><td>58</td><td>3.83</td><td>222</td><td>2.811</td></tr>
<tr><td>MM</td><td>58</td><td>5.14</td><td>298</td><td>3.841</td></tr>
<tr><td rowspan="3">Age</td><td>Teens</td><td>24</td><td>4.13</td><td>99</td><td>3.591</td><td rowspan="3">(F) 4.644</td><td rowspan="3"><u>0.011</u></td></tr>
<tr><td>20s-30s</td><td>158</td><td>4.64</td><td>733</td><td>3.470</td></tr>
<tr><td>Over 40s</td><td>37</td><td>2.81</td><td>104</td><td>2.093</td></tr>
</table>

Social Structural Factors	Occupation	Housewife	17	2.65	45	2.206	(F) 3.879	0.022
		Office worker	30	3.40	102	2.527		
		Student	172	4.59	789	3.502		
	Region	Metropolitan	122	4.52	552	3.589	(t) 1.243	0.215
		Non-metro	97	3.96	384	3.010		
Social Situational Factors	Number of Speakers	1:1	174	4.74	824	3.494	(t) 5.849	0.000
		Multi.	45	2.49	112	1.866		
	Topic	Impersonal	219	0.05	12	0.247	(t) -18.345	0.000
		Personal		4.22	924	3.345		
	Power	-	79	5.01	396	3.543	(t) 2.481	0.014
		+	140	3.86	540	3.173		
	Distance	-	174	4.38	762	3.320	(t) 0.915	0.361
		+	45	3.87	174	3.468		

Gender

Table 5-3 summarizes the results of the analysis of sociopragmatic variables of interactive sentence ender *-nuntey(yo)*[32]. First, I analyzed the social structural variable of gender. A total frequency of 936 *-nuntey(yo)* hedges were counted from my data via the search engine called *hanmalwu* of *Seycong* corpus. In addition, 483 uses of *-nuntey(yo)* by 112 females (i.e., 4.31 uses/female) and 453 uses of *-nuntey(yo)* by 107 males (i.e., 4.23 uses/male) were counted through investigating the gender of all the interlocutors, for a total of 936 uses of *-nuntey(yo)*. I subsequently investigated the frequency of *-nuntey(yo)* uses by individual interlocutors followed by the independent *t*-test statistical analysis in order to

32 *-nuntey* is used for verbs, *-(u)ntey* for adjectives in the present tense. With the anterior suffix *-ess/ass*, it is invariably *-nuntey regardless of verbs or adjectives* (H.S. Lee, 1999).

Table 5-4 Post-hoc Analysis of Age Associated with the Use of *-nuntey(yo)*

	I	J	I-J	Std. Error	P-Value
Dunnett T3	Teens	20s-30s	-0.514	0.783	0.883
		Over 40s	1.314	0.810	0.299
	20s-30s	Teens	0.514	0.783	0.883
		Over 40s	1.828*	0.441	0.000
	Over 40s	Teens	-1.314	0.810	0.299
		20s-30s	-1.828*	0.441	0.000

Table 5-5
Post-hoc Analysis of Occupation Associated with the Use of *-nuntey(yo)*

	I	J	I-J	Std. Error	P-Value
Dunnett T3	Housewife	Office worker	-0.753	0.707	0.641
		Student	-1.940*	0.598	0.010
	Office worker	Housewife	0.753	0.707	0.641
		Student	-1.187	0.533	0.088
	Student	Housewife	1.940*	0.598	0.010
		Office worker	1.187	0.533	0.088

investigate difference in usage by gender. As shown in Table 5-3, the standard deviation of females is 3.227 while that of males is 3.487. In addition, the t-value is 0.174 and the P-value is 0.862. According to the *t*-test analysis, there is no significant difference between two groups if the P-value is greater than 0.05. Hence, my data shows that there is no statistical difference between females and males in terms of the frequency of using the ISE (interactive sentence ender) *-nuntey(yo)*.

Gender composition

Second, an analysis of gender composition was conducted. According to the results of the search engine *hanmalwu* , there were 824 tokens of *-nuntey(yo)* used by 174 interlocutors (i.e., 4.74 tokens/person) in two-party conversations (two participants) while there were 112 tokens of *-nuntey(yo)* used by 45 interlocutors (i.e., 2.49 token/person) in multi- party conversations (more than two participants) among the total number of 936 tokens of *-nuntey(yo)*. Moreover, among two-party conversations there were 304 tokens used by 58 females (i.e., 5.24 tokens/ person) in female-female (FF) gender composition, 222 tokens used by 58 males and females (i.e., 3.83 tokens/ person) in male-female (MF) gender composition, and 298 tokens used by 58 males (i.e., 5.14 tokens/ person) in male-male (MM) gender composition. ANOVA was used in order to investigate the differences of gender composition. As shown in Table 5-3, the standard error deviation of female-female (FF) gender composition is 3,624, that of male-female (MF) gender composition is 2.881, and that of male-male (MM) gender composition is 3.841. In addition, the F-value is 3.020 and the P-value is 0.051. According to the ANOVA analysis, there is no significant difference among groups if the P-value is greater than 0.05. Hence, my data shows that there is no statistical difference among gender compositions (i.e., FF, MF, MM) in terms of the frequency of using the ISE *-nuntey(yo)*.

Age

Third, the age variable was analyzed. According to the results of the search engine *hanmalwu*, among 936 tokens in my data, there were 99 tokens used by 24 interlocutors of the age group in their teens (i.e., 4.13 tokens/person), 733 tokens used by 158 interlocutors in their 20s-30s (i.e., 4.64 tokens/person), and 104 tokens used by 37 interlocutors in the over 40 age group (i.e., 2.81 tokens/ person). ANOVA was used in order to investigate the difference of each age group. As shown in Table 5-3, the standard error deviation of the teenage group is 3.591, that of those in their 20s-30s is 3.470, and that of those over the age of 40 is 2.093. In addition, the F-value is 4.644 and the P-value is 0.011. According to the analysis of ANOVA, there is a significant difference among groups if the P-value is smaller than 0.05. The Dunnett T3 test for Post-hoc analysis was used in order to verify the result. According to the results of Post-hoc analysis in Table 5-4, the mean difference (I-J) of I group (20s-30s) and J group (over 40s) is 1.828 and the P-value is 0.000. Since the P-value is smaller than 0.05 and the mean difference is positive value, my data shows that the ISE -*nuntey (yo)*is used more by the age group of 20s-30s than by the age group of over 40s.

Occupation

Fourth, usage by occupational background was analyzed. According to the results of the search engine *hanmalwu*, among 936 tokens in my data, there were 45 tokens used by 17 housewives (i.e., 2.65 tokens/person), 102 tokens used by 30 office workers (i.e., 3.40 tokens/person), and 789 tokens used by 172 students (i.e., 4.59 tokens/person). ANOVA was used in order to investigate the differences by occupation. As shown in the Table 5-2, the standard error deviation of housewives is 2.206, that of office workers is 2.527, and that of students is 3.502. In addition, the F-value is 3.879 and the P-value is 0.022. According to the analysis of ANOVA, there is a significant difference between groups if the P-value is smaller than 0.05. The Dunnett T3 test for Post-hoc analysis was used in order to verify the result. According to the results of Post-hoc analysis in Table 5-5, the mean difference (I-J) of I group (student) and J group (housewife) is 1.940 and the P-value is 0.010. Since the P-value is smaller than 0.05 and the mean difference is a positive value, my data shows that the ISE -*nuntey (yo)*is used more by students than by housewives.

Region

Fifth, usage by the region was analyzed. According to the results of the search engine *hanmalwu*, among 936 tokens in my data, there were 552 tokens used by 122 interlocutors (i.e., 4.52 tokens /person) from metropolitan areas such as *Seoul* city and cities in *Kyengki* Province while there were 384 tokens used by 97 interlocutors (i.e., 3.96 tokens/person) from non-metropolitan areas such as several different Korean provinces such as *Kangwen, Cenla, Kyengsang, Chwungcheng*, and so on. The independent t-test was used in order to investigate the differences by region (metropolitan areas vs. non-metropolitan areas). As shown in Table 5-3, the standard deviation of metropolitan areas is 3.589 while that of non-metropolitan areas is 3.010. In addition, the *t*-value is 1.243 and the P-value is 0.215. According to the *t*-test analysis, there is no significant difference between two groups if the P-value is greater than 0.05. Hence, my data shows that there is no statistical difference between metropolitan areas and non-metropolitan areas in terms of the frequency of using the ISE *-nuntey (yo)*.

Number of Speakers

Sixth, the independent *t*-test was used in order to investigate the difference between two-party conversations (two participants) and multiple-party conversations (involving more than two participants). According to the result of search engine *hanmalwu*, there were 824 tokens of *-nuntey (yo)* used by 174 interlocutors (i.e., 4.74 tokens/person) in two-party conversations (two participants) while there were 112 tokens of *-nuntey(yo)* used by 45 interlocutors (i.e., 2.49 token/person) in multiple-party conversations (more than two participants) among the total number of 936 tokens of *-nuntey (yo)*. As shown in Table 5-3, the standard deviation of two-party conversations is 3.494 while that of multiple-party conversations is 1.866. In addition, the t-value is 5.849 and the P-value is 0.000. According to the t-test analysis, there is a significant difference between two groups if the P-value is smaller than 0.05. Hence, my data shows that there is a significant difference between two-party conversations and multiple-party conversations in terms of the frequency of using the ISE *-nuntey(yo)*. Since the t-value is a positive number (4.5.849) the result can be analyzed as showing that *-nuntey(yo)* is used more in two-party conversations than in multiple-party conversations.

Topic

Seventh, the topic (personal topics vs. impersonal topics) of conversation was analyzed. I distinguish personal topics (i.e., individual/

private topics such as boyfriend/girlfriend, grades, appearances, etc.) and impersonal topics (i.e., social, political topic such as the suicide of the former president, a college entrance exam, free trade agreement, Korea's unification, etc.). According to the results of the search engine *hanmalwu*, among 936 tokens in my data, there were 12 tokens used by 219 interlocutors (0.05 tokens/person) with impersonal topics while there were 924 tokens used by 219 interlocutors (i.e., 4.22 tokens/person) in conversations with personal topics. The paired *t*-test was used in order to investigate the difference between conversations with public topics and conversations with private topics. As shown in Table 5-3, the standard deviation of conversations with an impersonal topic is 0.247 while that of conversations with a personal topic is 3.345. In addition, the *t*-value is -18.345 and the P-value is 0.000. According to the paired *t*-test analysis, there is a significant difference between two groups if the P-value is smaller than 0.05. Hence, my data shows that there is a significant difference between conversations with an impersonal topic and conversations with a personal topic in terms of the frequency of using the ISE *-nuntey(yo)*. Since the *t*-value is a negative number (-18.345) the result can be analyzed as showing that *-nuntey(yo)* is used more in conversations with personal topics than in conversations with impersonal topics.

Power

Eighth, power relations between interlocutors were analyzed. According to the results of the search engine *hanmalwu*, among 936 tokens in my data, there were 396 tokens used by 79 interlocutors (i.e., 5.01 tokens/person) in conversations without power relations between interlocutors, while there were 540 tokens used by 140 interlocutors (i.e., 3.86 tokens/person) in conversations with power relations between interlocutors. The independent *t*-test was used in order to investigate the difference between conversations without power relations and conversations with power relations among interlocutors. As shown in Table 5-3, the standard deviation of conversations without power relations among interlocutors is 3.543 while that of conversations with power relations among interlocutors is 3.173. In addition, the *t*-value is 2.481 and P-value is 0.014. According to the *t*-test analysis, there is a significant difference

Table 5-6 Statistical Verification of *-ketun(yo)* (t-test and ANOVA)

Factors		Group	N	Mean	Frequency	Std. (Error) Deviation	t (F) Value	P-Value
Social Structural Factors	Gender	F	112	1.01	113	2.133	1.260	0.210
		M	107	0.72	77	1.139		
	Gender Composition	FF	58	1.24	72	2.536	1.141	0.322
		MF	58	1.05	61	1.711		
		MM	58	0.72	42	1.039		
	Age	Teens	24	0.83	20	1.404	0.106	0.899
		20s-30s	158	0.90	142	1.883		
		Over 40s	37	0.76	28	1.116		
	Occupation	Housewife	17	0.94	16	1.197	0.170	0.844
		Office worker	30	0.70	21	1.236		
		Student	172	0.89	153	1.840		
	Region	Metropolian	122	1.09	133	1.933	2.245	0.026
		Non-metro	97	0.59	57	1.375		
Social Situational Factors	Number of Speakers	1:1	174	1.01	175	1.867	3.637	0.000
		Multi	45	0.33	15	0.798		
	Topic	Impersonal	219	0.00	1	0.068	-7.376	0.000
		Personal		0.86	189	1.721		
	Power	-	79	0.91	72	2.027	0.282	0.778
		+	140	0.84	118	1.533		
	Distance	-	174	0.85	148	1.486	-0.287	0.775
		+	45	0.93	42	2.453		

between two groups if the P-value is smaller than 0.05. Hence, my data shows that there is a significant difference between conversation without power relations and conversation with power relations among interlocutors in terms of the frequency of using ISE *-nuntey(yo)*. Since the *t*-value is a positive number (2.481) the result can be analyzed as showing that *-nuntey (yo)* is used more in conversations without power relations than in conversations with power relations among interlocutors in terms of the frequency of using ISE *-nuntey(yo)*.

Distance

Ninth, distance relations between interlocutors were analyzed. According to the results of the search engine *hanmalwu*, among 936 tokens in my data, there were 762 tokens used by 174 interlocutors (i.e., 4.38 tokens/person) in conversations without distance relations between interlocutors while there were 174 tokens used by 45 interlocutors (i.e., 3.87 tokens/person) in conversations with distance relations between interlocutors. The independent *t*-test was used in order to investigate the difference between conversation without distance relations and conversation with distance relations among interlocutors. As shown in Table 5-3, the standard deviation of conversations without distance relations among interlocutors is 3.320 while that of conversations with distance relations among interlocutors is 3.468. In addition, the t-value is 0.915 and the P-value is 0.361. According to the *t*-test analysis, there is no significant difference between two groups if the P-value is greater than 0.05. Hence, my data shows that there is no statistical difference between conversations without distance relations among interlocutors and conversations with distance relations among interlocutors in terms of the frequency of using the ISE *-nuntey(yo)*.

5.1.3 *-ketun(yo)*

Gender

Table 5-6 summarizes the results of the analysis of the sociopragmatic variables of the interactive sentence ender *-ketun(yo)*. First, I analyzed the gender factor among many social structural variables. A total frequency of 190 *-ketun(yo)* hedges were counted from my data via the search engine called *hanmalwu* of *Seycong* corpus. In addition, 113 uses of *-ketun(yo)* by 112 females (i.e., 1.01uses/ female) and 77 uses of *-ketun(yo)* by 107 males (i.e., 0.72 uses/male) were counted by investigating the gender of all the interlocuters, for a total of 190 uses of *-ketun(yo)*. I subsequently investigated the frequency of *-ketun(yo)* uses by individual interlocutors followed by the independent *t*-test statistical analysis in order to investigate difference in usage by gender. As shown in Table 5-6, the standard deviation of females is 2.133 while that of males is 1.139. In addition, the *t*-value is 1.260 and the P-value is 0.210. According to the *t*-test analysis, there is no significant difference between two groups if the P-value is greater than 0.05. Hence, my data shows that there is no statistical difference between females and males in terms of the frequency of using the ISE (interactive sentence ender) *-ketun(yo)*.

Gender composition

Second, an analysis of gender composition was conducted. According to the results of the search engine *hanmalwu*, there were 175 tokens of *-ketun(yo)* used by 174 interlocutors (i.e., 1.01tokens/ person) in two-party conversations (two participants) while there were 15 tokens of *-ketun(yo)* used by 45 interlocutors (i.e., 0.33 token/person) in multiple-party conversations (more than two participants) among the total number of 190 tokens of *-ketun(yo)*. Moreover, among two-party conversations there were 72 tokens used by 58 females (i.e., 1.24 tokens/ person) in female-female (FF) gender composition, 61 tokens used by 58 males and females (i.e., 1.05 tokens/ person) in male-female (MF) gender composition, and 42 tokens used by 58 males (i.e., 0.72 tokens/ person) in male-male (MM) gender composition. ANOVA was used in order to investigate the differences of gender composition. As shown in Table 5-6, the standard error deviation of female-female (FF) gender composition is 2.536, that of male-female (MF) gender composition is 1.711, and that of male-male (MM) gender composition is 1.039. In addition, the F-value is 1.141 and the P-value is 0.322. According to the ANOVA analysis, there is no significant difference among groups if the P-value is greater than 0.05. Hence, my data shows that there is no statistical difference among gender composition (i.e., FF, MF, MM) in terms of the frequency of using the ISE *-ketun(yo)*.

Age

Third, the age variable was analyzed. According to the results of the search engine *hanmalwu*, among 190 tokens in my data, there were 20 tokens used by 24 interlocutors of the age group in their teens (i.e., 0.83 tokens/person), 142 tokens used by 158 interlocutors in their 20s-30s (i.e., 0.90 tokens/person), and 28 tokens used by 37 interlocutors in the over 40 age group (i.e., 0.76 tokens/ person). ANOVA was used in order to investigate the difference of each age group. As shown in Table 5-6, the standard error deviation of the teenage group is 1.404, that of those in their 20s-30s is 1.833, and that of those over the age of 40 is 1.116. In addition, the F-value is 0.106 and the P-value is 0.899. According to the analysis of ANOVA, there is no significant difference between groups if the P-value is greater than 0.05. Hence, my data shows that there is no statistical difference among age groups (i.e., teens, 20s-30s, and over 40s) in terms of the frequency of using the ISE *-ketun(yo)*.

Occupation

Fourth, usage by occupational background was analyzed. According to the results of the search engine *hanmalwu*, among 190 tokens in my data, there were 16 tokens used by 17 housewives (i.e., 0.94 tokens/person), 21 tokens used by 30 office workers (i.e., 0.70 tokens/person), and 153 tokens used by 172 students (i.e., 0.89 tokens/person). ANOVA was used in order to investigate the differences by occupation. As shown in Table 5-6, the standard error deviation of housewives is 1.197, that of office workers is 1.236, and that of students is 1.840. In addition, the F-value is 0.170 and the P-value is 0.844. According to the analysis of ANOVA, there is no significant difference between groups if the P-value is greater than 0.05. Hence, my data shows that there is no statistical difference by occupation (housewives, office workers, or students) in terms of the frequency of using the ISE *-ketun(yo)*.

Region

Fifth, usage by the region was analyzed. According to the results of the search engine *hanmalwu*, among 190 tokens in my data, there were 133 tokens used by 122 interlocutors (i.e., 1.09 tokens /person) from metropolitan areas such as *Seoul* city and cities in *Kyengki* Province while there were 57 tokens used by 97 interlocutors (i.e., 0.59 tokens/person) from non-metropolitan areas such as the Korean provinces of *Kangwen, Cenla, Kyengsang, Chwungcheng*, and so on. The independent *t*-test was used in order to investigate the differences by region (metropolitan areas vs. non-metropolitan areas). As shown in Table 5-6, the standard deviation of metropolitan areas is 1.933 while that of non-metropolitan areas is 1.375. In addition, the *t*-value is 2.245 and the P-value is 0.026. According to the *t*-test analysis, it is said that there is significant difference between two groups if the P-value is smaller than 0.05. Hence, my data shows that there is a significant difference between metropolitan areas and non-metropolitan areas. Since the *t*-value is a positive number (2.245) the result can be analyzed as showing that <u>*-ketun(yo)* is used more in metropolitan areas than non-metropolitan areas in terms of the frequency of using the ISE *-ketun(yo)*.</u>

Number of Speakers

Sixth, the independent *t*-test was used in order to investigate the difference between two-party conversations (two participants) and multiple-party conversations (involving more than two participants). According to the results of the search engine *hanmalwu*, there were 175 tokens of *-ketun(yo)* used by 174 interlocutors (i.e., 1.01tokens/person) in two-party conversations (two participants) while there were 15 tokens of *-ketun(yo)* used by 45 interlocutors (i.e., 0.33 token/person) in multiple-party conversations (more than two participants) among the total number of 190 tokens of *-ketun(yo)*. As shown in Table 5-6, the standard deviation of two-party conversations is 1.867 while that of multiple-party conversations is 0.798. In addition, the *t*-value is 3.637 and the P-value is 0.000. According to the *t*-test analysis, it is said that there is a significant difference between two groups if the P-value is smaller than 0.05. Hence, my data shows that there is a significant difference between two-party conversations and multiple-party conversations in terms of the frequency of using the ISE *-ketun(yo)*. Since the t-value is a positive number (3.637) the result can be analyzed as showing that *-ketun(yo)* is used more in two-party conversations than in multiple-party conversations.

Topic

Seventh, the topic (personal topics vs. impersonal topics) of conversation was analyzed. I distinguish personal topics (i.e., individual/private topics) and impersonal topics (i.e., social topics, political topics such as a suicide of the former president, a college entrance exam, free trade agreement, Korea's unification, etc.). According to the results of the search engine *hanmalwu*, among 190 tokens in my data, there was 1 token used by 219 interlocutors (0.00 tokens/person) with impersonal topics while there were 189 tokens used by 219 interlocutors (i.e., 0.86 tokens/person) in conversations with personal topics. The paired *t*-test was used in order to investigate the difference between conversations with impersonal topics and conversations with personal topics. As shown in Table 5-6, the standard deviation of conversation with impersonal topics is 0.068 while that of conversation with personal topics is 1.721. In addition, the t-value is -7.376 and the P-value is 0.0000. According to the t-test analysis, there is a significant difference between two groups if the P-value is smaller than 0.05. Hence, my data shows that there is a significant difference between conversations with personal topics and conversations with impersonal topics in terms of the frequency of using the ISE-*ketun(yo)*. Since the t-value is a negative number (-7.376) the result can be analyzed as showing that *-ketun(yo)* is used more in conversations with personal topic than in conversations with impersonal topic.

Power

Eighth, power relations between interlocutors were analyzed. According to the results of the search engine *hanmalwu*, among 190 tokens in my data, there were 72 tokens used by 79 interlocutors (i.e., 0.91 tokens/person) in conversations without power relations between interlocutors, while there were 118 tokens used by 140 interlocutors (i.e., 0.84 tokens/person) in conversations with power relations between interlocutors. The independent *t*-test was used in order to investigate the difference between conversations without power relations and conversations with power relations among interlocutors. As shown in Table 5-6, the standard deviation of conversations without power relations among interlocutors is 2.027 while that of conversations with power relations among interlocutors is 1.533. In addition, the *t*-value is 0.282 and the P-value is 0.778. According to the *t*-test analysis, there is no significant difference between two groups if the P-value is greater than 0.05. Hence, my data shows that there is no statistical difference between conversations without power relations among interlocutors and conversations with power relations among interlocutors in terms of the frequency of using the ISE *-ketun(yo)*.

Distance

Ninth, distance relations between interlocutors were analyzed. According to the results of the search engine *hanmalwu*, among 190 tokens in my data, there were 148 tokens used by 174 interlocutors (i.e., 0.85 tokens/person) in conversations without distance relations between interlocutors while there were 42 tokens used by 45 interlocutors (i.e., 0.93 tokens/person) in conversations with distance relations between interlocutors. The independent *t*-test was used in order to investigate the difference between conversations without distance relations and conversations with distance relations among interlocutors. As shown in Table 5-6, the standard deviation of conversations without distance relations among interlocutors is 1.486 while that of conversations with distance relations among interlocutors is 2.453. In addition, the t-value is -0.287 and the P-value is 0.775. According to the t-test analysis, there is no significant difference between two groups if the P-value is greater than 0.05. Hence, my data shows that there is no statistical difference between conversations without distance relations among interlocutors and conversations with distance relations among interlocutors in terms of the frequency of using ISE *-ketun(yo)*.

5.1.4 *-telako(yo)*[33]

Table 5-7 Statistical Verification of *-telako(yo)* (t-test and ANOVA)

Factors		Group	N	Mean	Frequency	Std. (Error) Deviation	t (or F)-Value	P-Value
Social Structural Factors	Gender	F	112	0.35	39	1.327	1.266	0.207
		M	107	0.18	19	0.511		
	Gender Composition	FF	58	0.26	15	0.890	0.870	0.421
		MF	58	0.45	26	1.602		
		MM	58	0.19	11	0.476		
	Age	Teens	24	0.08	2	0.408	2.561	0.080
		20s-30s	158	0.22	34	0.717		
		Over 40s	37	0.59	22	1.936		
	Occupation	Housewife	17	0.12	2	0.332	5.046	0.007
		Office worker	30	0.80	24	2.219		
		Student	172	0.19	32	0.640		
	Region	Metropolitan	122	0.31	38	1.220	0.762	0.447
		Non-metro	97	0.21	20	0.676		
	Number of Speakers	1:1	174	0.30	52	1.092	0.975	0.331
		Multi	45	0.13	6	0.625		

33 The allomorph of *-telakwu (yo)*of *-telako(yo)* was considered when counting the frequency.

Social Situational Factors	Topic	Imper-sonal	219	0.01	3	0.117	-3.566	0.000
		Personal		0.25	55	0.994		
	Power	-	79	0.19	15	0.681	-0.820	0.413
		+	140	0.31	43	1.162		
	Distance	-	174	0.25	44	1.028	-0.342	0.732
		+	45	0.31	14	0.973		

Table 5-8
Post-hoc Analysis of Occupation Associated with the Use of *-telako(yo)*

	I	J	I-J	Std. Error	P-Value
LSD	housewife	office worker	-0.682	0.303	0.025
		student	-0.068	0.253	0.787
	office worker	housewife	0.682	0.303	0.025
		student	0.614	0.197	0.002
	student	housewife	0.068	0.253	0.787
		office worker	-0.614	0.197	0.002

Gender

Table 5-7 summarizes the results of analysis of sociopragmatic variables of interactive sentence ender *-telako(yo)*. First, I analyzed the gender factor among many social variables. A total frequency of 58 *-telako(yo)* hedges were counted from my data via the search engine called *hanmalwu* of *Seycong* corpus. In addition, 39 uses of *-telako(yo)* by 112 females (i.e., 0.35 uses/ female) and 19 uses of *-telako(yo)* by 107 males (i.e., 0.18 uses/male) were counted through investigating the gender of all the interlocutors, for a total of 58 uses of *-telako(yo)*. I subsequently investigated the frequency of *-telako(yo)* uses by individual interlocutors followed by the independent *t*-test statistical analysis in order to investigate difference in usage by gender. As shown in Table 5-7, the standard deviation of females is 1.327 while that of males is 0.511. In addition, the *t*-value is 1.266 and the P-value is 0.207. According to the t-test analysis, there is no significant difference between two groups if the P-value is greater than 0.05. Hence, my data shows that there is no statistical difference between females and males in terms of the frequency of using the ISE *-telako(yo)*.

Gender composition

Second, an analysis of gender composition was conducted. According to the results of the search engine *hanmalwu*, there were 52 tokens of *-telako(yo)* used by 174 interlocutors (i.e., 0.30 tokens/ person) in two-party conversations (two participants) while there were 6 tokens of *-telako(yo)* used by 45 interlocutors (i.e., 0.13 token/person) in multiple-party conversations (more than two participants) among the total number of 58 tokens of *-telako(yo)*. Moreover, among two-party conversations there were 15 tokens used by 58 females (i.e., 0.26 tokens/ person) in female-female (FF) gender composition, 26 tokens used by 58 males and females (i.e., 0.45 tokens /person) in male-female (MF) gender composition, and 11 tokens used by 58 males (i.e., 0.19 tokens/ person) in male-male (MM) gender composition. ANOVA was used in order to investigate the differences of gender composition. As shown in Table 5-7, the standard error deviation of female-female (FF) gender composition is 0.890, that of male-female (MF) gender composition is 1.602, and that of male-male (MM) gender composition is 0.476. In addition, the F-value is 0.870 and the P-value is 0.421. According to the ANOVA analysis, there is no significant difference among groups if the P-value is greater than 0.05. Hence, my data shows that there is no statistical difference among gender compositions (i.e., FF, MF, MM) in terms of the frequency of using the ISE *-telako(yo)*.

Age

Third, the age variable was analyzed. According to the results of the search engine *hanmalwu*, among 58 tokens in my data, there were 2 tokens used by 24 interlocutors of the age group in their teens (i.e., 0.08 token/person), 34 tokens used by 158 interlocutors in their 20s-30s (i.e., 0.22 tokens/person), and 22 tokens used by 37 interlocutors in the over

40 age group (i.e., 0.59 tokens/ person). ANOVA was used in order to investigate the difference of each age group. As shown in Table 5-7, the standard error deviation of the teenage group is 0.408, that of those in their 20s-30s is 0.717, and that of those over the age of 40 is 1/836. In addition, the F-value is 2.561 and the P-value is 0.080. According to the analysis of ANOVA, there is no significant difference between groups if the P-value is greater than 0.05. Hence, my data shows that there is no statistical difference among age groups (i.e., teens, 20s-30s, and over 40s) in terms of the frequency of using the ISE *-telako(yo).*

Occupation

Fourth, usage by occupational background was analyzed. According to the results of the search engine *hanmalwu*, among 58 tokens in my data, there were 2 tokens used by 17 housewives (i.e., 0.12 tokens/person), 24 tokens used by 30 office workers (i.e., 0.80 tokens/person), and 32 tokens used by 172 students (i.e., 0.19 tokens/person). ANOVA was used in order to investigate the differences by occupation. As shown in Table 5-7, the standard error deviation of housewives is 0.332, that of office workers is 2.219, and that of students is 0.640. In addition, the F-value is 5.046 and the P-value is 0.007. According to the analysis of ANOVA, there seems to be difference between groups if the P-value is smaller than 0.05. The LSD (Least Significant Difference) test for post-hoc analysis was used in order to verify the result. According to the results of post-hoc analysis shown in Table 5-8, there is no statistical difference between housewives and students in terms of the frequency of using the ISE *-telako(yo)*since the P-value in LSD test is greater than 0.05. However, the mean difference (I-J) of group I (office worker) and group J (house wife/student) is 0.682/0.614 and the P-value is 0.025/0.002. Moreover, the mean difference (I-J) of group I (house wife/student) and group J (office worker) is -0.682/-0.614 and the P-value is 0.025/0.002. Since the P-value is smaller than 0.05 and the mean difference (I-J) is a negative number, the result can be analyzed as showing that *-telako(yo)* is used more by office workers than housewives and students.

Region

Fifth, usage by region was analyzed. According to the results of the search engine *hanmalwu*, among 58 tokens in my data, there were 38 tokens used by 122 interlocutors (i.e., 0.31 tokens/ person) from metropolitan areas such as *Seoul* city and cities in *Kyengki* Province while there were 20 tokens used by 97 interlocutors (i.e., 0.21 tokens/ person) from non-metropolitan areas including the Korean provinces such as *Kangwen, Cenla, Kyengsang, Chwungcheng*, and so on. The independent *t*-test was used in order to investigate the differences by region (metropolitan areas vs. non-metropolitan areas). As shown in Table 5-7, the standard deviation of metropolitan areas is 1.220 while that of non-metropolitan areas is 0.676. In addition, the t-value is 0.762 and the P-value is 0.447. According to the *t*-test analysis, there is no significant difference between two groups if the P-value is greater than 0.05. Hence, my data shows that there is no statistical difference between metropolitan areas and non-metropolitan areas in terms of the frequency of using the ISE *-telako(yo)*.

Number of Speakers

Sixth, the independent *t*-test was used in order to investigate the difference between two-party conversations (two participants) and multiple-party conversations (involving more than two participants, i.e., three or four). According to the results of the search engine *hanmalwu*, there were 52 tokens of *-telako(yo)* used by 174 interlocutors (i.e., 0.30 tokens/ person) in two-party conversations (two participants) while there were 6 tokens of *-telako(yo)* used by 45 interlocutors (i.e., 0.13 tokens/ person) in multiple-party conversations (more than two participants) among the total number of 58 tokens of *-telako(yo)*. As shown in Table 5-7, the standard deviation of two-party conversations is 1.092 while that of multiple-party conversations is 0.625. In addition, the *t*-value is 0.975 and the P-value is 0.331. According to the *t*-test analysis, there is no significant difference between two groups if the P-value is greater than 0.05. Hence, my data shows that there is no statistical difference between two-party conversations and multiple-party conversations in terms of the frequency of using the ISE *-telako(yo)*.

Topic

Seventh, the topic (personal topics vs. impersonal topics) of conversation was analyzed. I distinguish personal topics (i.e., individual/private topics such as boyfriend/girlfriend, grades, appearances, etc.) and impersonal topics (i.e., social topics, political topics such as the suicide of the former president, a college entrance exam, free trade agreement, Korea's unification, etc.). According to the results of the search engine *hanmalwu*, among 58 tokens in my data, there were 3 tokens used by 219 interlocutors (0.01 tokens /person) with impersonal topics while there were 55 tokens used by 219 interlocutors (i.e., 0.25 tokens / person) in conversations with personal topics. The paired *t*-test was used in order to investigate the difference between conversations with impersonal topics and conversations with personal topics. As shown in Table 5-7, the standard deviation of conversations with an impersonal topic is 0.117 while that of conversations with a personal topic is 0.994. In addition, the *t*-value is -3.566 and the P-value is 0.000. According to the *t*-test analysis, there is a significant difference between two groups if the P-value is smaller than 0.05. Hence, my data shows that there is a significant difference between conversations with impersonal topics and conversations with personal topics in terms of the frequency of using the ISE-*telako(yo)*. Since the *t*-value is a negative number (-3.566) the result can be analyzed as showing that -*telako(yo)* is used more in conversations with personal topics than in conversations with impersonal topics.

Power

Eighth, power relations between interlocutors were analyzed. According to the results of the search engine *hanmalwu*, among 58 tokens in my data, there were 15 tokens used by 79 interlocutors (i.e., 0.19 tokens/person) in conversations without power relations between interlocutors, while there were 43 tokens used by 140 interlocutors (i.e., 0.31tokens/person) in conversations with power relations between interlocutors. The independent *t*-test was used in order to investigate the difference between conversations without power relations and conversations with power relations among interlocutors. As shown in Table 5-7, the standard deviation of conversation without power relations among interlocutors is 0.681 while that of conversation with power relations among interlocutors is 1.162. In addition, the t-value is -0.820 and the P-value is 0.413. According to the *t*-test analysis, there is no significant difference between two groups if the P-value is greater than 0.05. Hence, my data shows that there is no statistical difference between conversations without power relations among interlocutors and conversations with power relations among interlocutors in terms of the frequency of using the ISE *-telako(yo)*.

Distance

Ninth, distance relations between interlocutors were analyzed. According to the results of the search engine *hanmalwu*, among 58 tokens in my data, there were 44 tokens used by 174 interlocutors (i.e., 0.25 tokens/person) in conversations without distance relations between interlocutors while there were 14 tokens used by 45 interlocutors (i.e., 0.31 tokens/person) in conversations with distance relations between interlocutors. The independent *t*-test was used in order to investigate the difference between conversations without distance relations and conversations with distance relations among interlocutors. As shown in Table 5-7, the standard deviation of conversations without distance relations among interlocutors is 1.028 while that of conversation with distance relations among interlocutors is 0.973. In addition, the *t*-value is -0.342 and the P-value is 0.732. According to the *t*-test analysis, there is no significant difference between two groups if the P-value is greater than 0.05. Hence, my data shows that there is no statistical difference between conversations without distance relations among interlocutors and conversations with distance relations among interlocutors in terms of the frequency of using the ISE *-telako(yo)*.

5.1.5 *-ci(yo)*

Table 5-9 Statistical Verification of *-ci(yo)* (t-test and ANOVA)

Factors		Group	N	Mean	Fre-quency	Std. (Error) Deviation	t (F) Value	P-Value
Social Structural Factors	Gender	F	112	4.64	520	4.080	-0.224	0.823
		M	107	4.77	510	4.081		
	Gender Compo-sition	FF	58	4.57	265	3.681	0.452	0.637
		MF	58	5.16	299	4.384		
		MM	58	5.22	303	4.138		
	Age	Teens	24	3.67	88	3.332	3.388	0.036
		20-30	158	4.52	714	3.827		
		Over 40	37	6.16	228	5.134		
	Occupa-tion	House-wife	17	7.53	128	5.789	6.879	0.001
		Office worker	30	5.87	176	4.524		
		Student	172	4.22	726	3.642		
	Region	Metro-politan	122	4.83	589	4.250	0.507	0.612
		Non-metro	97	4.55	441	3.851		
Social Situational Factors	Number of Speakers	1:1	174	4.98	867	4.065	2.012	0.045
		Multi	45	3.62	163	3.956		
	Topic	Imper-sonal	219	0.15	32	0.695	-16.034	0.000
		Personal		4.56	998	4.011		
	Power	-	79	4.87	385	3.364	0.500	0.618
		+	140	4.61	645	4.430		
	Distance	-	174	5.07	882	4.140	2.650	0.009
		+	45	3.29	148	3.488		

Table 5-10 Post-hoc Analysis of Age Associated with the Use of *-ci(yo)*

	I	J	I-J	Std. Error	P-Value
LSD	teens	20s-30s	-0.852	0.882	0.335
		Over 40s	-2.495	1.056	0.019
	20s-30s	teens	0.852	0.882	0.335
		Over 40s	-1.643	0.736	0.027
	Over 40s	teens	2.495	1.056	0.019
		20s-30s	1.643	0.736	0.027

Table 5-11 Post-hoc Analysis of Occupation Associated with the Use of *-ci(yo)*

	I	J	I-J	Std. Error	P-Value
LSD	Housewife	office worker	1.663	1.204	0.169
		student	3.308	1.008	0.001
	Office worker	housewife	-1.663	1.204	0.169
		student	1.646	0.785	0.037
	Student	housewife	-3.308	1.008	0.001
		office worker	-1.646	0.785	0.037

Gender

Table 5-9 summarizes the results of the analysis of the sociopragmatic variables of the interactive sentence ender *-ci(yo)*. First, I analyzed the gender factor among many social structural variables. A total frequency of 1,030 *-ci(yo)* hedges were counted from my data via the search engine called *hanmalwu* of *Seycong* corpus. In addition, 520 uses of *-ci(yo)* by 112 females (i.e., 4.64 uses/ female) and 510 uses of *-ci(yo)* by 107 males (i.e., 4.77 uses/male) were counted through investigating all the interlocutors, for a total of 1,030 uses of *-ci(yo)*. I subsequently investigated the frequency of *-ci(yo)* uses by individual interlocutors followed by the independent t-test statistical analysis in order to investigate difference in usage by gender. As shown in Table 5-9, the standard deviation of females is 4.080 while that of males is 4.081. In addition, the t-value is -0.224 and the P-value is 0.823. According to the t-test analysis, there is no significant difference between two groups if the P-value is greater than 0.05. Hence, my data shows that there is no statistical difference between females and males in terms of the frequency of using the ISE (interactive sentence ender) *-ci(yo)*.

Gender composition

Second, an analysis of gender composition was conducted. According to the results of the search engine *hanmalwu*, there were 867 tokens of *-ci(yo)* used by 174 interlocutors (i.e., 4.98 tokens/ person) in two-party conversations (two participants) while there were 163 tokens of *-ci(yo)* used by 45 interlocutors (i.e., 3.62 tokens/person) in multiple-party conversations (more than two participants) among the total number of 1030 tokens of *-ci(yo)*. Moreover, among two-party conversations there were 265 tokens used by 58 females (i.e., 4.57 tokens/person) in female-female (FF) gender composition, 299 tokens used by 58 males and females (i.e., 5.16 tokens/person) in male-female (MF) gender composition, and 303 tokens used by 56 males (i.e., 5.22 tokens/person) in male-male (MM) gender composition. ANOVA was used in order to investigate the differences of gender composition. As shown in Table 5-9, the standard error deviation of female-female (FF) gender composition is 3.681, that of male-female (MF) gender composition is 4.384, and that of male-male (MM) gender composition is 4.138. In addition, the F-value is 0.452 and the P-value is 0.637. According to the ANOVA analysis, there is no significant difference among groups if the P-value is greater than 0.05. Hence, my data shows that there is no statistical difference among gender compositions (i.e., FF, MF, MM) in terms of the frequency of using the ISE *-ci(yo)*.

Age

Third, the age variable was analyzed. According to the results of the search engine *hanmalwu*, among 1030 tokens in my data, there were 88 tokens used by 24 interlocutors of the age group in their teens (i.e., 3.67 token/person), 714 tokens used by 158 interlocutors in their 20s-30s (i.e., 4.52 tokens/person), and 228 tokens used by 6.16 interlocutors in the over 40 age group (i.e., 6.16 tokens/ person). ANOVA was used in order to investigate the difference of each age group. As shown in Table 5-9, the standard error deviation of the teenage group is 3.332, that of those in their 20s-30s is 3.827, and that of those over the age of 40 is 5.134. In addition, the F-value is 3.388 and the P-value is 0.036. According to the analysis of ANOVA, there seems a significant difference between groups if the P-value is smaller than 0.05. The LSD (Least Significant Difference) test for Post-hoc analysis was used in order to verify the result. According to the results of post-hoc analysis shown in Table 5-10, there is no statistical difference between teens and 20s-30s in terms of the frequency of using the ISE *-ci(yo)* since the P-value in the LSD test is greater than 0.05. However, the mean difference of group I (over 40s) and group J (teens/20s-30s) is 2.495/1.643 and the P-value is 0.019/0.027. Moreover, since the P-value is smaller than 0.05 and the mean difference (I-J) is a positive number, the result can be analyzed as showing that <u>*-ci(yo)* is used more by interlocutors over the age of 40 than interlocutors of teens and 20s-30s</u>.

<u>Occupation</u>

Fourth, usage by occupational background was analyzed. According to the results of the search engine *hanmalwu*, among 1030 tokens in my data, there were 128 tokens used by 17 housewives (i.e., 7.53 tokens/ person), 176 tokens used by 30 office workers (i.e., 5.87 tokens/person), and 726 tokens used by 172 students (i.e., 4.22 tokens/person). ANOVA was used in order to investigate the differences by occupation. As shown in Table 5-9, the standard error deviation of housewives is 5.789, that of office workers is 4.524, and that of students is 3.642. In addition, the F-value is 6.879 and the P-value is 0.001. According to the analysis of ANOVA, there is a difference between groups if the P-value is smaller than 0.05. The LSD (Least Significant Difference) test for post-hoc analysis was used in order to verify the result. As shown in Table 5-11, there is no statistical difference between housewives and office workers in terms of the frequency of using the ISE *-ci(yo)* since the P-value in the LSD test is greater than 0.05. However, the mean difference

(I-J) of group I (housewives) and group J (students) is 2.991 and the P-value is 0.000, and the mean difference (I-J) of group I (student) and group J (housewives/office workers) is -3.308/-1.646 and the P-value is 0.001/0.037. Moreover, since the P-value is smaller than 0.05 and the mean difference (I-J) is a negative number, the result can be analyzed as showing that <u>*-ci(yo)* is used more by housewives/office workers than students</u>.

<u>Region</u>

Fifth, usage by region was analyzed. According to the results of the search engine *hanmalwu*, among 1030 tokens in my data, there were 589 tokens used by 122 interlocutors (i.e., 4.83 tokens /person) from metropolitan areas such as *Seoul* city and cities in *Kyengki* Province while there were 441 tokens used by 97 interlocutors (i.e., 4.55 tokens/ person) from non-metropolitan areas including the Korean provinces such as *Kangwen, Cenla, Kyengsang, Chwungcheng*, and so on. The independent *t*-test was used in order to investigate the differences by region (metropolitan areas vs. non-metropolitan areas). As shown in Table 5-9, the standard deviation of metropolitan areas is 4.250 while that of non-metropolitan areas is 3.851. In addition, the t-value is 0.507 and the P-value is 0.612. According to the t-test analysis, there is no significant difference between two groups if the P-value is greater than 0.05. Hence, my data shows that there is no statistical difference between metropolitan areas and non-metropolitan areas in terms of the frequency of using the ISE *-ci(yo)*.

<u>Number of Speakers</u>

Sixth, the independent *t*-test was used in order to investigate the difference between two-party conversations (two participants) and multiple-party conversations (involving more than two participants). According to the results of the search engine *hanmalwu*, there were 867 tokens of *-ci(yo)* used by 174 interlocutors (i.e., 4.98 tokens/ person) in two-party conversations (two participants) while there were 163 tokens of *-ci(yo)* used by 45 interlocutors (i.e., 3.62 tokens/person) in multiple-party conversations (more than two participants) among the total number of 1030 tokens of *-ci(yo)*. As shown in Table 5-9, the standard deviation of two-party conversations is 4.065 while that of multiple-party conversations is 3.956. In addition, the *t*-value is 2.012 and the P-value is 0.045. According to the *t*-test analysis, there is a significant difference between two groups if the P-value is smaller than 0.05. Hence, my data shows that there is a significant difference between two-party conversations and multiple-party conversations in terms of the frequency of using the ISE *-ci(yo)*. Since the t-value is a positive number (2.012) the result can be analyzed as showing that <u>-ci(yo) is used more in two-party conversations than in multiple-party conversations</u>.

<u>Topic</u>

Seventh, the topic (personal topics vs. impersonal topics) of conversation was analyzed. I distinguish personal topics (i.e., individual/private topics such as boyfriend/girlfriend, grades, appearances, etc.) and impersonal topics (i.e., social topics, political topics such as the suicide of the former president, a college entrance exam, free trade agreement, Korea's unification, etc.). According to the results of the search engine *hanmalwu*, among 1030 tokens in my data, there were 32 tokens used by 219 interlocutors (0.15 tokens/person) with impersonal topics while there 998 tokens used by 219 interlocutors (i.e., 4.56 tokens/person) in conversations with personal topics. The paired *t*-test was used in order to investigate the difference between conversations with impersonal topics and conversations with personal topics. As shown in Table 5-9, the standard deviation of conversation with impersonal topic is 0.695 while that of conversations with personal topics is 4.011. In addition, the t-value is -16.034 and the P-value is 0.000. According to the *t*-test analysis, there is a significant difference between two groups if the P-value is smaller than 0.05. Hence, my data shows that there is a significant difference between conversations with impersonal topics and conversations with personal topics in terms of the frequency of using the ISE *-ci(yo)*. Since the t-value is a negative number (-16.031) the result can be analyzed as showing that *-ci(yo)* <u>is used more in conversations with personal topics</u>

than in conversations with impersonal topics.

Power

Eighth, power relations between interlocutors were analyzed. According to the results of the search engine *hanmalwu*, among 1030 tokens in my data, there were 385 tokens used by 79 interlocutors (i.e., 4.87 tokens/person) in conversations without power relations between interlocutors, while there were 645 tokens used by 140 interlocutors (i.e., 4.61 tokens/person) in conversations with power relations between interlocutors. The independent *t*-test was used in order to investigate the difference between conversations without power relations and conversations with power relations among interlocutors. As shown in Table 5-9, the standard deviation of conversations without power relations among interlocutors is 3.364 while that of conversations with power relations among interlocutors is 4.430. In addition, the *t*-value is 0.500 and P-value is 0.618. According to the t-test analysis, there is no significant difference between two groups if the P-value is greater than 0.05. Hence, my data shows that there is no statistical difference between conversations without power relations among interlocutors and conversations with power relations among interlocutors in terms of the frequency of using the ISE *-ci(yo)*.

Distance

Ninth, distance relations between interlocutors were analyzed. According to the results of the search engine *hanmalwu*, among 1030 tokens in my data, there were 882 tokens used by 174 interlocutors (i.e., 5.07 tokens/person) in conversations without distance relations between interlocutors while there were 148 tokens used by 45 interlocutors (i.e., 3.29 tokens/person) in conversations with distance relations between interlocutors. The independent *t*-test was used in order to investigate the difference between conversations without distance relations and conversations with distance relations among interlocutors. As shown in the Table 5-9, the standard deviation of conversations without distance relations among interlocutors is 4.140 while that of conversations with distance relations among interlocutors is 3.488. In addition, the *t*-value is 2.650 and the P-value is 0.009. According to the *t*-test analysis, there is a significant difference between two groups if the P-value is smaller than 0.05. Hence, my data shows that there is a significant difference between conversations without distance relations and conversations with distance relations among interlocutors. Since the t-value is a positive number (5.264) the result can be analyzed as showing that *-ci(yo)* is used more in conversations without distance relations than conversations with distance relations among interlocutors.

5.1. 6 *-ney (yo)*

Table 5-12 Statistical Verification of *-ney(yo)* (t-test and ANOVA)

Factors		Group	N	Mean	Frequency	Std. (Error) Deviation	t (F) Value	P-Value
Social Situational Factors	Gender	F	112	0.93	104	1.299	-0.665	0.507
		M	107	1.06	113	1.535		
	Gender Composition	FF	58	0.88	51	1.093	0.633	0.532
		MF	58	1.10	64	1.619		
		MM	58	1.16	67	1.449		
	Age	Teen	24	0.58	14	0.830	1.469	0.232
		20-30	158	1.00	158	1.476		
		Over 40	37	1.22	45	1.436		
	Occupation	Housewife	17	1.53	26	1.875	1.620	0.200
		Office worker	30	0.77	23	0.858		
		Student	172	0.98	168	1.439		
	Region	Metropolitan	122	1.08	132	1.541	1.067	0.287
		Non-metro	97	0.88	85	1.244		
	Number of Speakers	1:1	174	1.05	182	1.401	1.132	0.259
		Multi	45	0.78	35	1.475		

Social Situational Factors	Topic	Imper-sonal	219	0.00	1	0.068	-10.204	**0.000**
		Personal		0.99	216	1.419		
	Power	-	79	0.95	75	1.250	-0.325	0.746
		+	140	1.01	142	1.508		
	Distance	-	174	1.07	186	1.484	1.609	0.109
		+	45	0.69	31	1.083		

Gender

Table 5-12 summarizes the results of the analysis of the sociopragmatic variables of the interactive sentence ender *-ney (yo)*. First, I analyzed the gender factor among many social structural variables. A total frequency of 217 *-ney (yo)* hedges were counted from my data via the search engine called *hanmalwu* of *Seycong* corpus. In addition, 104 uses of *-ney (yo)* by 112 females (i.e., 0.93 uses/ female) and 113 uses of *-ney (yo)* by 107 males (i.e., 1.06 uses /male) were counted through investigating the gender of all the interlocutors appeared for a total of 217 uses of *-ney (yo)*. I subsequently investigated the frequency of *-ney (yo)* uses by individual interlocutors followed by the independent *t*-test statistical analysis in order to investigate difference in usage by gender. As shown in Table 5-12, the standard deviation of females is 1.299 while that of males is 1.535. In addition, the t-value is -0.655 and the P-value is 0.507. According to the *t*-test analysis, there is no significant difference between two groups if the P-value is greater than 0.05. Hence, my data shows that there is no statistical difference between females and males in terms of the frequency of using the ISE *-ney (yo)*.

Gender composition

Second, an analysis of gender composition was conducted. According to the results of the search engine *hanmalwu*, there were 182 tokens of *-ney (yo)* used by 174 interlocutors (i.e., 1.05 tokens/ person) in two-party conversations (two participants) while there were 35 tokens of *-ney (yo)* used by 45 interlocutors (i.e., 0.78 tokens/person) in multiple-party conversations (more than two participants) among the total number of 217 tokens of *-ney (yo)*. Moreover, among two-party conversations there were 51 tokens used by 58 females (i.e., 0.88 tokens/person) in female-female (FF) gender composition, 64 tokens used by 58 males and females (i.e., 1.10 tokens /person) in male-female (MF) gender composition, and 67 tokens used by 58 males (i.e., 1.16 tokens/person) in male-male (MM) gender composition. ANOVA was used in order to investigate the differences of gender composition. As shown in Table 5-12, the standard error deviation of female-female (FF) gender composition is 1.093, that of male-female (MF) gender composition is 1.619, and that of male-male (MM) gender composition is 1.449. In addition, the F-value is 0.633 and the P-value is 0.532. According to the ANOVA analysis, there is no significant difference among groups if the P-value is greater than 0.05. Hence, my data shows that there is no statistical difference among gender compositions (i.e., FF, MF, MM) in terms of the frequency of using the ISE *-ney (yo)*.

Age

Third, the age variable was analyzed. According to the results of the search engine *hanmalwu*, among 217 tokens in my data, there were 14 tokens used by 24 interlocutors of the age group in their teens (i.e., 0.58 token/person), 158 tokens used by 158 interlocutors in their 20s-30s (i.e., 1.00 tokens/person), and 45 tokens used by 37 interlocutors in the over 40 age group (i.e., 1.22 tokens/ person). ANOVA was used in order to investigate the difference of each age group. As shown in Table 5-12, the standard error deviation of the teenage group is 0.830, that of those in their 20s-30s is 1.476, and that of those over the age of 40 is 1.436. In addition, the F-value is 1.469 and the P-value is 0.232. According to the analysis of ANOVA, there is no significant difference between groups if the P-value is greater than 0.05. Hence, my data shows that there is no statistical difference among age groups (i.e., teens, 20s-30s, and over 40s) in terms of the frequency of using the ISE *-ney (yo)*.

Occupation

Fourth, usage by occupational background was analyzed. According to the results of the search engine *hanmalwu*, among 217 tokens in my data, there were 26 tokens used by 17 housewives (i.e., 1.53 tokens/person), 23 tokens used by 30 office workers (i.e., 0.77 tokens/person), and 168 tokens used by 172 students (i.e., 0.98 tokens/person). ANOVA was used in order to investigate the differences by occupation. As shown in Table 5-12, the standard error deviation of housewives is 1.875, that of office workers is 0.858, and that of students is 1.439. In addition, the F-value is 1.620 and the P-value is 0.200. According to the analysis of ANOVA, there is no significant difference between groups if the P-value is greater than 0.05. Hence, my data shows that there is no statistical difference by occupation (housewives, office workers, or students) in terms of the frequency of using the ISE *-ney (yo)*.

Region

Fifth, usage by region was analyzed. According to the results of the search engine *hanmalwu*, among 217 tokens in my data, there were 132 tokens used by 122 interlocutors (i.e., 1.08 tokens /person) from metropolitan areas such as *Seoul* city and cities in *Kyengki* Province while there were 85 tokens used by 97 interlocutors (i.e., 0.88 tokens/person) from non-metropolitan areas including the Korean provinces such as *Kangwen, Cenla, Kyengsang, Chwungcheng*, and so on. The independent *t*-test was used in order to investigate the differences by region (metropolitan areas vs. non-metropolitan areas). As shown in Table 5-12, the standard deviation of metropolitan areas is 1.541 while that of non-metropolitan areas is 1.244. In addition, the *t*-value is 1.067 and the P-value is 0.287. According to the t-test analysis, there is no significant difference between two groups if the P-value is greater than 0.05. Hence, my data shows that there is no statistical difference between metropolitan areas and non-metropolitan areas in terms of the frequency of using the ISE *-ney (yo)*.

Number of Speakers

Sixth, the independent *t*-test was used in order to investigate the difference between two-party conversations (two participants) and multiple-party conversations (involving more than two participants). According to the results of the search engine *hanmalwu*, there were 182 tokens of *-ney (yo)* used by 174 interlocutors (i.e., 1.05 tokens/person) in two-party conversations (two participants) while there were 35 tokens of *-ney (yo)* used by 45 interlocutors (i.e., 0.78 tokens/person) in multiple-party conversations (more than two participants) among the total number of 217 tokens of *-ney (yo)*. As shown in Table 5-12, the standard deviation of two-party conversations is 1.401 while that of multiple-party conversations is 1.475. In addition, the *t*-value is 1.132 and the P-value is 0.259. According to the t-test analysis, there is no significant difference between two groups if the P-value is greater than 0.05. Hence, my data shows that there is no statistical difference between two-party conversations and multiple-party conversations in terms of the frequency of using the ISE *-ney (yo)*.

Topic

Seventh, the topic (personal topics vs. impersonal topics) of conversation was analyzed. I distinguished personal topics (i.e., individual/private topics such as boyfriend/ girlfriend, grades, appearances, etc.) and impersonal topics (i.e., social topics, political topics such as the suicide of the former president, a college entrance exam, the free trade agreement, Korea's unification, etc.). According to the results of the search engine *hanmalwu*, among 217 tokens in my data, there was 1 token used by 219 interlocutors (0.00 token/person) with impersonal topics while there were 216 tokens used by 219 interlocutors (i.e., 0.99 tokens/person) in conversations with personal topics. The paired *t*-test was used in order to investigate the difference between conversations with impersonal topics and conversations with personal topics. As shown in Table 5-12, the standard deviation of conversation with impersonal topics is 0.068 while that of conversation with personal topics is 1.49. In addition, the t-value is -10.204 and the P-value is 0.000. According to the *t*-test analysis, there is a significant difference between two groups if the P-value is smaller than 0.05. Hence, my data shows that there is a significant difference between conversations with impersonal topic and conversations with personal topic in terms of the frequency of using the ISE *-ney (yo)*. Since the *t*-value is a negative number (-10.204) the result can be analyzed as showing that <u>*-ney (yo)* is used more in conversations with personal topics than in conversations with impersonal topics</u>.

<u>Power</u>

Eighth, power relations between interlocutors were analyzed. According to the results of the search engine *hanmalwu*, among 217 tokens in my data, there were 75 tokens used by 79 interlocutors (i.e., 0.95 tokens/person) in conversations without power relations between interlocutors, while there were 142 tokens used by 140 interlocutors (i.e., 1.01 tokens/person) in conversations with power relations between interlocutors. The independent *t*-test was used in order to investigate the difference between conversations without power relations and conversations with power relations among interlocutors. As shown in Table 5-12, the standard deviation of conversations without power relations among interlocutors is 1.250 while that of conversations with power relations among interlocutors is 1.508. In addition, the t-value is -0.325 and the P-value is 0.746. According to the *t*-test analysis, there is no significant difference between two groups if the P-value is greater than 0.05. Hence, my data shows that there is no statistical difference between conversations without power relations among interlocutors and conversations with power relations among interlocutors in terms of the frequency of using the ISE *-ney (yo)*.

<u>Distance</u>

Ninth, distance relations between interlocutors were analyzed. According to the results of the search engine *hanmalwu*, among 217 tokens in my data, there were 186 tokens used by 174 interlocutors (i.e., 1.07 tokens/person) in conversations without distance relations between interlocutors while there were 31 tokens used by 45 interlocutors (i.e.,

0.69 tokens/person) in conversations with distance relations between interlocutors. The independent *t*-test was used in order to investigate the difference between conversations without distance relations and conversations with distance relations among interlocutors. As shown in Table 5-12, the standard deviation of conversations without distance relations among interlocutors is 1.484 while that of conversations with distance relations among interlocutors is 1.083. In addition, the *t*-value is 1.609 and the P-value is 0.109. According to the *t*-test analysis, there is no significant difference between two groups if the P-value is greater than 0.05. Hence, my data shows that there is no statistical difference between conversation without distance relations among interlocutors and conversation with distance relations among interlocutors in terms of the frequency of using the ISE *-ney (yo)*.

5.1.7 *-tay(yo)*

Table 5-13 Statistical Verification of -tay(yo) (t-test and ANOVA)

Factors		Group	N	Mean	Frequency	Std. (Error) Deviation	t (or F) Value	P-Value
Social Structural Factors	Gender	F	112	1.38	155	2.145	3.309	0.001
		M	107	0.63	67	1.103		
	Gender Composition	FF	58	1.57	91	2.333	3.759	0.025
		MF	58	1.17	68	1.808		
		MM	58	0.64	37	1.180		
	Age	Teen	24	1.04	25	2.074	0.074	0.929
		20-30	158	0.99	156	1.700		
		Over 40	37	1.11	41	1.807		
	Occupation	Housewife	17	0.71	12	1.312	2.827	0.061
		Office worker	30	1.70	51	2.184		
		Student	172	0.92	159	1.689		

	Region	Metro-politan	122	1.08	132	1.892	0.645	0.520
		Non-metro	97	0.93	90	1.570		
Social Situational Factors	Number of Speakers	1:1	174	1.13	196	1.864	2.460	0.015
		Multi	45	0.58	26	1.158		
	Topic	Imper-sonal	219	0.07	15	0.371	-8.069	0.000
		Personal		0.95	207	1.641		
	Power	-	79	1.25	99	1.945	1.522	0.129
		+	140	0.88	123	1.629		
	Distance	-	174	1.10	191	1.820	1.396	0.164
		+	45	0.69	31	1.443		

Table 5-14
Post-hoc Analysis of Gender Composition Associated with the Use of -tay(yo)

	I	J	I-J	Std. Error	P-Value
Dunnett T3	FF	MF	0.397	0.388	0.667
		MM	0.931	0.343	**0.024**
	MF	FF	-0.397	0.388	0.667
		MM	0.534	0.283	0.175
	MM	FF	-0.931	0.343	**0.024**
		MF	-0.534	0.283	0.175

Gender

Table 5-13 summarizes the results of the analysis of the sociopragmatic variables of the interactive sentence ender *-tay (yo)*. First, I analyzed the gender factor among many social structural variables. A total frequency of 222 *-tay(yo)* hedges were counted from my data via the search engine called *hanmalwu* of *Seycong* corpus. In addition, 155 uses of *-tay* by 112 females (i.e., 1.38 uses/ female) and 67 uses of *-tay (yo)* by 107 males (i.e., 0.63 uses / male) were counted through investigating the gender of all the interlocutors, for a total of 222 uses of *-ney (yo)*. I subsequently investigated the frequency of *-ney (yo)* uses by individual interlocutors followed by independent *t*-test statistical analysis in order to investigate differences in usage by gender. As shown in Table 5-13, the standard deviation of females is 2.145 while that of males is 1.103. In addition, the *t*-value is 3.309 and the P-value is 0.001. According to the *t*-test analysis, there is a significant difference between two groups if the P-value is smaller than 0.05. Hence, my data shows that there is a significant difference between females and males in terms of the frequency of using the ISE *-tay(yo)*. Since the *t*-value is a positive number (3.309) the result can be analyzed as showing that <u>*-tay (yo)* is used more by females than by males</u>.

<u>Gender composition</u>

Second, an analysis of gender composition was conducted. According to the results of the search engine *hanmalwu*, there were 196 tokens of *-tay(yo)* used by 174 interlocutors (i.e., 1.13 tokens/ person) in two-party conversations (two participants) while there were 26 tokens of *-tay(yo)* used by 45 interlocutors (i.e., 0.58 tokens/person) in multiple-party conversations (more than two participants) among the total number of 222 tokens of *-tay(yo)*. Moreover, among two-party conversations there were 91 tokens used by 58 females (i.e., 1.57 tokens/person) in female-female (FF) gender composition, 68 tokens used by 58 males and females (i.e., 1.17 tokens/ person) in male-female (MF) gender composition, and 37 tokens used by 58 males (i.e., 0.64 tokens/person) in male-male (MM) gender composition. ANOVA was used in order to investigate the differences of gender composition. As shown in Table 5-13, the standard error deviation of female-female (FF) gender composition is 2.333, that of male-female (MF) gender composition is 1.808, and that of male-male (MM) gender composition is 1.180. In addition, the F-value is 3.759 and the P-value is 0.025. According to the ANOVA analysis, there seems to be a significant difference among groups if the P-value is smaller than 0.05. The Dunnett T3 test for Post-hoc analysis was used in order to verify the result. According to the results of Post-hoc analysis in Table 5-14, the mean difference (I-J) of I group (FF) and J group (MM) is 0.931 and the P-value is 0.024. Since the P-value is smaller than 0.05 and the mean difference is positive value, my data shows that the ISE *-tay(yo)* is used more in female-female gender composition than in male-male gender composition.

Age

Third, the age variable was analyzed. According to the results of the search engine *hanmalwu*, among 222 tokens in my data, there were 25 tokens used by 24 interlocutors of the age group in their teens (i.e., 1.04 tokens/person), 156 tokens used by 158 interlocutors in their 20s-30s (i.e., 0.99 tokens/person), and 41 tokens used by 37 interlocutors in the over 40 age group (i.e., 1.11 tokens/ person). ANOVA was used in order to investigate the difference of each age group. As shown in Table 5-13, the standard error deviation of the teenage group is 2.074, that of those in their 20s-30s is 1.700, and that of those over the age of 40 is 1.807. In addition, the F-value is 0.074 and the P-value is 0.929. According to the analysis of ANOVA, there is no significant difference between groups if the P-value is greater than 0.05. Hence, my data shows that there is no statistical difference among age groups (i.e., teens, 20s-30s, and over 40s) in terms of the frequency of using the ISE *-tay (yo)*.

Occupation

Fourth, usage by occupational background was analyzed. According to the results of the search engine *hanmalwu*, among 222 tokens in my data, there were 12 tokens used by 17 housewives (i.e., 0.71 tokens/person), 51 tokens used by 30 office workers (i.e., 1.70 tokens/person), and 159 tokens used by 172 students (i.e., 0.92 tokens/person). ANOVA was used in order to investigate the differences by occupation. As shown in Table 5-13, the standard error deviation of housewives is 1.312, that of office workers is 2.184, and that of students is 1.689. In addition, the F-value is 2.827 and the P-value is 0.061. According to the analysis of ANOVA, there is no significant difference between groups if the P-value is greater than 0.05. Hence, my data shows that there is no statistical difference by occupation (housewives, office workers, or students) in terms of the frequency of using the ISE *-tay(yo)*.

Region

Fifth, usage by region was analyzed. According to the results of the search engine *hanmalwu*, among 222 tokens in my data, there were 132 tokens used by 122 interlocutors (i.e., 1.08 tokens/ person) from metropolitan areas such as *Seoul* city and cities in *Kyengki* Province while there were 90 tokens used by 97 interlocutors (i.e., 0.93 tokens/ person) from non-metropolitan areas including several different Korean provinces such as *Kangwen, Cenla, Kyengsang, Chwungcheng*, and so on. The independent *t*-test was used in order to investigate the differences by region (metropolitan areas vs. non-metropolitan areas). As shown in Table 5-13, the standard deviation of metropolitan areas is 1.892 while that of non-metropolitan areas is 1.570. In addition, the *t*-value is 0.645 and the P-value is 0.520. According to the *t*-test analysis, there is no significant difference between two groups if the P-value is greater than 0.05. Hence, my data shows that there is no statistical difference between metropolitan areas and non-metropolitan areas in terms of the frequency of using the ISE *-tay(yo)*.

Number of Speakers

Sixth, the independent *t*-test was used in order to investigate the difference between two-party conversations (two participants) and multiple-party conversations (involving more than two participants). According to the results of the search engine *hanmalwu*, there were 196 tokens of *-tay(yo)* used by 174 interlocutors (i.e., 1.13 tokens/ person) in two-party conversations (two participants) while there were 26 tokens of *-tay(yo)* used by 45 interlocutors (i.e., 0.58 tokens/person) in multiple-party conversations (more than two participants) among the total number of 222 tokens of *-tay(yo)*. As shown in Table 5-13, the standard deviation of two-party conversations is 1.864 while that of multiple-party conversations is 1.158. In addition, the t-value is 0.645 and the P-value is 0.015. According to the t-test analysis, there seems to be a significant difference between two groups if the P-value is smaller than 0.05. Hence, my data shows that there is a significant difference between two-party conversations and multiple-party conversations in terms of the frequency of using the ISE *-tay(yo)*. Since the t-value is a positive number (0.645) the result can be analyzed as showing that *-tay (yo)* is used more in two-party conversations than in multiple-party conversations.

Topic

Seventh, the topic (personal topics vs. impersonal topics) of conversation was analyzed. I distinguish personal topics (i.e., individual/private topics such as boyfriend/girlfriend, grades, appearances, etc.) and impersonal topics (i.e., social topics, political topics such as the suicide of the former president, a college entrance exam, the free trade agreement, Korea's unification, etc.). According to the results of the search engine *hanmalwu*, among 222 tokens in my data, there were 15 tokens used by 219 interlocutors (0.07 tokens/person) with impersonal topics while there 207 tokens used by 219 interlocutors (i.e., 0.95 tokens /person) in conversations with personal topics. The paired t-test was used in order to investigate the difference between conversations with impersonal topics and conversations with personal topics. As shown in Table 5-13, the standard deviation of conversations with impersonal topics is 0.371 while that of conversations with personal topics is 1.641. In addition, the t-value is -8.069 and the P-value is 0.000. According to the *t*-test analysis, there is a significant difference between two groups if the P-value is smaller than 0.05. Hence, my data shows that there is a significant difference between conversations with impersonal topics and conversations with personal topics in terms of the frequency of using the ISE *-tay(yo)*. Since the t-value is a negative number (-8.069) the result can be analyzed as showing that *-tay(yo)* is used more in conversations with personal topics than in conversations with impersonal topics.

Power

Eighth, power relations between interlocutors were analyzed. According to the results of the search engine *hanmalwu*, among 222 tokens in my data, there were 99 tokens used by 79 interlocutors (i.e., 1.25 tokens/person) in conversations without power relations between interlocutors, while there were 123 tokens used by 140 interlocutors (i.e., 0.88 tokens/person) in conversations with power relations between interlocutors. The independent *t*-test was used in order to investigate the difference between conversations without power relations and conversations with power relations among interlocutors. As shown in Table 5-13, the standard deviation of conversations without power relations among interlocutors is 1.945 while that of conversations with power relations among interlocutors is 1.629. In addition, the *t*-value is 1.522 and the P-value is 0.129. According to the *t*-test analysis, there is no significant difference between two groups if the P-value is greater than 0.05. Hence, my data shows that there is no statistical difference between conversations without power relations among interlocutors and conversations with power relations among interlocutors in terms of the frequency of using the ISE *-tay(yo)*.

Distance

Ninth, distance relations between interlocutors were analyzed. According to the results of the search engine *hanmalwu*, among 222 tokens in my data, there were 191 tokens used by 174 interlocutors (i.e., 1.10 tokens/person) in conversations without distance relations between interlocutors while there were 31 tokens used by 45 interlocutors (i.e., 0.69 tokens/person) in conversations with distance relations between interlocutors. The independent *t*-test was used in order to investigate the difference between conversations without distance relations and conversations with distance relations among interlocutors. As shown in Table 5-13, the standard deviation of conversations without distance relations among interlocutors is 1.820 while that of conversations with distance relations among interlocutors is 1.433. In addition, the *t*-value is 1.396 and the P-value is 0.164. According to the *t*-test analysis, there is no significant difference between two groups if the P-value is greater than 0.05. Hence, my data shows that there is no statistical difference between conversations without distance relations among interlocutors and conversations with distance relations among interlocutors in terms of the frequency of using the ISE *-tay(yo)*.

5.2 Summary of Sociopragmatic Analysis of Seven ISEs

Table 5-15 summarizes the results of the sociopragmatic analysis of selected hedge items, which are seven interactive sentence enders, *-canha(yo), -nuntey(yo), -ketun(yo), -telako(yo), -ci(yo), -ney(yo), tay(yo)* in Section 5.1. The current study investigates the correlation between the frequency of each hedge item and sociopragmatic factors after t-test analysis or ANOVA analysis of seven hedge items, which has a total of 3,445 frequencies in my data.

1. Statistical analysis illustrates that *-canha(yo)* is used more in two-party conversations than in multiple-party conversations.
2. Statistical analysis illustrates that *-canha(yo)* is used more in conversations with personal topics (i.e., individual/private topics such as boyfriend/girlfriend, grades, appearances, etc.) than in conversations with impersonal topics (i.e., social topics, political topics such as the suicide of the former president, a college entrance exam, the Free Trade Agreement, Korea's unification, etc.).
3. Statistical analysis illustrates that *-nuntey(yo)* is used more by interlocutors of age group of the 20s-30s than by interlocutors of the age group of over 40s.
4. Statistical analysis illustrates that *-nuntey(yo)* is used more by students than by housewives.
5. Statistical analysis illustrates that *-nuntey(yo)* is used more in two-party conversations than in multiple-party conversations.
6. Statistical analysis illustrates that *-nuntey(yo)* is used more in conversations with personal topics than in conversations with impersonal topics.
7. Statistical analysis illustrates that *-nuntey(yo)* is used more in conversations without power relations than in conversations with power relations among interlocutors.
8. Statistical analysis illustrates that *-ketun(yo)* is used more in metropolitan areas than in non-metropolitan areas.

Table 5-15 Summary of Findings of Sociopragmatic Analysis

	Social Structural Factors					**Social Situational Factors**			
	Gender	Gender Comp.	Age	Occupation	Region	Num. of Speakers	Topic	Power	Distance
ISE(1) -canha (yo)						1:1 > Multi.	Personal > Impersonal		
ISE(2) -nuntey (yo)			20s-30s > 40s	Student > Housewife		1:1 > Multi.	Personal > Impersonal	-P > +P	
ISE(3) -ketun (yo)					Metro> Non-metro	1:1 > Multi.	Personal > Impersonal		
ISE(4) -telako (yo)				Office worker > Student = Housewife			Personal > Impersonal		
ISE(5) -ci(yo)			40s > 20s-30s = teens	Housewife = Office worker > Student		1:1 > Multi.	Personal > Impersonal		-D > +D
ISE(6) -ney(yo)							Personal > Impersonal		
ISE(7) -tay(yo)	F > M	FF > MM				1:1 > Multi.	Personal > Impersonal		

9. Statistical analysis illustrates that *-ketun(yo)* is used more in two-party conversations than in multiple-party conversations.
10. Statistical analysis illustrates that *-ketun(yo)* is used more in conversations with personal topics than in conversations with impersonal topics.
11. Statistical analysis illustrates that *-telako(yo)* is used more by office workers than by housewives or students.
1.2 Statistical analysis illustrates that *-telako (yo)* is used more in conversations with personal topics than in conversations with impersonal topics.
13. Statistical analysis illustrates that *-ci(yo)* is used more by interlocutors of the age group of over 40 than by interlocutors of the age group of 20s-30s.
14. Statistical analysis illustrates that *-ci(yo)* is used more by housewives and office workers than by students.
15. Statistical analysis illustrates that *-ci(yo)* is used more in two-party conversations than in multiple-party conversations.
16. Statistical analysis illustrates that *-ci(yo)* is used more in conversations with personal topics than in conversations with impersonal topics.
17. Statistical analysis illustrates that *-ci(yo)* is used more in conversations without distance relations than conversations with distance relations among interlocutors.
18. Statistical analysis illustrates that *-ney(yo)* is used more in conversations with personal topics than in conversations with impersonal topics.
19. Statistical analysis illustrates that *-tay(yo)* is used more by females than by males.
20. Statistical analysis illustrates that *-tay(yo)* is used more in female-female gender composition than in male-male gender composition.
21. Statistical analysis illustrates that *-tay(yo)* is used more in two-party conversations than in multiple-party conversations.
22. Statistical analysis illustrates that *-tay(yo)* is used more in conversations with personal topics than in conversations with impersonal topics.

In short, the meaning of findings in Section 5.1 (Sociopragmatic Analysis of ISEs) is summarized as follows. First, one of the most predominant meaningful variables is the number of speakers in conversations (two-party conversations vs. multiple-party conversations). The analysis showed that there was correlation between the number of speakers in conversation and the hedge items such as *-canha(yo), -nuntey(yo),-ketun(yo), -ci(yo), -tay(yo)*. The number of speakers in conversation is especially correlated with five items among seven ISEs (interactive sentence enders). Hence, according to the results of the current study, I propose the hypothesis that hedge items are used more in two-party conversations than in multiple-party conversations in contemporary Korean discourse.

I assume that this study is the first empirical analysis based on statistical method to verify my hypothesis.

Why are more hedges used in two-party conversations than in multiple-party conversations? Or why are relatively fewer hedges used in multiple-party conversations than in two-party conversations? This study is not able to provide a solid answer. However, there might be several possible assumptions[34] about the a correlation between hedges and the size of a group. The fact that interlocutors use more hedges in two-party conversations than in multiple-party conversations might be related to collective psychology or collective dynamism. An individual is prone to have less responsibility in a group and to avoid responsibility than in one-on-one conversations. Therefore, the result of this study is meaningful in that it provides a step towards proving collective psychology and collective dynamism through language use. I infer that interlocutors use relatively more hedges to facilitate or promote interpersonal relations in two-party conversations than in multiple-party conversations.

[Hypothesis1] Number of Speakers in Conversation

More hedges are used in two-party conversations than in multiple-party conversations in Korean spoken discourse.

Second, one of the most predominant meaningful variables is the topic of conversation. The analysis showed that there were correlations between the topic of conversation and hedge items such as *-canha(yo),*

34 One of several possible assumptions might be related to the topic of conversation since there were more conversations with personal topics than conversations with impersonal topics in my corpus.

-nuntey(yo), -ketun(yo), telako(yo), -ci(yo), -ney(yo), and *-tay(yo).* Specifically, the topic of conversation (personal topics vs. impersonal topics) is correlated with all seven ISEs (interactive sentence enders). In this study, I distinguished personal topics (i.e., individual/private topics such as boyfriend/girlfriend, grades, appearances, etc.) and impersonal topics (i.e., social topics, political topics such as the suicide of the former president, a college entrance exam, the free trade agreement, Korea's unification, etc.). According to the results of this study, I can propose the hypothesis that hedge items are used more in conversations with personal topics than in conversations with impersonal topics in contemporary Korean discourse. To my knowledge, this study is the first empirical analysis based on statistical methods to verify my hypothesis.

[Hypothesis 2] Topics of Conversation

More hedges are used in conversations with personal topics than with impersonal topics in Korean spoken discourse.

Third, the results of this study criticize the sociolinguistic overgeneralization of the previous research on hedges. The previous research on hedges (Lakoff, 1975; Mulac et al., 1988; Carli, 1990; Grob and Allen, 1996) claims that hedges are more used by females or are considered as powerless language. However, the results of this study show that an individual hedge item has a different correlation with various social variables such as gender, age, occupation, region, power relations, distance relations, topic, etc. According to the results of analysis, for example, the ISE *-tay(yo)* is used more by females than by males and the ISE *-ci(yo)* is used more by older generations than younger generations but not for every hedge item. There is only one case among my data that shows correlation between power relations and hedge usage between interlocutors (e.g., *-nuntey(yo)*) and that shows the correlation between distance relations and hedge use(e.g., *-ci(yo)*). Hence, this study criticizes the overgeneralization of macro analysis of sociolinguistics related to hedges and suggests micro analysis on hedges for further studies.

5.3 Re-examination of Two Major Findings

In this section I will re-examine two major findings on social situational factors such as number of speakers (two-party conversations vs. multiple-party conversations) and topics of conversation (personal topics vs. impersonal topics) and hedge items.

Re-examination will be done by analyzing the correlation between the numbers of speakers as well as topics of conversation and hedge items (seven auxiliary verbs) and contrasting analysis with seven interactive sentence enders (ISEs). Seven auxiliary verbs (AV) to be analyzed among lexical hedges in my data are *-kes kath-, -ci molu-, -tus ha-, -na po-, -e/a-to toy-, -e/a cwu-,-e/a po-.*

5.3.1 Re-examination on number of speakers in conversation and hedge use

The results of the statistical analysis in Table 5-16 summarize the correlation between the number of speakers in conversations and hedge items such as the seven interactive sentence enders (ISEs) and seven auxiliary verbs (AVs). The independent *t*-test was used in order to investigate the difference between two-party conversations (two participants) and multiple-party conversations (involving more than two participants). The results of the statistical analysis are as follows.

First, according to the results of the search engine *hanmalwu*, there were 342 tokens of *-kes kath-* used by 174 interlocutors (i.e., 1.97 tokens/ person) in two-party conversations (two participants) while there were 38 tokens of *-kes kath-* used by 45 interlocutors (i.e., 0.84 tokens/ person) in multiple-party conversations (more than two participants) among the total number of 380 tokens of *-kes kath-*. As shown in Table 5-16, the standard deviation of two-party conversations is 2.270 while that of multiple-party conversations is 1.278. In addition, the *t*-value is

Table 5-16 Contrastive Analysis of ISEs and AVs on Number of Speakers

Hedge Items	Num. of Speakers	N	Mean	Standard Deviation	t-value	P-value	Interpreta-tion
ISE1 *-canha(yo)*	1:1	174	3.90	3.356	2.415	0.017	**1:1>Multi**
	Multi	45	2.53	3.448			
ISE2 *-nuntey(yo)*	1:1	174	4.74	3.494	5.849	0.000	**1:1>Multi**
	Multi	45	2.49	1.866			
ISE3 *-ketun(yo)*	1:1	174	1.01	1.867	3.637	0.000	**1:1>Multi**
	Multi	45	0.33	0.798			
ISE4 *-telako(yo)*	1:1	174	0.30	1.092	0.975	0.331	
	Multi	45	0.13	0.625			
ISE5 *-ci(yo)*	1:1	174	4.98	4.065	2.012	0.045	**1:1>Multi**
	Multi	45	3.62	3.956			
ISE6 *-ney(yo)*	1:1	174	1.05	1.401	1.132	0.259	
	Multi	45	0.78	1.475			
ISE7 *-tay(yo)*	1:1	174	1.13	1.864	2.460	0.015	**1:1>Multi**
	Multi	45	0.58	1.158			
AV1 *-kes kath-*	1:1	174	1.97	2.270	4.366	0.000	**1:1>Multi**
	Multi	45	0.84	1.278			
AV2 *-ci molu-*	1:1	174	0.13	0.382	0.248	0.804	
	Multi	45	0.11	0.318			
AV3 *-tus ha-*	1:1	174	0.01	0.107	0.720	0.472	**N/A**
	Multi	45	0.00	0.000			
AV4 *-na po-*	1:1	174	0.28	0.693	0.128	0.898	
	Multi	45	0.27	0.720			
AV5 *-e/a to toy-*	1:1	174	0.04	0.197	2.693	0.008	**1:1>Multi**
	Multi	45	0.00	0.000			
AV6 *-e/a cwu-*	1:1	174	0.08	0.330	0.261	0.794	
	Multi	45	0.07	0.252			
AV7 *-e/a po-*	1:1	174	0.43	0.740	3.615	0.000	**1:1>Multi**
	Multi	45	0.13	0.405			

4.366 and the P-value is 0.000. According to the *t*-test analysis, there is a significant difference between two groups if the P-value is smaller than 0.05. Hence, my data shows that there is a significant difference between two-party conversations and multiple-party conversations in terms of the frequency of using the AV (auxiliary verb) *-kes kath-*. Since the *t*-value is a positive number (4.366) the result can be analyzed as showing that <u>*-kes kath-* is used more in two-party conversations than in multiple-party conversations</u>.

Second, according to the results of the search engine *hanmalwu*, there were 22 tokens of *-ci molu-* used by 174 interlocutors (i.e., 0.13 tokens/ person) in two-party conversations (two participants) while there were 5 tokens of *-ci molu-* used by 45 interlocutors (i.e., 0.11 token/person) in multiple-party conversations (more than two participants) among the total number of 27 tokens of *-ci molu-*. As shown in the Table 5-16, the standard deviation of two-party conversations is 0.382 while that of multiple-party conversations is 0.318. In addition, the t-value is 0.248 and the P-value is 0.804. According to the *t*-test analysis, there is no significant difference between two groups if the P-value is greater than 0.05. Hence, my data shows that there is no significant difference between two-party conversations and multiple-party conversations in terms of the frequency of using AV (auxiliary verb) *-ci molu-*.

Third, according to the results of the search engine *hanmalwu*, there were only two tokens of *-tus ha-*counted in my data. Thus, the result of statistical analysis of *-tus ha-* will not be quoted in this re-examination although statistical analysis of *-tus ha-* was obtained.

Fourth, according to the results of the search engine *hanmalwu*, there were 49 tokens of *-na po-* used by 170 interlocutors (i.e., 0.28 tokens/ person) in two-party conversations (two participants) while there were 12 tokens of *-na po-* used by 45 interlocutors (i.e., 0.27 tokens/ person) in multiple-party conversations (more than two participants) among the total number of 61 tokens of *-na po-*. As shown in Table 5-16, the standard deviation of two-party conversations is 0.693 while that of multiple-party conversations is 0.720. In addition, the t-value is 0.128 and the P-value is 0.898. According to the *t*-test analysis, there is no significant difference between two groups if the P-value is greater than 0.05. Hence, my data shows that there is no statistical difference between two-party conversations and multiple-party conversations in terms of the frequency of using the AV (auxiliary verb) *-na po.*

Fifth, according to the results of the search engine *hanmalwu* , there were 7 tokens of *-e/a-to toy-* used by 174 interlocutors (i.e., 0.04 tokens/ person) in two-party conversations (two participants) while there were 0 token of *-e/a-to toy-* used by 45 interlocutors (i.e., 0.00 tokens/ person) in multiple-party conversations (more than two participants) among the total number of 7 tokens of *-e/a-to toy-*. As shown in Table 5-16, the standard deviation of two-party conversations is 0.197 while that of multiple-party conversations is 0.000. In addition, the *t*-value is 2.693 and the P-value is 0.008. According to the *t*-test analysis, there is a significant difference between two groups if the P-value is smaller than 0.05. Hence, my data shows that there is a significant difference between two-party conversations and multiple-party conversations in terms of the frequency of using the AV (auxiliary verb) *-e/a-to toy-*. Since the t-value is a positive number (2.693) the result can be analyzed as showing that <u>*-e/a-to toy-* is used more in two-party conversations than in multiple-party conversations.</u>

Sixth, according to the results of the search engine *hanmalwu*, there were 14 tokens of *-e/a cwu-* used by 174 interlocutors (i.e., 0.08 tokens/ person) in two-party conversations (two participants) while there were 3 token of *-e/a cwu-* used by 45 interlocutors (i.e., 0.07 tokens/ person) in multiple-party conversations (more than two participants) among the total number of 17 tokens of *-e/a cwu-*. As shown in Table 5-16, the standard deviation of two-party conversations is 0.330 while that of multiple-party conversations is 0.252. In addition, the t-value is 0.261 and the P-value is 0.794. According to the *t*-test analysis, there is no significant difference between two groups if the P-value is greater than 0.05. Hence, my data shows that there is no statistical difference between two-party conversations and multiple-party conversations in terms of the frequency of using the AV (auxiliary verb) *-e/a cwu-*.

Seventh, according to the results of the search engine *hanmalwu*, there were 75 tokens of *-e/a po-* used by 174 interlocutors (i.e., 0.43 tokens/ person) in two-party conversations (two participants) while there were 6 token of *-e/a po-* used by 45 interlocutors (i.e., 0.13 tokens/ person) in multiple-party conversations (more than two participants) among the total number of 81 tokens of *-e/a po-*. As shown in Table 5-16, the standard deviation of two-party conversations is 0.740 while that of multiple-party conversations is 0.405. In addition, the t-value is 3.615 and the P-value is 0.000. According to the *t*-test analysis, there is a significant difference between two groups if the P-value is smaller than 0.05. Since the *t*-value is a positive number (3.615) the result can be analyzed as showing that *-e/a po-* is used more in two-party conversations than in multiple-party conversations.

In short, the results of statistical analysis in Table 5-16 show that three hedge items such as the AVs *-kes kath-, -e/a-to toy-*, and *-e/a po-*among seven auxiliary verbs were used more in two-party conversations than in multiple-party conversations. Hence, my hypothesis concerning the number of speakers in conversation (More hedges are used in two-party conversations than in multiple-party conversations in Korean spoken discourse) appears to be valid since it is verified statistically in both seven ISEs and seven AVs. Hence, according to the results of statistical analysis, I can claim that hedge items are used more in two-party conversations than in multiple-party conversations in contemporary Korean discourse.

5.3.2 Re-examination of topics of conversations and hedge use

The results of statistical analysis in Table 5-17 summarize the correlation between the topic (personal topics vs. impersonal topics) of conversation and hedge items such as seven interactive sentence enders (ISEs) and seven auxiliary verbs (AVs). The independent *t*-test was used in order to investigate the difference between personal and impersonal topics in conversations. The results of statistical analysis are as follows.

First, according to the results of the search engine *hanmalwu*, among 380 tokens in my data, there were 41 tokens of *-kes kath-* used by 219

Table 5-17 Contrastive Analysis of ISEs and AVs on Topic of Conversations

Hedge Items	Mean	N	Standard Deviation	Paired Differences		t-value	P-value	Interpretation
				Mean	Std. Deviation			
ISE1_Impersonal	0.12	219	0.823	-3.370	3.519	-14.173	0.000	Personal > Impersonal
ISE1_Personal	3.49	219	3.367					
ISE2_Impersonal	0.05	219	0.247	-4.164	3.359	-18.345	0.000	Personal > Impersonal
ISE2_Personal	4.22	219	3.345					
ISE3_Impersonal	0.00	219	0.068	-0.858	1.722	-7.376	0.000	Personal > Impersonal
ISE3_Personal	0.86	219	1.721					
ISE4_Impersonal	0.01	219	0.117	-0.237	0.985	-3.566	0.000	Personal > Impersonal
ISE4_Personal	0.25	219	0.994					
ISE5_Impersonal	0.15	219	0.695	-4.411	4.071	-16.034	0.000	Personal > Impersonal
ISE5_Personal	4.56	219	4.011					
ISE6_Impersonal	0.00	219	0.068	-0.982	1.424	-10.204	0.000	Personal > Impersonal
ISE6_Personal	0.99	219	1.419					
ISE7_Impersonal	0.07	219	0.371	-0.877	1.608	-8.069	0.000	Personal > Impersonal
ISE7_Personal	0.95	219	1.641					
AV1_Impersonal	0.19	219	0.828	-1.361	2.281	-8.827	0.000	Personal > Impersonal
AV1_Personal	1.55	219	2.057					
AV2_Impersonal	0.00	219	0.000	-0.123	0.369	-4.945	0.000	Personal > Impersonal
AV2_Personal	0.12	219	0.369					
AV3_Impersonal	0.00	219	0.000	-0.009	0.095	-1.417	0.158	N/A
AV3_Personal	0.01	219	0.095					
AV4_Impersonal	0.01	219	0.135	-0.260	0.704	-5.468	0.000	Personal > Impersonal
AV4_Personal	0.27	219	0.688					
AV5_Impersonal	0.00	219	0.000	-0.032	0.176	-2.683	0.008	Personal > Impersonal
AV5_Personal	0.03	219	0.176					
AV6_Impersonal	0.00	219	0.000	-0.078	0.315	-3.643	0.000	Personal > Impersonal
AV6_Personal	0.08	219	0.315					
AV7_Impersonal	0.00	219	0.000	-0.370	0.694	-7.885	0.000	Personal > Impersonal
AV7_Personal	0.37	219	0.694					

interlocutors (0.19 tokens/person) with impersonal topics while there were 339 tokens of *-kes kath-* used by 219 interlocutors (i.e., 1.55 tokens/person) in conversations with personal topics. The paired *t*-test was used in order to investigate the difference between conversations with impersonal topics and conversations with personal topics. As shown in Table 5-17, the standard deviation of conversations with impersonal topics is 0.828 while that of conversations with personal topics is 2.057. In addition, the *t*-value is -8.927 and the P-value is 0.000. According to the *t*-test analysis, there is a significant difference between two groups if the P-value is smaller than 0.05. Hence, my data shows that there is a significant difference between conversations with impersonal topics and conversations with personal topics in terms of the frequency of using the AV (auxiliary verb) *-kes kath-*. Since the *t*-value is a negative number (-8.927) the result can be analyzed as showing that <u>*-kes kath-* is used more in conversations with personal topics than in conversations with impersonal topics</u>.

Second, according to the results of the search engine *hanmalwu*, among 27 tokens in my data, there were 0 tokens of *-ci molu-* used by 219 interlocutors (0 tokens/person) with impersonal topics while there were 27 tokens of *-ci molu-* used by 219 interlocutors (i.e., 0.12 tokens /person) in conversations with personal topics. The paired *t*-test was used in order to investigate the difference between conversations with impersonal topics and conversations with personal topics. As shown in Table 5-17, the standard deviation of conversation with impersonal topics is 0.000 while that of conversations with personal topics is 0.369. In addition, the t-value is -4.945 and the P-value is 0.000. According to the *t*-test analysis, there is a significant difference between two groups if the P-value is smaller than 0.05. Hence, my data shows that there is a significant difference between conversations with impersonal topics and conversations with personal topics in terms of the frequency of using the AV (auxiliary verb) *-ci molu-*. Since the *t*-value is a negative number (-4.945) the result can be analyzed as showing that <u>*-ci molu-* is used more in conversations with personal topics than in conversations with impersonal topics</u>.

Third, according to the results of the search engine *hanmalwu*, there were only two tokens of *-tus ha-* counted in my data. Thus, the result of statistical analysis of *-tus ha-* will not be quoted in this re-examination although statistical analysis of *-tus ha-* was obtained.

Fourth, according to the results of the search engine *hanmalwu*, among 61 tokens in my data, there were 2 tokens of *-na po-* used by 219 interlocutors (0.01 tokens/person) with impersonal topics while there were 59 tokens of *-na po-* used by 219 interlocutors (i.e., 0.27 tokens /person) in conversations with personal topics. The paired *t*-test was used in order to investigate the difference between conversations with impersonal topics and conversations with personal topics. As shown in Table 5-17, the standard deviation of conversation with impersonal topics is 0.135 while that of conversation with personal topics is 0.688. In addition, the t-value is -5.468 and the P-value is 0.000. According to the *t*-test analysis, there is a significant difference between two groups if the P-value is smaller than 0.05. Hence, my data shows that there is a significant difference between conversations with impersonal topics and conversations with personal topics in terms of the frequency of using the AV (auxiliary verb) *-na po-*. Since the *t*-value is a negative number (-5.468) the result can be analyzed as showing that <u>*-na po-* is used more in conversations with impersonal topics than in conversations with personal topics</u>.

Fifth, according to the results of the search engine *hanmalwu*, among 7 tokens in my data, there were 0 token of *-e/a-to toy-* used by 219 interlocutors (0.00 token/person) with impersonal topics while there were 7 tokens of *-e/a-to toy-* used by 219 interlocutors (i.e., 0.03 tokens /person) in conversations with personal topics. The paired *t*-test was used in order to investigate the difference between conversations with impersonal topics and conversations with personal topics. As shown in the Table 5-17, the standard deviation of conversation with impersonal topics is 0.000 while that of conversation with personal topics is 0.176. In addition, the *t*-value is -2.683 and the P-value is 0.008. According to the *t*-test analysis, there is a significant difference between two groups if the P-value is smaller than 0.05. Hence, my data shows that there is a significant difference between conversations with impersonal topics and conversations with personal topics in terms of the frequency of using the AV (auxiliary verb) *-e/a-to toy-* . Since the t-value is a negative number (-2.683) the result can be analyzed as showing that *-e/a-to toy-* is used more in conversations with personal topics than in conversations with impersonal topics.

Sixth, according to the results of the search engine *hanmalwu*, among 17 tokens in my data, there were 0 tokens of *-e/a cwu-* used by 219 interlocutors (0.00 tokens/person) with impersonal topics while there were 17 tokens of *-e/a cwu-* used by 219 interlocutors (i.e., 0.08 tokens/person) in conversations with personal topics. The paired *t*-test was used in order to investigate the difference between conversations with impersonal topics and conversations with personal topics. As shown in the Table 5-17, the standard deviation of conversations with impersonal topics is 0.000 while that of conversations with personal topics is 0.315. In addition, the t-value is -3.643 and the P-value is 0.000. According to the *t*-test analysis, there is a significant difference between two groups if the P-value is smaller than 0.05. Hence, my data shows that there is a significant difference between conversations with impersonal topics and conversations with personal topics in terms of the frequency of using the AV (auxiliary verb) *-e/a cwu-*. Since the *t*-value is a negative number (-3.643) the result can be analyzed as showing that *-e/a cwu-* is used more in conversations with personal topics than in conversations with impersonal topics.

Seventh, according to the results of the search engine *hanmalwu*, among 81 tokens in my data, there were 0 tokens of *-e/a po-* token used by 219 interlocutors (0.00 tokens/person) with impersonal topics while there were 81 tokens of *-e/a po-* used by 219 interlocutors (i.e., 0.37 tokens /person) in conversations with personal topics. The paired *t*-test was used in order to investigate the difference between conversations with impersonal topics and conversations with personal topics. As shown in Table 5-17, the standard deviation of conversations with impersonal topics is 0.000 while that of conversations with personal topics is 0.694. In addition, the t-value is -7.885 and the P-value is

0.000. According to the *t*-test analysis, there is a significant difference between two groups if the P-value is smaller than 0.05. Hence, my data shows that there is a significant difference between conversations with impersonal topics and conversations with personal topics in terms of the frequency of using the AV (auxiliary verb) *-e/a po-*. Since the *t*-value is a negative number (-7.885) the result can be analyzed as showing that *-e/a po-* is used more in conversations with private topics than in conversations with impersonal topics.

In short, the results of statistical analysis in Table 5-17 show that seven hedge items such as auxiliary verbs *-kes kath-, -ci molu-, -tus ha-, -na po-, -e/a-to toy-, -e/a cwu-,-e/a po-* were used more in conversations with personal topics than in conversations with impersonal topic. Hence, my hypothesis of topics in conversation (More hedges are used in conversations with personal topics than with impersonal topics in Korean spoken discourse) could be valid since it is verified statistically in both seven ISEs and seven AVs. Hence, according to the results of statistical analysis, I can claim that hedge items are used more in conversations with personal topics than with impersonal topics in contemporary Korean discourse.

5.4 Summary

First, the results of the statistical analysis of seven interactive sentence enders (ISEs) among lexical hedges show that there are correlations between hedge use and sociopragmatic factors. Twenty-two findings in the sociopragmatic analysis of seven ISEs were illustrated in detail in Section 5.2.

Second, one of the most meaningful findings is that the number of speakers in conversation (two-party conversations vs. multiple-party conversations) affects hedge use. The result of analysis revealed that there were correlation between the number of speakers in conversation and the hedge items such as *-canha(yo), -nuntey(yo),-ketun(yo), -ci(yo), -tay(yo)* among seven ISEs (interactive sentence enders). According to this result, I propose the hypothesis that hedges are used more in two-party conversations than in multiple-party conversations in contemporary Korean discourse. Furthermore, in Section 5.3 similar results from the statistical analysis of the re-examination of the correlation between the number of speakers in conversations and hedge use were obtained. The results of the statistical analysis showed that three hedge items such as the auxiliary verbs (AVs) *-kes kath-, -e/ato toy-*, and *-e/a po-*among six AVs were used more in two-party conversations than in multiple-party conversations. Hence, my hypothesis concerning the number of speakers in conversation (More hedges are used in two-party conversations than in multiple-party conversations in Korean spoken discourse) was not falsified since it is verified statistically both with respect to the use of the seven ISEs and the use of the three AVs.

Third, another meaningful finding is that the topic of conversation affects hedge use. The results of the analysis revealed that there were correlations between the topic of conversation (personal topics vs. impersonal topics) and the hedge items such as the seven ISEs *-canha(yo), -nuntey(yo), -ketun(yo), -telako(yo), -ci(yo), -ney(yo), tay(yo)*. According to this result, I propose the hypothesis that hedges are used more in conversations with personal topics than in conversations with impersonal topics in contemporary Korean discourse. Furthermore, in Section 5.3 similar results from the statistical analysis of the re-examination of the correlation between the topic of conversation and hedge use were obtained. The results of statistical analysis showed that all six hedge items such as the auxiliary verbs *-kes kath-, -ci molu-, -na po-, -e/a-to toy-, -e/a cwu-,-e/a po-* were used more in conversations with personal topics than in conversations with impersonal topics. Hence, my hypothesis concerning the topic of conversation (More hedges are used in conversations with personal topics than with impersonal topics in Korean spoken discourse) was not falsified since it is verified statistically both with respect to the use of the seven ISEs and the use of three AVs.

CHAPTER 6

PRAGMALINGUISTIC ANALYSIS OF SELECTED HEDGES

In this Chapter I will examine hedge use in terms of a pragmalinguistic perspective. In order to employ pragmalinguistic analysis, the two interactive sentence enders (ISEs) *-canha(yo)* and *-ketun(yo)* were chosen among seven ISEs in lexical hedges and they will be analyzed qualitatively as well as quantitatively. The reasons for selecting these two items are as follows. First, it is necessary for qualitative analysis to narrow down the number of items. Second, in contemporary Korean spoken discourse both *-canha(yo)* 'you know' and *-ketun(yo)* 'you see' share similar hedge functions such as enhancing interpersonal rapport, establishing solidarity, seeking agreement, and so forth. Also, they are both concerned with the speaker's degree of knowledge about the propositional content of the utterance (M. Park, 2003). Third, they had similar results from the statistical analysis on sociopragmatic variables in Chapter 5. The results show that both *-canha(yo)* and *-ketun(yo)* are used more in two-party conversations than in multiple-party conversation and more in personal topic conversations than in impersonal topic conversation. Neither *-canha(yo)* nor *-ketun(yo)* had differences in terms of other sociopragmatic factors such as gender, gender composition of conversations, age, occupation except for region.[35].

In Section 6.1 I will examine the development of the ISE *-canha(yo)*, summarize the speech act types associated with the use of *-canha(yo)* and give examples based on speech acts types, and analyze *-canha(yo)* in terms of politeness perspectives. In particular, this study will analyze

35 Note that *-ketun(yo)* are used more in metropolitan areas than in nonmetropolitan areas.

the frequency of speech act types as well as politeness strategies, present the findings as hypotheses, and verify the hypotheses statistically.

In Section 6.2, I will examine the development of the ISE *-ketun(yo)*, summarize the speech act types associated with the use of *-ketun(yo)* and give examples based on speech acts types, and analyze *-ketun(yo)* in terms of politeness perspectives. In particular, this study will analyze the frequency of speech act types as well as politeness strategies, present the findings as hypotheses, and verify the hypotheses statistically. Section 6.3 will compare the results of analysis and findings of 6.1 and 6.2.

Hedges are especially related to speech act illocutionary force in discourse. Speakers employ hedges in order to attenuate any negative effects such as harshness or hurt, to offer hospitality to listeners, and to communicate effectively. Hedges in speech acts are important factors in an interactive context since speech acts involve the relationship between the speaker and the listener as well as the relationship between a speaker and a proposition. Thus, this chapter will attempt to analyze the two ISEs *-canha(yo)* and *-ketun(yo)* in relation to speech act types and politeness strategies.

6.1 Pragmalinguistic Analysis of the ISE *-canha(yo)*

6.1.1 Development of the ISE *-canha(yo)*

Let me briefly summarize the theoretical background of grammaticalization in order to explain the development of the ISE *-canha(yo)*. Grammaticalization refers to the dynamic linguistic process of deriving grammatical forms or structures out of lexical, phrasal, or clausal constructions, as well as from other grammatical entities (Sohn 1999a, p. 152). The mechanism of linguistic change involves three essential elements- meaning shift, grammatical restructuring, and phonological change. The meaning shift and grammatical restructuring occur simultaneously while phonological change usually occurs later and optionally.

Furthermore, a functional shift means there is a shift in the composition of meaning shift and grammatical restructuring. Many words and affixes have developed from other words or larger constructions through a long period of evolution (Sohn 1999b, p.261). Moreover, Traugott and Konig (1991) claim that grammaticalization is unidirectional in the process of a meaning shift from the propositional to the textual to the expressive level. In this developmental path, concrete referential meanings develop toward more abstract and subjective meanings. Hence, the pragmatic meaning of grammaticalizing material, which indexes the speaker's subjective attitudes and beliefs, is strengthened in the process of grammaticalization while its semantic content may decrease. In other words, meaning shifts move away from objective, referential meaning towards subjective, speaker-oriented attitudes (*subjectification*). Also, such speaker-based semantic pragmatic change conforms to the unidirectional principle but not vice versa. The prerequisites for grammaticalization are (i) semantic suitability of the source concepts, (ii) typological salience, (iii) syntagmatic contiguity (two or more forms must be contiguous in order to merge and form a grammatical element), and (iv) frequency of use (i.e., the form has to be used frequently in order to be grammaticalized). Along with those general characteristics, major characteristics of grammaticalization suggested by Hopper (1991, p. 22) are summarized as follows:

(a) *Layering*: Within a broad functional domain,[36] a variety of different forms and constructions (i.e. older layers and newer layers) may coexist and serve similar functional purposes.
(b) *Divergence* (or *split*): When a lexical form undergoes grammaticalization to a clitic or affix, the original lexical form may remain as an autonomous element and undergo the same changes as an ordinary lexical item.
(c) *Specialization*: Within a functional domain, as grammaticalization takes place, the variety of formal choices narrows and the smaller number of forms selected assume more general grammatical meanings.

---

36 According to Givon (1984, p.325) functional domain means some general functional area such as tense-aspect-modality (TAM), case, reference, etc.

(d) *Persistence*: The attributes of the original lexical item constrain the distribution of its grammaticalized form.
(e) *Decategorization*: The categorical change triggered by grammaticalization tends to be from a major category (e.g. noun and verb) to a minor category (e.g. preposition and clausal connectives).

In Contemporary Korean, *-canha(yo)* is predominantly used as one of the interactive sentence enders (ISEs) in spoken discourse. The newly innovated sentence ender *-canha(yo)* 'you see!, as you know' has evolved from *-ci anha(yo)* , which is the long-form negation in Korean. Moreover, the long form negation *-ci anha(yo)* is originally from *-ci ani*[37] *hay-yo* (NOM[38] not do/be-POL) 'Isn't it the case that⋯.' (H. Sohn, 199b). The long-form negation *-ci anha(yo)* in Contemporary Korean occurs in pure negative context; on the other hand, the reduced form *-canha(yo)* has special purposes for interactive functions such as enhancing interpersonal rapport, establishing solidarity, or seeking agreement, and so forth (S. Sohn, 2005).

For example,

(1) *ku* *moca-nun* *Mia-eykey* *ewulli-**ci-anha-yo***.
that hat-TC Mia-DAT look good- NOM **not** do-POL
'That hat does **not** look good on Mia.'

(2) *ku* *moca-un* *Mia -eykey* *ewulli-**canh-ayo***.
that hat-TC Mia-DAT look good-**CANH**-POL
'That hat does look good on Mia (**as you know**).'

The only overt difference between sentences (1) and (2) is phonological reduction which occurs in the sentence (2). However, there is also semantic difference between two sentences. The sentence (1) has

37 The negation marker *an* in *anh-ayo* has its origin in *ani-hay-yo* which was used in the early Modern Korean (17C-18C) and started being replaced with *an* in the late 19th century (Lee, 1993).

38 The suffix *-ci* is called aspectual marker, nominalizer, complementizer, or committal suffix depending on the author. Following H. Sohn (1999, p.262), this is glossed as NOM (nominalizer) in this paper.

pure negative meaning whereas the sentence (2) does not have negative meaning at all. There is a semantic shift towards subjectivity from the full form *-ci anha(yo)* to the reduced form *-canha(yo)* via the process of grammaticalization. According to Kawanishi and S.Sohn, *ci* + *anh-* is reduced to *canh-* via the grammaticalization process, by which "the meaning of *-cahn-* moves toward an interactive function and a speaker-centered situation, denoting the speaker's subjective evaluation (cf. Traugott 1989)" (1993, p.552). That is, the semantic changes are observed in *-ci anha(yo)* towards subjectivity[39] in that the reduced form *-canha(yo)* codes new interactive functions which were not coded in its original form *-ci anha(yo)* (Kawanishi & S. Sohn, 1993). Let us exemplify the interactive or interpersonal functions of *-canha(yo)* observed in spoken discourse, excerpted from Kawanishi & S.Sohn (1993), as in (3).

(3) 1.Y: → *cinan khwethe kkaci-nun kyohwan haksayng-i*
last quarter until-TC exchange student-NM
mahn-ci anh-ass-eyo.
many-**ci** **anh**-PAST-POL
'Until last quarter, there were not many exchange students.'

2. J: *cepen-ey.*
Last time-at
'Last time.'

3. Y: → *senpay-tul-i-***canh***-ayo, ta-tul.*
Senior-PL-be-CANH-POL all-PL
'(As you know) they are all my seniors. All of them are.'

4. J: ung.
yeah
'Yeah'

5.Y: → *Ta senpay-tul-i-nikka manna-myen*
all senior-PL-be-since meet-if
*amwulayto com pwulliha-***canh***-ayo.*
anyhow a bit disadvantageous-**CANH**-POL

39 Traugott (1995) suggests the notion of 'subjectification' in which meanings tend to change from objective, referential to subjective and speaker-based situation.

'Since all of them are my seniors, when I see them, (as you would agree with me), I would be in a disadvantageous situation.

The long-form negation *-ci anh-* in line 1 is simply used for negating the propositional content while *-canh-* in line 3 and line 5 has the effect of interactive alignment. In other words, *-ci anha(yo)* concerns the informational content while the reduced form *-canha(yo)* concerns the interactive function. The newly innovated sentence ending *-canha(yo)* functions to indicate interactive focus on speaker-provided information (Schiffrin 1987, p.267). Thus, the function of *-canha(yo)* is to mark the common knowledge and it is known as a device that elicits the addressee's agreement or confirmation. Also, *-canha(yo)* is more often used in informal situations since the use of *-canha(yo)* indexes a lower degree of formality and it narrows the communicative distance (i.e., improves solidarity) between the speaker and the listener in terms of sociopragmatics.

As observed above, the direction of the semantic shift in the process of the grammaticalization of *-canha(yo)* is from propositional meaning to a speaker's subjective belief; this shift is consistent with typical patterns of grammaticalization phenomena in Korean (cf. H. Sohn, 1990). Also, Traugott (1991) focuses on meaning change in the process of grammaticalization and suggests that semantic-pragmatic change moves from propositional to an expressive[40] meaning via a textual function. According to this view the semantic shift in the process of grammaticalization is always unidirectional.

Furthermore, there is a syntactic reanalysis in that the full form *-ci anha(yo)* occurs in a variety of constructions (conjunctive, embedded, and main clauses) while *-canha(yo)* is strictly limited to a sentence-final position. *-canha(yo)* loses the ability to occur with various morphosyntactic categories and limits its occurrence to a sentence-final position, causing syntactic restructuring in the process of grammaticalization.

40 He expressive function of language serves in the expression and development of the speaker attitude and interaction with others.

The syntactic shift to a sentence-final modal in grammaticalization is quite common in Korean.

According to H. Sohn (1990), the development of the sentence-final modals in Korean is typically associated with historical deletion with semantic-pragmatic changes. As a result, grammaticalized forms often create decategorization. Moreover, in the course of the transition from a negation marker to the sentence-final modal marker, there is an intermediate stage where the nongrammaticalized full form *-ci anh-ayo* and the grammaticalized reduced form *-canh-ayo* coexist. At the first stage, *-ci anh-ayo* and *-canha(yo)* are interchangeable without a meaning shift. At the second stage, two forms are no longer interchangeable, as in the fossilized form *iss-canha(yo)* 'you know that?, well'. In short, the reduced form *-canha(yo)* acquires a new textual function as a sentence-final modal with an interactive effect whose function is not coded in the long form negation *-ci anha(yo)*.

6.1.2 Usage of the ISE *-canha(yo)*

Table 6-1 is the summary of examples of each speech act types associated with the use of the ISE *-canha(yo)*.

Table 6-1
Examples of Each Speech Act Type Associated with the Use of ISE-*canha(yo)*

Speech Act Type	Examples	Strategy Type
P-1 (Seeking agreement)	*phansa-lul hataka-to ku lamyencip-ul mwullye pat-nun kes-ey tayhan kelikkim-i wulinala-pota cokum tel han kes-un sasil-i-**canha**-yo.*	P
P-2 (Informing)	*kyelsungcen-i-**canha**, kukey.*	P
P-3 (Reminiscing)	*kotunghakkyo tani-l ttay hangsang cip-eyse pap mek-ko ka-ss-**canha**.*	P
N-1 (Stating an opinion)	*kulayse kuntey kyoyukhakkwa himtul-**canha**. kongpwu cal hha-nun ay-tul ka-ko sensaeng toy-nun ke-nikka.*	N
N-2 (Telling a problem)	*na-to ttel-e-ciko sihem ta ccik-ko naw-ass-**canha** kunyang.*	N

N-3 (Complaining)	*kulenikkan hyeng-i pap com cal chayngki-e mek-ula-ko hay-ss-**canha**.*	N
N-4 (Requesting)	*an-tul-li-myen kuman po-lako ha-**canha**.*	N
N-5 (Suggesting)	*a ne pesu tha-ya toy-canha.*	N
N-6 (Criticizing)	*ahu cwuk-keyss-e himtul-ese. Ahu yocum cepen-ey hanpen pi w-ass-ess-**canha**.*	N
N-7 (Expressing emotions)	*nen kulay-to kiswuksa-**canha**.*	N
N-8 (Bragging)	*na cal sayng-ky-ess-**canha**.*	N
N-9 (Opposing)	*an-ssis-ese nankey ani-**canha**.*	N
N-11 (Apologizing)	*cinan-pen-ey nay-ka ne cikum kyeysok kkamek-ko mos cw-ess-**canha**.*	N

(1) The Example of P-1 (Seeking Agreement)

File number 21: Artisan spirit (Craftsmanship)

M1: *cangin-ul ettehkey palapo-nunya ku kwancem-uy*
atisan-AC how look-PLN that view-GN
chai-nun iss-ul-ci molu-keyss-nuntey.
difference-TC have-RL-whether don't know-PRS-ENDER
'How we view an artisan··· Well, there might be a different point of view.'

M2: *kule-myen wuli-ka icey palapo-nun cangin*
yes-if we-NOM now look-RL artisan
cengsin-i-la-nun key ilpon-eyse ttacinta-myen phansa-lul
spirit-be-QT-TC thing Japan-in determine-if judge-AC
ha-taka-to ku lamyencip-ul mwullye-pat-nun
do-while-even DM ramen house-AC inherit-receive-RC
kes-ey tayha-n kelikkim-i wuli nala-pota
thing-to regard-RL hesitation-NM our country-more
→ *cokum tel ha-n kes-un sasil-i-**canha**-yo.*
a little less do-RL thing-TC truth-NM-CANHA-POL
'Then, how we view an artisan···. You know, compared to Koreans, Japanese are less hesitant about inheriting their family business such as ramen house (for example, even a judge can inherit the running of

his/her ramen house business) than in Korea.'
M1: *kuleh-ci*
so-ENDER
'That's right'

Two male students in their 20s (M1 is older than M2) are discussing the artisan spirit (craftsmanship). M2 compares the situation between Korea and Japan but he thinks that M1 might have a different point of view from him. So, M2 doesn't want to assert his opinion and rather seeks agreement from M1 by employing the ISE *-cahnha.* M1 responds that he agrees with M2's opinion. Therefore, we can conclude that the hedge ISE *-canha(yo)* functions as a positive politeness strategy in this conversation.

(2) The Example of P-2 (Informing)
File number 8: Soccer game
O1: *e, e a onul-i mokyoil-i-canha.*
um um ah today-NM Thursday-be-CANHA
nayilmoley-canha.
day after tomorrow-CANHA
'Um, today is Thursday. It (the game) is the day after tomorrow, isn't it?'
O2: *a, nayilmoley-myen kuke-canha.*
ah, day after tomorrow-if that thing-CANHA
phulimiey liku macimak kyengki.
premier league last game
'The day after tomorrow is the last game of premier league, isn't it?'
O1: → *kyelsungcen-i-**canha**, kukey.*
final game-be-CANHA
'That is the final game CANHA, you know'
O2: *a, kulay?*
ah so
'Is that so?'

Two office workers in their 30s are talking about the soccer game. O1 says that today is Thursday and he realizes that the day after tomorrow is the big game. O2 says that the day after tomorrow is the last day of premier league. But O1 informs O2 that it is the final game by employing the ISE *-cahnha* as a positive politeness strategy in order to enhance their solidarity.

(3) The Example of P-3 (Reminiscing)

File number 50: Breakfast

M: *achim-ey ilccik wuntong-hako pap chayngky-e mek-ko*
morning-in early exercise-do meal get-INF eat-and
kuleko hakkyo ka-ko hay-ya-ci.
and school go-and do-must-ENDER
'You should exercise early in the morning, have breakfast, and then go to school.'

S: *kulay-to swuep-I ta ocen-ey iss-e kackwu.*
but-even class-NM all morning-in have-INF because
'But even so, I have all my classes in the morning.'

M: *kunikka pap-un mek-ko swuep-ul kongpwu-lul ha-ko*
so meal-TC eat-and class-AC study-AC do-and
hay-ya-ci. kotunghakkyo tani-l ttay
do-must-ENDER high school attend-RL time
*hangsang cip-eyse pap mek-ko ka-ss-**canha***
always home-at meal eat-and go-PST-CANHA
'So, that's why you should eat breakfast and then study. You know, you always went to (high) school after you had breakfast."

S: *ani-ya an-mek-un nal-to iss-ess-e.*
no-be-INT not-eat-RL day-also be-PST-INT
'No, there were days I didn't have breakfast.'

M: *myech pen-ina tway?*
how many times-or become-INF.
Emma-ka ne pap an-chayngky-e-cwu-myen
Mom-NM you meal no-prepare-INF-give-if
ohilye appahanthey honna-nuntey.
rather dad-from scold-ENDER
'How many times did you not have breakfast? (That's nonsense) because if I didn't (prepare breakfast for you) then your dad rather scolded me."

A mother in her 40s and a son in his 20s are talking about breakfast.

The mother is advising her son to have breakfast (for his health) every morning. Her son says that he can't have breakfast every morning because he has so many classes in the morning. His mother is reminiscing about his high school days saying that he had breakfast every day back then (even though he had a busy schedule in the morning). The mother is concerned about her son's health so she wants him to have breakfast but she does not want to scold or preach at him regarding his breakfast but rather, she wants him to reminisce about his high school days so that he doesn't have an excuse. By employing the ISE *-canha*, the mother wants to confirm the shared knowledge with her son in order to enhance rapport with her son.

(4) The Example of N-1 (Stating an Opinion)

File number 35: Major at college

S1: *ne kulem kochi-ka etieti ponay-cwul-swu-issta kule-ni?*
you then coach-NM where send-give-can yes-PLN
'Did your coach tell you which school he could recommend you to?'

S2: *ponay-cwul-swu-iss-nun ken acik an-malha-ko.*
send-give-can-RL thing yet not-say-and.
'Well, he didn't say anything about it yet.'

S1: e
'Hum'

S2: *nay-ka wuntong···. icey-nun casin eps-tako.*
I-NM sports now-TC confidence don't have-QT
'Well, I told him I don't have confidence any more in doing sports.'

S1: e
'Hum'

S2: *ka-l-kke-myen kyoyyukhakkwa-na ilen-tey ka-ko siph-tako.*
go-will-thing-if education major-or like this-place go-and wish-QT
'If I have to go, I would rather apply for the education program or something.'

S1: um
'Hum'

S2: → *kulayse kuntey kyoyukhakkwa himtul-**canha**.*
so But education major hard-CANHA
kongpwu cal ha-nun ay-tul ka-ko

study well do-RL student-PL go-and
sensayng toy-nun ke-nikka.
teacher become-RL thing-because
'But, you know that being an education major is really hard. Smart students usually apply for that major and they become teachers, you know.'

Two high school senior students (S1 is a male student and S2 is a female student) are talking about S2's major at college (S2 is a member of the school's athletic team). S2 is saying that she is not confident in doing sports and applying for a major in sports. She tells her friend that she told this to the coach of her sports team and wanted to apply for an education major. Furthermore, she is stating her opinion about the education major by employing the ISE *-cahna* in order to elicit her friend in conversation. That is, the ISE *-cahna* was used to express the speaker's effort to mitigate illocutionary force when stating his/her opinion or talking about a problem, as a negative politeness strategy.

(5) The Example of N-2 (Telling a Problem)

File number 23: Certificate

M1: *Philyo eps-e.*
necessity don't have-INF
kanpwu-tul-pakkey cey.e-lul hay-ya toy-canha.
executive-PL-only control-AC must become-CANHA.
kanpwu-nun thongceykwan.
executives-NM controller.
ku-kes-pota-n hanca.
that-thing-rather-TC Chinese character
'I don't think it is necessary. Only executives need to have the (proficiency) certificate because they need to be in control.'

M2: *cakyekcung tta-kaciko, hana-ssik tta-ya-ha-nuntey.*
certificate obtain-DM one by one obtain-must-but.
Cakyekcung hanahana-ssik
certificate one by one
'I have to get the certificates one by one.'

M1: *ani, nay-ka yopen-ey sihem-ul po-ass-nuntey.*
DM I-NM this time-at test-ACtake-but.
kuke mwe-ya···. yuthongkwanlisa sihem po-ass-nuntey
that thing DM distribution manger test take-PST-but
ay-tul ta ttel-e-c-ess-e.
student-PL all fail-become-INT.
na-to tteleci-ko sihem ta ccik-ko
I-also fail-and test all guess-and
naw-ass-canha kunyang.
come out-PST-CANHA DM
'Well, I took the test this time. What was that···. the distribution manager test but all the other students failed. I failed too. I guessed all the answers.'

M2: *a yuthongkwanlisa-na tta-lkka?*
ah distribution manager-or get-will?
'Should I get a distribution manager certificate?'

Two male friends (college students) are talking about obtaining a certificate. F1 says that there is no need to get a distribution manager certificate because it is only necessary for executives. And he says to his friend, who thinks that he should get a certificate, that he failed the test and even guessed all the answers. By employing the ISE *-canha* he mitigates the illocutionary force of telling his friend his problem.

(6) The Example of N-3 (Complaining)

File number 18: Illness

S1 :*kuntey, onul-un moksoli-ka com mom-i manhi*
but today-TC voice-NM a little Body-NM a lot
aph-un-ke kath-untey?
sick-RL thing seems-ENDER
'Well, your voice sounds a little bit weird. It seems like you really don't feel well.'

S2: *ehyu, yocum mom-i pyellu manhi an-coh-ase.*
whew recently body-NM especially much not-good-because
pheylyem choki-ketun-yo.
pneumonia first stage-ENDER
'I have been sick recently. I have the first stage of pneumonia.'

akka *swuep-ul* *com* *tut-taka*
while ago class-AC a little listen-and then
swuep *ta* *kkuthna-ko*
class all finish-and
palo *cip-ey* *ka-ss-ci-yo.*
immediately home-at go-PST-ENDER-POL
'I was in class but when it was finished I went home immediately.'

S1: *ewu,* *kulehkey* *cakku* *apha-kaciko* *ettek-hana?*
gee like that repeatedly sick-because how-do-ENDER?
Namca-ka.
Male-NM
kulenikkan *hyeng-i* *pap* *com* *cal* *chayngki-e*
so older brother-NM meal DM well prepare-INF
mek-ula-ko *hay-ss-**canha**.*
eat-intend-and do- PST-CANHA
way *ilehkye* *hyeng* *mal-ul* *an-tul-e,* *e?*
why like this older brother saying-AC not-listen-INT huh.
'Gee, what are you going to do with yourself as a man if you get sick that easily? That's why you should eat better. Why didn't you listen to me, huh?'

S2: *hakkwan* *pap* *mek-umyen* *sal* *ppaci-e.yo.*
dormitory meal eat-if fat lose-POL
kulayto *pap* *manhi* *mek-ko* *iss-nuntey*
however meal a lot eat-and stay-but
wenlay *kikwanci-ka* *an-coh-a-kaciko.*
originally bronchus-NM not-good-because
'I usually lose weight if I eat dormitory meals. But I have been eating a lot. I have problems with my respiratory system.

Two male college students (S1 is senior to S2, A junior student calls his senior *hyeng*, which means an elder brother, literally) are talking about the junior's illness. The senior student is concerned about his junior and his health. So, he is complaining about S2 and why he did not listen to him because he has been worried and told him to eat better before. He is mitigating the illocutionary force of his complaining by employing the ISE *-canha*.

(7) The Example of N-4 (Requesting)

File number 65: Comic book

F1: *cikum ta tul-li-myense an-tul-li-nun chek*
now all listen-PAS-while not-listen-PAS-RL pretending
ha-ko iss-ci?
do-and stay-ENDER
'You are pretending not to hear anything, right?'

F2: *cincca an-tul-ly-e?*
really not-hear-PAS-INT
'Really I didn't hear you.'

F3: *uhahahahaha kuman kuman po-myen ett-ay?*
(Laughing) stop stop see-if how-INT
'(Laughing) How about you stop reading a comic book.'

F1: *an-tul-li-myun kuman po-lako ha-**canha.***
→ not listen-PAS-if stop see-QT do-CANHA
'If you can't hear anything, I am asking you to stop reading the comic book.'

Three high school senior students are talking together. But F2 is distracted by his comic book and he is saying that he can't concentrate on what the other two friends are talking about. So, F3 tells him not to read it. In addition to that, F1 is telling him that F3 is asking him to stop reading it so that they can talk together. By using the ISE *-cahna* he can mitigate the illocutionary force of requesting.

(8) The Example of N-5 (Suggesting)

File number 6: Bus

S1 :*ili-lo wa Sunghyo-ya eti ka?*
here-to come Sunghyo-VOC where go
a i-ke emcheng himt-untey.
ah this-thing extremely hard-ENDER
'Sunghyo, come here. Where are you going? Man, this is really difficult to do.'

S2: → *a ne pesu tha-ya toy-**canha.***
ah, you bus ride-must become-CANHA
'Ah, you have to take the bus, don't you?'

S1: *ah acik sikan iss-e 6-si-kkaci-la-se.*
ah yet time have-INT six- hour-by-be-because
cikum 52-pwun-i-nikkan com-man te
now 52minute-be-because a little-only more
yayki-ha-ca wuli.
story-do-PR we
'Oh, we still have time. Since the bus is coming at 6 o'clock and it is only 5:52. We can talk a little longer.'

S2: *mwusun yayki-lul te hay-ya ha-l-ci*
what story-AC more do-must do-RL-whether
molu-keyss-nuntey na-n.
don't know-PRS-ENDER I-TC
'I don't know what more to tell you.'

Two male college students are talking together. S1 wants to talk with his friend and record their conversation. But S2 suggests that S1 should take the bus to go home by using the ISE *-cahna* to mitigate the illocutionary force of his suggestion since he does not want to hurt S1 by refusing his request to talk more.

(9) The Example of N-6 (Criticizing)

File number 8: Contract

S: *w-ass-e? yosay kakey ha-ko iss-nun ke*
come-PST-INT nowadays store do-and stay-RL thing
ettehkey toyss-e?
how become-INT
'You are here. How is your store going?'

O: *ahu cwuk-keyss-e himtul-ese.*
phew die-PRS-INT hard-because

→ *ahu yocum cepen-ey han-pen pi w-ass-ess-**canha.***
phew recently that time-at one time rain come-PST-CANHA
'Phew, it is too rough to work. Gee, it has been raining recently.'

S : uu
yah

O: *ah, pi w-ass-ul ttay kakey chenceng-eyse mwul*
ah rain come-PST-RL time store ceiling-from water

tteleci-ko.
leak-become-and.
ya, kamcen tanghay-ss-e son.
hey electric shock cause-PST-INT hand
cwuk-nun-cwul al-ass-e.
die-RL-the way know-PST-INT
'When it rained, the ceiling at the store leaked. Because of the flooding I got an electric shock to my hand. I thought it almost killed me.'
S : *ya ku-ke cheum-ey kyeyyakha-l-ttay*
hey that-thing first-time contract-RL-time
pi an-say-nta-ko
rain not-leak-QT-and
→ *hay-se ha-n-ke-**canha.***
do-because do-RL thing-CANHA
'Hey, you contracted for that store because there was no leaking, didn't you?'

Two friends in their late 20s (S is a male student and O is a female office worker) are talking about her store space she recently rented. But the ceiling is leaking unlike what the contract had described. O seeks agreement on recent weather conditions from S by employing the ISE *–cahnha.* On the other hand, when she is complaining about the situation of her store, he was carefully criticizing that she did not double-check the contract and the building, by employing the ISE *–cahna* because he is concerned about her feelings although he is also criticizing her carelessness.

(10) The Example of N-7 (Expressing Emotions)
File number 6: Rain
S1: *way pi-ka o-nya? a··· na*
why rain-NM come-PLN? ah··· I
'Why is it raining? Ah···I'
S2: *maynnal yeki-nun maynnal pi o-canha*
everyday here-TC everyday rain come-CANHA
wenlay huhuhuhu
originally (laughing)
'It is almost always raining here.'

S1: *nalssi-ka* *maliya* *nemwu pyenteksulewe*
weather-NM you know really unpredictable
'You know, the weather is too unpredictable here.'
S2: → *Nen* *kulay-to* *kiswuksa-**canha.***
You but dormitory-CANHA
'But you are living in the dormitory.'

Two male college students in their 20s are talking together about the weather. S1 is talking about the bad weather in *Chwunchen* (a city in Korea). S2 is saying that it rains in *Chwunchen* almost every day. S2 is envious because S1 is living in the dormitory and is expressing his desire to live in the dorm like S1.

(11) The Example of N-8 (Bragging)
File number 53: Good-looking
S1: *ani* *seeping* *ku-ke* *mak* *cal* *sayngki-n* *ay-tul* *ha-nun*
well, serving that thing DM good looking-RL guy-PL do-RL
ke *ani-ya?*
thing no-PLN
'Well, waiting on tables is just for good-looking guys, isn't it?'
S2: *mol-la.*
don't know-PLN
'I don't know'
S1: *kuntey* *way* *ne-hanthey* *hay-ss-ci?*
but why you-to do-PST-ENDER?
'But, why did they assign you to wait on tables?'
S2: → *na* *cal* *sayngky-ess-**canha.***
I well look-PST-CANHA
'Come on, you know, I am a good-looking guy.

Two male college students are talking about S2's part time job which is working as a waiter at a café. S1 is wondering why the employer hired S2 because he thinks that only good-looking guys are usually hired for serving. Then S2 is kind of bragging about himself being a good-looking guy but by employing the ISE-*canha* he does not offend the listener by employing ISE -*canha* to hedge the illocutionary force of bragging.

(12) The Example of N-9 (Opposing)

File number 43: Eye Trouble

F1: *na nwun-ey mwe na-ss-e.*
I eye-at something get-PST-INT
'I have something in my eye.'

F2: *an-ey? ceypal ssis-e kulenikkan.*
in-at? please wash-INT so
'Inside? That's why you should wash your eyes.'

F1: → *an-ssis-ese na-n key ani-**canha.***
not-wash-because get-RL thing not-CANHA
'It is not because of not washing my eyes.'

F2: *com ssis-ela telepkey cincca haha.*
Please wash-PLN filthy really laughing
'Why don't you wash your eyes? Man, they are really dirty, Ha Ha.'

Two female college students (freshmen) are talking about F1's problem with her eye. Regarding F1's problem F2 suggests that she should wash her eyes clean. But F1 protests her comment because she thinks that it is not related to not washing her eyes. F2 used the ISE *-canha* in order to mitigate the illocutionary force of her opposition.

(13) The Example of N-11 (Apologizing)

File number 7: Money

M1: *akka e samman-wen pilly-ess-nuntey.*
some time ago well thirty-thousand-won borrow-PST-but
e kulem iman-wen cwe-ya-ci, heyheyhey
well then twenty-thousand-won give-must-ENDER (laughing)
'I borrowed thirty dollars a while ago. So I ought to give you twenty. Ha Ha.'

M2: *a omanwen cw-ess-e?*
Oh fifty-thousand-won give-PST-INT?
Cengseki-ka kongyen hay-ss-tako?
Cengseki-NM performance do-PST-QT?
'Did Cengseok give you fifty dollars for the performance?

M1: *ani ani nay-ka Sengyuni-hanthey path-ass-ess-e.*
no no I-NM Sengyuni-from receive-PST-PST-INT.

→ *cina-n* *pen-ey* *nay-ka* *ne* *cikum* *kyeysok* *kkamek-ko*
Pass-RL time-at I-NM you now continuously forget-and
mos *cw-ess-canha.* *cwu-lkkey.*
not able give-PST-CAHNA. Give-will.
'No, no, I received money from Sengyun. I kept forgetting to give you the money I borrowed. I'll pay you back.'

Two male college students are friends talking to each other about money. M1 borrowed some money from M2 but he did not pay it back. Therefore, he is sorry to keep forgetting and apologizes by employing the ISE *-canha* for mitigation.

As we have seen from the examples, the ISE *-canha(yo)* has various hedge functions. For example, it is used to elicit the listener's agreement or confirmation, to confirm shared knowledge, to soften the force of a criticism or complaint for effective communication, and so forth. In short, the ISE *-canha(yo)* is used as a positive politeness strategy involving interactive alignment such as seeking agreement and confirmation while *-canha(yo)* is used as a negative politeness strategy involving speaker's attitude towards mitigating force when complaining, telling a problem, opposing, or criticizing. The ISE *-canha(yo)* is more often used in informal situations since the use of *-canha(yo)* indexes a lower degree of formality and it narrows the communicative distance (i.e., improves solidarity) between the speaker and the listener in terms of sociopragmatics.

6.1.3 Analysis of the ISE *-canha(yo)* from the politeness perspective

Table 6-2 shows the frequency of each speech act type and strategies (positive politeness strategies vs. negative politeness strategies). As shown in Table 6-2, the frequency of P-1 (Seeking agreement) is 275, that of P-2 (Informing) is 220, and that of P-3 (Reminiscing) is 19. On the other hand, the frequency of N-1 (Stating an opinion) is 136, that of N-2 (Telling a problem) is 14, that of N-3 (Complaining) is 74, that of N-4 (Requesting) is 2, that of N-5 (Suggesting) is 19, that of N-6 (Criticizing) is 11, that of N-7 (Expressing emotions) is 3, that of N-8

Table 6-2 Frequency by Speech Act Type and Strategy Associated with the Use of the ISE -canha(yo)

Speech Act Type		Frequency by Type	Frequency by Strategies
P-1	Seeking agreement	275	513
P-2	Informing	220	
P-3	Reminiscing	19	
N-1	Stating an opinion	136	279
N-2	Telling a problem	14	
N-3	Complaining	74	
N-4	Requesting	2	
N-5	Suggesting	19	
N-6	Criticizing	11	
N-7	Expressing emotions	3	
N-8	Bragging	9	
N-9	Opposing	6	
N-11	Apologizing	2	
Total		792	792

(Bragging) is 9, that of N-9 (Opposing) is 6, and that of N-11 (Apologizing) is 2. Furthermore, the frequency of positive politeness strategies (P) is 513 whereas that of negative politeness strategies (N) is 279.

Figure 6-1 and Figure 6-2 indicate the frequency of each speech act type and of each politeness strategy, respectively. As shown in Figure 6-1, P-1 (Seeking agreement) appeared most frequently among speech act types using positive politeness strategy, followed by P-2 (Informing), N-1 (Stating an opinion), and N-3 (Telling a problem). As shown in Figure 6-2, the frequency of positive politeness strategies is considerably greater than that of negative politeness strategies. Hence, I will propose two hypotheses regarding politeness strategies as well as speech act type, and verify those hypotheses statistically.

Figure 6-1 Frequency by Speech Act Type of *-canha(yo)*

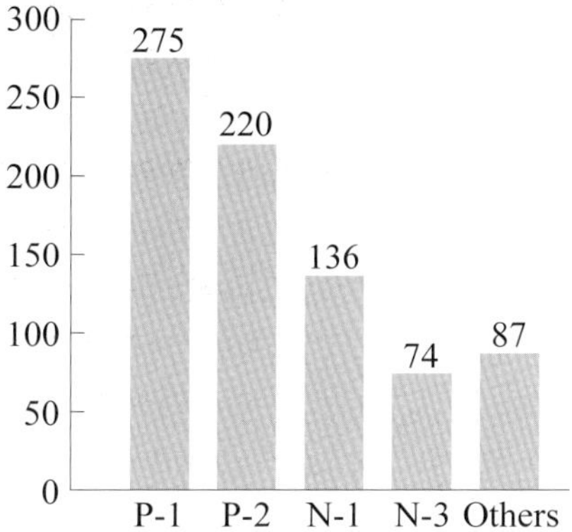

Figure 6-2 Frequency by Politeness Strategies of *-canha(yo)*

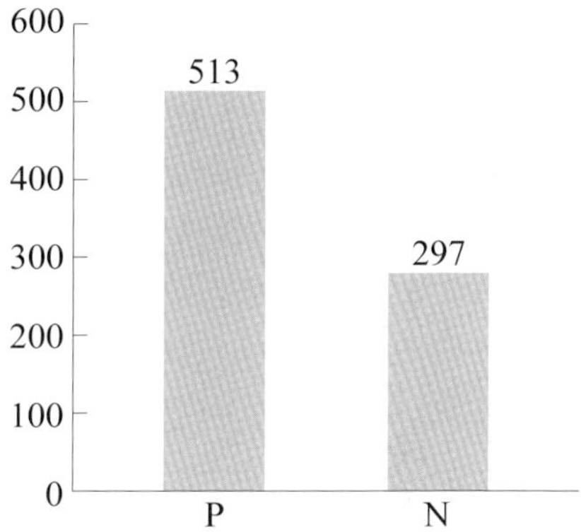

Hypothesis 1:

The ISE ***-canha(yo)*** is used more as a positive politeness strategy than as a negative politeness strategy.

Table 6-3
Statistical Analysis of Politeness Strategies Associated with the Use of *-canha(yo)*

Strategy	Frequency	Mean	Number	Std. Deviation	t-value	P-value	Interpretation
Positive politeness strategy	513	2.343	219	2.512	6.276	0.000	P>N
Negative politeness strategy	279	1.274	219	1.639			

Table 6-3 shows the results of the statistical analysis of politeness strategies in the case of *-canha(yo)*. According to the results of the search engine *hanmalwu*, among the total number of 792 tokens of *-canha(yo)* in my data, there were 513 uses as a positive politeness strategy by 219 interlocutors (i.e., 2.343 tokens/person) while there were 279 uses as a negative politeness strategy by 219 interlocutors (i.e., 1.274 tokens/

person). The paired t-test was used in order to investigate the difference between use as a positive politeness strategy and use as a negative politeness strategy. As shown in Table 6-3, the standard deviation for positive politeness strategies is 2.512 while that of negative politeness strategies is 1.639. In addition, the *t*-value is 6.276 and the P-value is 0.000. According to the *t*-test analysis, there is a significant difference between two groups if the P-value is smaller than 0.05. Hence, my data shows that there is a significant difference between positive politeness strategies and negative politeness strategies in terms of using the ISE *-canha(yo)*. Since the *t*-value is a positive number (6.276) the result can be analyzed as showing that <u>*-canha(yo)* is used more as a positive politeness strategy than as a negative politeness strategy.</u>

Hypothesis 2:

The ISE ***-canha (yo)*** is used the most frequently in speech act type P-1 (Seeking agreement) followed by P-2(Informing), N-1(Stating an opinion).

Table 6-4 Statistical Verification of Speech Act Type of *-canha(yo)*

Speech Act Type	Fre-quency	Mean	Std. Error Deviation	F-value	P-value	Interpreta-tion
P-1 (Seeking agreement)	275	1.256	0.082	15.198	0.000	P1 > P2 > N1
P-2 (Informing)	220	1.005	0.082			
N-1 (Stating an opinion)	136	0.621	0.082			

Table 6-4 shows the results of the statistical analysis of the frequency by speech act type in the case of *-canha(yo)*. According to the results of the search engine *hanmalwu*, the frequency of P-1 speech acts (Seeking agreement) used by 219 interlocutors is 275 (i.e., 1.256/person), that of P-2 speech acts (Informing) used by 219 interlocutors is 220 (i.e.,

1.005/person), and that of N-1 speech acts (Stating an opinion) used by 219 interlocutors is 136 (i.e., 0.621/person). One-way ANOVA was used in order to investigate the differences among speech act types in case of using *-canha(yo)*. The results of statistical analysis show that the standard error deviation of P-1, P-2, and N-1 is all 0.082. In addition, the F-value is 15. 198 and the P-value is 0.000. According to one-way ANOVA analysis, there is a significant difference among groups if the P-value is smaller than 0.05. Hence, we can say that there is a difference among speech act types associated with the use of *-canha(yo).* Moreover, when analyzing the mean value, the bigger the mean value is, the more frequently *-canha(yo)* was employed in the speech act with that mean value. However, we need to verify the difference among groups by the mean difference of multiple comparison and meaningful probability. As shown in Table 6-4, *-canha(yo)* is used the most frequently in P-1 speech acts (Seeking agreement), followed by P-2 speech acts (Informing) and N-1 speech acst (Stating an opinion).

6.2 Pragmalinguistic Analysis of Selected the ISE *-ketun(yo)*

6.2.1 Development of the ISE *-ketun(yo)*

In spoken corpus, *-ketun* is used as a sentence ender more frequently than as a conjunctive suffix. For example, in CETConc (Web-based concordances, Korea University) there are 267 uses of *-ketun* as a sentence ender while there are 170 uses of *-ketun* as a conjunctive suffix; in KORTERM (KAIST Korean corpus, 1998) there are 1,062 instances of *-ketun* as a sentence ender while there are 555 instances of *-ketun* as a conjunctive suffix. Moreover, in contemporary Korean, the usage of the conjunctive suffix is limited to written expressions or archaic expression in spoken discourse. In my corpus, all 190 tokens of *-ketun* were sentence enders. There were no usage as a conjunctive suffix.

The newly innovated sentence ender *-ketun(yo)* has developed from a conditional complex construction through main clause omission. One motivation of main clause omission is to mitigate the assertiveness of various speech acts in terms of indirect speech acts since the main clause usually carries the speaker's assertion. Hence, by omitting a main clause, the speaker can give the addressee the option of making the final decision on the basis of the background information expressed in the unomitted clause (H. Sohn 1999b, p.418). The sentence ender *-keten (yo)*, which was originally a subordinate clausal ender, became a sentence ender via grammaticalization with the diachronic omission of the main clause. When an identical form is used as a sentence ender after main clause deletion *(Principle of Persistence)*, the original meaning still remains and it functions as an illocution-mitigating device to reduce the speaker's assertiveness. We should note that grammaticalization is motivated by speaker-hearer interactions and communicative strategies.

Let us observe the data excerpted from Sohn's (1999a) in (1).

(1) *pi-ka* *o-**keten**-yo.*
Rain-NM come-KETUN-POL
'It's raining, (that's why.)'

Sohn (1999) argues that the sentence ender *-ketun(yo)* in (1) is the result of functional transfer, following unrecoverable main clause omission in conversation. That is, the subordinate clause has become a complete sentence via grammaticalization process where the subordinate clause-final element has been functionally transferred into sentence-final ender.

The structural reanalysis of grammaticalization might be stated in (2).

(2) [Clause 1 + Clause 2] S → [Clause 1 + polite particle *yo*] S

The statement (2) indicates that the main clause in an original complex sentence is diachronically deleted: the original subordinate clause (Clause 1) has been restructured as a main clause (*Structural Reanalysis*). According to Sohn (1999a), the newly innovated sentence has been restructured from originally complex sentences. First, the last elements other than the polite particle *yo* occur as the last element of a subordinate clause and are followed by a main clause although de-categorized, which is the conjunctive particle *-keten*. Second, the ender still retains its original syntactic and morphological properties (per the persistence principle). It cannot take verbal suffixes other than *yo*. (For example, * *pi ka o-keten-p-ni-ta*). Third, diachronic omission is suggested by the existence of syntactically parallel forms with an unomitted main clause (per the divergence principle) (p.164). As H. Sohn (2007) asserted, the form *-ketun* is an inherent conjunctive suffix with the meaning of the conditional or mild reason 'since, (even) if, provided that, given that.' When the form *-ketun* is used as a conjunctive suffix, it usually signals a conditional and rarely reason. As a conditional, the suffix *-ketun* is used only when the following main clause denotes the speaker's intention (e.g., imperative, propositive, and intentive) (H. Sohn, 2007).

As a sentence ender, it does not carry a conditional sense but the sense of mild justification. Basically, there are two different uses of *-ketun* in contemporary Korean: as a clause conjunctive suffix as exemplified in (3) and as a sentence ending as exemplified in (4).

(3) *Kim kwacang o-**ketun** selyu kac-ko nay pang-ulo com*
Kim chief come-if documents bring-and my room-to DM
o-la-ko malhay cwu-key
come-IM-CNJ tell-INF give-BLN
'If the chief Kim comes, then tell him to come to my office with the documents.'

The form *-ketun* in example (3) is used as a conjunctive suffix whose meaning is 'if'. The clause connective *-ketun* is still used by the older generation in spoken discourse or in written texts. On the other hand, the sentence ender *-ketun(yo)* in example (4) is used when the speaker expresses his/her disagreement with universally-held ideas. The sentence ender *-ketun(yo)* functions as an illocution-mitigating device when the speaker has a psychological burden. In other words, people might think that he/she is bragging about his/her knowledge.

(4) *hunhi kwahak-i kachi-cwunglipcek-ila-ko*
usually science-NOM value-neutral-to be-QT
sayngkakha-ko iss-ciman
think-and stay-but
sasil kwahak-uy yeksa-lul salphy-e po-myen
actually science-GN history-AC speculate-INF try-if
*kulehci-ka anh-**ketun**-yo.*
so-NOM-NM not-KETUN-POL
'People usually consider that science is value-neutral, but it is not like that if we speculate about the history of science.'

The sentence ender *-ketun* in example (5) is used as a mitigating device when interlocutor B is refusing interlocutor A's request to be loaned some money because the speech act of refusal contradicts the requester's expectation.

(5) A: *Swuci-ya, kuphay-se kulentey ton com*
Swuci-VOC hurry-because DM money a little
kkw-e cwu-myen an-toy-lkka? (request)
lend-INF give-if not-become-INT
'Suji, can you lend me some money because I really need it right now.'
B : *kulssey, na-to yocum saceng-i an-coh-ketun.*
(refusal with falling tone)
Well I -too recently situation-NM not-good-KETUN.
'Well, I am not in a good situation, either.'

As seen above, the sentence ender *-ketun* is used as a hedge to mitigate the illocutionary force and /or directness level of the utterances in terms of politeness strategies in (4) & (5).

Koo and Rhee (2001) speculated about the process of grammaticalization of *-ketun* from the conditional marker to the sentence ender based on a historical corpus including the 16th century *Penyek Nokeltay*, 17th century *Nokeltay Enhay*, the 18th century *Mong.e Nokeltay*, and the

20th century *Yekcwu Penyek Nokeltay*. *Nokeltay* was a foreign language textbook used to train translators of Chinese and Mongolian. Historical data shows that *-keten* has undergone a functional shift from a clause connective suffix 'if, when, since' to a sentence-final marker. In contemporary Korean, *-umyen* usually used to indicate conditionality while *-ketun* has lost its prototypical function as a conditional marker, which was once widely used. Furthermore, Koo (2002, 2005) showed that the function of the conditional marker shifted to the politeness marker through analyzing the spoken data. Also, she asserted that it is derived from conditionality and unreality.

According to other researchers, such as S. Sohn & M. Park (2002), historical data show that the *-ketun* has undergone a functional shift from a clause connective suffix 'if, when, since' to a sentence-final marker. Also, they argue that *-ketun* has undergone a process of grammaticalization from a textual function to an interpersonal marker which highlights the speaker's epistemic stance[41]. The *-ketun* in middle Korean was used as a clause connective, whose function was to express conditional, concessive, temporal, or causal relationship between two events and to signal a background for the proposition made in the main clause (cf. S.Sohn & M. Park, 2002). In modern Korean, however, *-ketun* is used predominantly as a sentence ender.

Let me summarize the evidence of the grammaticalization of *-ketun*: (i) *Principle of Divergence* (A>A/ B): the sentence ender *-ketun* is also used as a subordinate clause suffix in contemporary Korean, (ii) *Principle of persistence*: the newly innovated sentence ender *-ketun* still retains its original syntactic and morphological properties (Cf. Sohn 1999, p.164). For example, *-ketun* cannot take verbal suffixes other than *yo*[42] (* *pi ka o-keten-p-ni-ta*), (iii) *Decategorization*: the conjunctive suffix *-ketun* has become decategorized as a modal suffix. The sentence ender *-keten(yo)* originally developed from a subordinate clause suffix becomes a sentence

41 The term 'epistemic' is used to indicate degrees of commitment by the speaker to what the speaker says (Park & S.Sohn & M. Park, 2002).

42 *yo* can occur in any sentence type or sentence fragments.

ender through main clause omission, as illustrated in (6):

(6) Development of *-ketun*
  (a) [subordinate clause + *ketun*] S1 + [main clause + (*yo*)] S2
  (b) Main clause omission
  (c) [subordinate clause + *ketun* + (*yo*)]
  (d) New main clause +*ketun* + (*yo*)

It is interesting that the function of *-ketun,* which was the original conditional marker in Korean, has been shifted to the marking of discourse-pragmatic functions such as mild justification and addressee confirmation in Modern Korean through grammaticalization.

6.2.2 Usage of ISE *-ketun(yo)*

Table 6-5
Examples of Each Speech Act Type Associated with the Use of *-ketun(yo)*

Speech Act Type	Examples	Strategies
P-1 (Seeking Agreement)	*mwulka-ka olu-nun-ke-n ani-**ketun.***	P
P-2 (Informing)	*na-to ce pen hakki-ey ayey phyo-lul mantul-ess-**ketun**.*	P
P-3 (Reminiscing)	*ani-l-kke-ya. Yen-ha-yess-**ketun**.*	P
P-4 (Complimenting)	*nay pang salam-tul nemwu coh-**ketun**.*	P
N-1 (Stating Opinion)	*com, hakswul palphyo cwunpiha-l ttay-to himtu-l kes kath-tako sayngkak hay-ss-**ketun**yo.*	N
N-8 (Bragging)	*kyeyney-tul-un a a ilay. Mal-ul nay-ka nemwu cal ha-**ketun**.*	N
N-9 (Opposing)	*pangkum ankulay-ss-**ketun**-yo.*	N
N-10 (Refusing)	*toy-ss-**ketun**.*	N

(1) The Example of P-1 (Seeking Agreement)
File number 95: Economy

M: *kuntey cikum-to mwe ton-ul an-phwul-myen*
  But now-also DM money-AC not-distribute-if

kiep-tul-i *cenpwu* *ta* *pwuto*
enterprise-PL-NM every all bankrupt
cikcen-i *toy-nikka.*
just before-NM become-because
'Even now, if the government doesn't distribute funds, the companies will be in bankruptcy.'

F: *kunikka* *mwe* *cwuthayk-i* *namaton-tako* *ha-ciman-un*
So DM housing-NM excessive-QT do-but-TC
kuke-l *sayngkak-ha-myen* *tto* *cipkaps-i*
that-AC think-do-if again housing cost-NM
olul-kes kath-ko
increase-seems-and.
'That's why even though there is surplus housing, housing costs seem to increase if we consider inflation.'

M: *kuchi* *kyelkwuk-ey-n* *mwe* *mwulka-nun* *hwaphyey*
Yes after all-at-TC DM price TC monetary
kachi-ey ttala *tallaci-nun ke-ci.*
value-according to change-RL thing- ENDER
→ *mwulka-ka* *olu-nun* *ke-n* *ani-**ketun.***
Price-NM increase-RL thing-TC no-KETUN
'Yes, the prices depend on monetary value. It is not that the price itself increases.'

F: *mac-ayo.*
Correct-POL.
'That's right.'
kulayto *icey* *kongkup-i* *swuyo-pota* *te* *manh-umyen*
But DM supply-NM demand-than more many-if
tteleci-l-swu *pakkey* *eps-ci* *an-ayo?*
decrease-RL-way besides don't have-NOM NEG-POL
'That's right. However, don't you think the price can't help decreasing if the supply exceeds the demand.'

Two office workers (male in his 50s and female in her 40s) are talking about the economic situation in Korea. M is talking about government relief funds which he knows could cause inflation. Since otherwise, companies may go bankrupt, F agrees with his thoughts. M talks about the situation regarding prices and seeks agreement from F by using the ISE *-canha* in order to facilitate the success of interaction between the interlocutors and to express the speaker's solidarity with the addressee.

(2) The Example of P-2 (Informing)

File number 71: Final Exam

F1: *kuntey kimalkosa-nun ettehkey cwunpiha-cyo?*
but final exam-TC how prepare-ENDER-POL
'Well, how should I prepare for the final exam?'

F2: *kimalkosa-nun ssu-nun ke-canha.*
final exam-TC write-RC thing-CANHA.
kunikkan han hakki-tongan payw-ess-ten ke-l
So one semester-during learn-PST-RT thing-AC
cengli-lul hay.
summary-AC do
→ *na-to ce pen hakki-ey a.yey phyo-lul mantul-ess-**ketun.***
I-too that time semester-at even table-AC make-PST-KETUN
'The final is a written test, you know. So just prepare what you studied over the semester. I made a table of everything from last semester, too'

F2: *ce pen-ey cal po-ass-eyo, sihem?*
That time-at well see-PST-POL exam
'Did you do well on the final exam?'

F1: *a ce pen-ey manghay-kacikwu tane sihem po-canha.*
ah that time-at ruin-because word test see-CANHA
'Oh, because I failed the test last time I have to take the vocabulary test, you know.'

Two female college students (Fl is a junior, F2 is a sophomore) are talking about a final exam. F1 is asking F2 about how to take the final exam. F2 is advising how to prepare for the final exam. The ISE *-ketun* was employed in order to enhance their solidarity and express a positive attitude toward F 1 when F2 gave the information and told her experience to her junior.

(3) The Example of P-3 (Reminiscing)

File number 77: Boyfriend

F1: *kyay* *namca-chinkwu* *ku ttay-to* *iss-ess-na?*
That-girl boy-friend that-time-also have-PST-ENDER
ne-lang *lwummeyithu* *ha-l ttay-to?*
you-with roommate do-RL time-also
'Did she have a boyfriend at that time even when you guys were roommates?'

F2: *ney, kuntey ku ttay ku salam-i cikum ku*
Yes but that time that person-NM present that
salam-i-n-cwul-un molu-keyss-kwu.
person-be-RL-TC don't know-PRS-POL
'Well, I am not sure if the previous boyfriend is the same person as the present boyfriend.

Fl: → *ani-l-kke-ya* *yenha-y-ess-**ketun.***
No-RL-thing-INT younger-be-PST-KETUN
'I don't think so. The previous boyfriend was younger than her.'

F2: *a cikum cikum-un-yo?*
ah now now-TC-POL
'How about now?'

Two female college students (F1 is a senior student and F2 is a junior student) are talking about a third person's boyfriend. F1 asks if that person had a boyfriend when she was F2's roommate. F2 says to F 1 that she doesn't know whether or not that person previous boyfriend is the same one as before as the present one. Then F1 remembers that the previous boyfriend of the third person was younger than she was. So it implies that the previous boyfriend is different from the present boyfriend of the third person. The ISE *-ketun* was employed as a positive politeness strategy when F1 reminisced about the past event as a positive politeness strategy in order to elicit conversation with F2.

(4) The Example of P-4 (Complimenting)

File number 6: Roommate

MI : *keuy* *kulayto* *lwummeyithu* *kule-n* *lwummey*
almost but roommate yes-RL roommate
eti *iss-nya?* *solcikhi.*
where have-PLN honestly
'I mean, where you can find another roommates like them. (i.e., they

are the best.)

M2 : *a na-to solcikhi mancokha-ko iss-e.*
ah I-also honestly satisfy-and stay-INT
→ *nay pang salam-tul nemwu coh-**ketun.***
my room people-PL really good-KETUN
'Yeah, actually I'm happy with my roommates. All of them are great.'

Two male college students are talking about M2's roommates. M1 says that they are the nicest guys. M2 agrees with M1 and even compliments them but he does not want to brag so he uses the ISE *-ketun*.

(5) The Example of N-1 (Stating Opinion)

File number 45: Conference

M: *maksang nwuna selmyeng tul-epo-myen-un kulehkey*
actually sister explanation listen-try-if-TC that much
palphyo-ka pwulphyenha-ci anh-ul kes kath-ayo.
presentation-NM uncomfortable-NOM not-RL seems-POL.
'If I listen to your explanation, then it seems like doing a presentation is not that difficult.'

F: *Ung*
'Yes'

M: *com, hakswul palphyo cwunpiha-l ttay-to himtu-l*
DM academic presentation prepare-RL time-also difficult-RL
→ *kes kath-tako sayngkakhay-ss-**ketun**-yo.*
seems-QT think-PST-KETUN-POL
'I thought that an academic conference would be a little bit difficult.'

Two college students are talking about a conference presentation. F is a female student who is senior to M and thus M calls her *nwuna*, which literally means 'sister' in Korean. M is concerned about the upcoming conference and he is stating his opinion about the conference presentation which might be difficult for him. By employing the ISE *-ketun* he can mitigate the illocutionary force of stating his opinion which might be different from that of his senior.

(6) The Example of N-8 (Bragging)

File number 31: Bragging

S: *hwupay-tul hantey nay-ka ile-n kotung.hakkyo*
junior-PL to I-NM this-RL high school
kyenghemtam-ul yayki-lul hay-cwe.
experience-AC story-AC do-give
kyeyney-tul-un a a ilay.
Those-guys-PL-TC oh oh say.
→ *mal-ul nay-ka nemwu cal ha-**ketun.***
tell-AC I-NM really well do-KETUN
'I tell about my high school experiences to my juniors. Then my juniors are impressed because I am so good at talking.'

M: *kongpwu-lul kongpwu-lul?*
study-AC study-AC
'Do you mean that you were good at studying?'

S: *na mal toykey cal ha-y.*
I story really well do-INT
'I mean I am really convincing and a good speaker.'

A mother in her 40s and a son in his 20s are talking about his college life. A son is bragging that his juniors at his college are so impressed when he talks about his experience in his high school life. By employing the ISE *-ketun* he can mitigate the illocutionary force of his bragging so that it is not overdoing it.

(7) The Example of N-9 (Opposing)

File number 55: Economy

M: *ni-ka pangkum kulay-ss-canha.*
you -NM just now say-PST-CANHA
'You said that just now.'

S: → *pangkum an-kulay-ss-**ketun**-yo.*
just now not-say-PST-KETUN-POL
'I didn't say that just now'

M: *eikwu kotung haksaeng mac-a?*
ouch high school studen right-INT
'Ouch! Are you really a high school student?'

S: *mac-ci*
correct-ENDER
'It's true.'

A mother in her 40s and a son in his teens are arguing about the son's behavior. The mother is telling him not to keep whining. But he protests to his mother that he did not keep whining. Although he is opposing his mom, his opposing statement is mitigated by employing the ISE *–ketun*.

(8) The Example of N-10 (Refusing)
File number 12: Money
S1: *pomwulsem-un kal ton-un iss-e?*
pomwulsem-TC go-RL money-TC have-INT
'Do you have money for Pomwulsem (The amusement Park)?'
S2: *ni man-ochen-won*
you fifteen thousand wen (Korean currency)
'You can pay 15 dollars.'
S1: → *toy-ss-**ketun.***
become-PST-KETUN
'That's fine. (Implied meaning is 'Never mind, I don't want to give you my money').

Two sisters (S1 is a college student and S2 is a high school student) are talking together. S2, a younger sister, wants to go to the amusement park with her friends. So, S2 asks S1, her elder sister, if she has money for that and S2 expects her elder sister give her money for the amusement park. However, S1 is refusing saying *toy-ss-ketun*, which is mitigated in its illocutionary force through S1's use of the ISE *–ketun* instead of saying *toy-ss-e* 'No' *or an-tway* 'No' with the same tone, both of which are direct refusals.

As we have seen from the examples, the ISE *-ketun(yo)* has various hedge functions. For example, it is used to elicit the listener's agreement as well as to soften the force of a face-threatening act for effective communication. In short, the ISE *-ketun(yo)* used as a 'positive politeness' strategy involves interactive alignment such as seeking agreement and informing or complementing, while *-ketun(yo)* used as a 'negative politeness' involves the speaker's desire to mitigate force when stating an opinion, bragging, opposing, or refusing, in my corpus. Like the ISE *-canha(yo)*, the ISE *-ketun(yo)* is also more often used in informal situations since the use of *-ketun(yo)* indexes a lower degree of formality and it narrows the communicative distance (i.e., improve solidarity) between the speaker and the listener in terms of sociopragmatics.

6.2.3 Analysis of the ISE *-ketun(yo)* from Politeness Perspective

Table 6-6 Frequency by Speech Act Type and Strategy Associated with the Use of *-ketun(yo)*

Speech Act Type		**Frequency by Type**	**Frequency by Strategies**
P-1	Seeking agreement	11	134
P-2	Informing	119	
P-3	Reminiscing	3	
P-4	Complimenting	1	
N-1	Stating an opinion	20	57
N-2	Telling a problem	5	
N-3	Complaining	6	
N-4	Requesting	0	
N-5	Suggesting	3	
N-6	Criticizing	6	
N-7	Expressing emotions	0	
N-8	Bragging	6	
N-9	Opposing	10	
N-10	Refusing	1	
N-11	Excusing	0	
Total		191	191

Table 6-6 shows the frequency of each speech act type and strategies (positive politeness strategies vs. negative politeness strategies). As shown in Table 6-6, the frequency of P-1 (Seeking agreement) is 11, that of P-2 (Informing) is 119, that of P-3 (Reminiscing) is 3, and that of P-4 (Complimenting) is 1. On the other hand, the frequency of N-1 (Stating an opinion) is 20, that of N-2 (Telling a problem) is 5, that of N-3 (Complaining) is 6, that of N-4 (Requesting) is 0, that of N-5 (Suggesting) is 3, that of N-6 (Criticizing) is 6, that of N-7 (Expressing emotions) is 0, that of N-8 (Bragging) is 6, that of N-9 (Opposing) is 10, that of N-10 (Refusing) is 1, that of N-11 (Apologizing) is 0. Furthermore, the frequency of positive politeness strategies (P) is 134 whereas that of negative politeness strategies (N) is 57.

Figure 6-3 and Figure 6-4 indicate the frequency of each speech act type and that of politeness strategies, respectively. As shown in Figure 6-3, P-2(Informing) appeared most frequently among speech act types using positive politeness strategies, followed by N-1 (Stating an opinion), and P-1(Seeking agreement). As shown in Figure 6-4, the frequency of positive politeness strategies is considerably greater than that of negative politeness strategies. Hence, I will propose two hypotheses regarding politeness strategies as well as speech act type, and verify those hypotheses statistically.

Figure 6-3 Frequency by Speech Act Type of *-ketun(yo)*

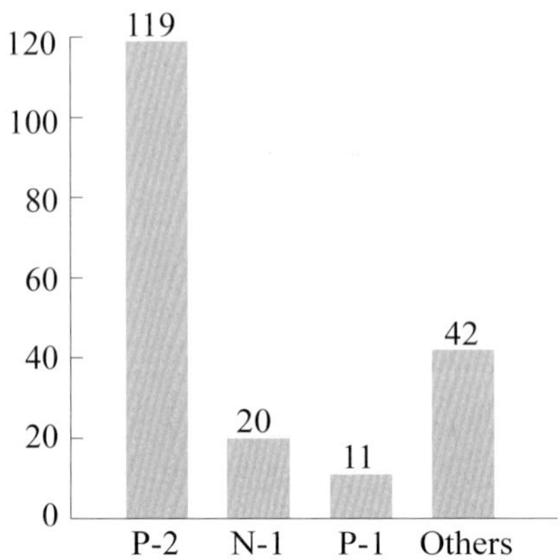

Figure 6-4 Frequency by Politeness Strategies of *-ketun(yo)*

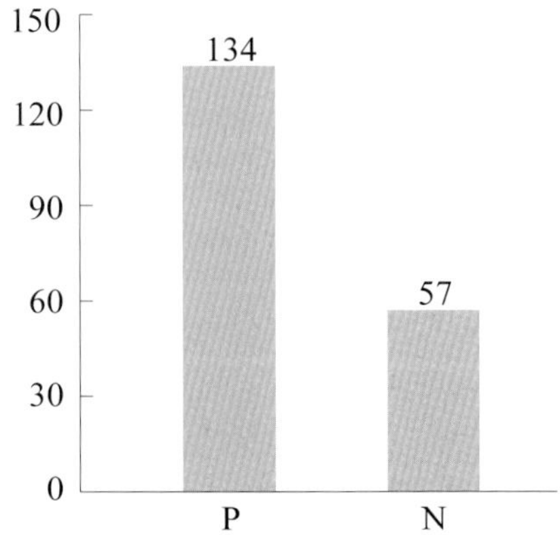

Hypothesis 1:
The ISE ***–ketun(yo)*** is used more as a positive politeness strategy than as a negative politeness strategy.

Table 6-7
Statistical Analysis of Politeness Strategies Associated with the Use of *-ketun(yo)*

Strategy	Fre-quency	Mean	Number of speakers	Std. Deviation	t-value	P-value	Interpreta-tion
Positive politeness strategy	134	0.607	219	1.375	3.710	0.000	P>N
Negative politeness strategy	57	0.260	219	0.742			

Table 6-7 shows the results of the statistical analysis of politeness strategies in the case of *-ketun(yo)*. According to the results of the search engine *hanmalwu*, among the total number of 192 tokens of *-ketun(yo)* in my data, there were 135 uses of positive politeness strategies used by 219 interlocutors (i.e., 0.61 tokens/person) while there were 57 uses of negative politeness strategies used by 219 interlocutors (i.e., 0.26 tokens/person). The paired *t*-test was used in order to investigate the difference between positive politeness strategies and negative politeness strategies. As shown in Table 6-7, the standard deviation of positive politeness strategies is 1.375 while that of negative politeness strategies is 0.742. In addition, the t-value is 3.710 and the P-value is 0.000. According to the *t*-test analysis, there is a significant difference between two groups if the P-value is smaller than 0.05. Hence, my data shows that there is a significant difference between positive politeness strategy and negative politeness strategy in terms of using the ISE *-ketun(yo)*. Since the *t*-value is a positive number (3.710) the result can be analyzed as showing that *-ketun(yo)* is used more as a positive politeness strategy than as a negative politeness strategy.

Hypothesis 2:
The ISE *–ketun(yo)* is used the most frequently in speech act type P2 (Informing) followed by P-1(Seeking agreement) and N-1(Stating an opinion).

Table 6-8 Statistical Verification of Speech Act Type of *-ketun(yo)*

Speech Act Type	Fre-quency	Mean	Std. Error Deviation	F-value	P-value	Interpreta-tion
P1 (Seeking Agreement)	11	0.050	0.051	28.535	0.000	P2 > P1=N1
P2 (Informing)	119	0.543	0.051			
N1 (Stating an opinion)	20	0.091	0.051			

Table 6-8 shows the results of the statistical analysis of frequency by speech act type in the case of *-ketun(yo)*. According to the results of the search engine *hanmalwu*, the frequency of a P-1 speech act (Seeking agreement) used by 219 interlocutors is 11 (i.e., 0.05/person), that of a P-2 speech act (Informing) used by 219 interlocutors is 119 (i.e., 0.543/person), and that of an N-1 speech act (Stating an opinion) used by 219 interlocutors is 20 (i.e., 0.091/person). ANOVA was used in order to investigate the differences among speech act types in the case of using *-ketun(yo)*. The results of the statistical analysis show that the standard error deviation of P-1, P-2, and N-1 is all 0.051. In addition to that, the F-value is 28.535 and the P-value is 0.000. According to ANOVA analysis, there is a significant difference among groups if the P-value is smaller than 0.05. Hence, we can say that there is a difference among speech act types associated with the use of *-ketun(yo)*. Moreover, when analyzing the mean value, the bigger the mean value is the more frequently *-ketun(yo)* was employed in a speech act with that mean value. However, we need to verify the difference among groups by the mean difference of multiple comparison and meaningful probability. As shown in Table 6-8, *-ketun(yo)* is used the most frequently in P-2 speech acts (Informing), followed by P-1 speech acts (Seeking agreement) and N-1 speech acts (Stating an opinion).

6.3 Summary

One of the major findings in this chapter is related to the correlation between hedge use and politeness strategies. The result of statistical analysis reveals that the ISE *-canha(yo)* 'you know' is used more as a positive politeness strategy than as a negative politeness strategy. Furthermore, the ISE *-canha(yo)* is used the most frequently in P-1 speech acts (Seeking agreement), followed by P-2 speech acts (Informing) and N-1 speech acts (Stating an opinion). Similarly, the result of statistical analysis reveals that the ISE *-ketun(yo)* 'you see' is used more as a positive politeness strategy than as a negative politeness strategy. Furthermore, the ISE *-ketun(yo)* is used the most frequently in P-2 speech acts (Informing), followed by P-1 speech acts (Seeking agreement) and N-1 speech acts (Stating an opinion).

Hedges were viewed traditionally in terms of a negative politeness strategy in order to mitigate the face-threatening effects of those speech acts that might damage interpersonal relationships between interlocutors. However, the results of the statistical analysis of my data elucidate that hedges in Korean spoken discourse are employed more as a positive politeness strategy than a negative politeness strategy. In other words, these results confirm that the function of hedges is to facilitate the success of interactions between interlocutors and to express a speaker's solidarity with the addressee or a positive attitude toward the addressee in the case of the ISE *-canha(yo)* ' you know' and the ISE *-ketun(yo)* 'you see.'

CHAPTER 7

CONCLUSION

7.1. General Remarks

This book has performed an empirical analysis of Korean hedges in contemporary spoken discourse. In this study, I defined a hedge as a linguistic device that softens or mitigates the illocutionary force of a proposition as well as expresses a speaker's concern for the addressee's feelings. Furthermore, I defined a hedge as an interactive strategy for facilitating the success of interactions between interlocutors, for expressing the speaker's solidarity with an addressee or a positive attitude towards the addressee, and for protecting face for self and/or others in terms of politeness. The data analyzed was drawn from my corpus based on approximately 17 hours of spoken discourse, composed of unplanned, naturally-occurring conversations in order to answer the research questions I identified. This study classified possible lexical hedges and syntactic hedges in my corpus and investigated the frequency of individual hedge items. In addition, it also provided an analysis of the correlation between hedge use and sociopragmatic factors as well as pragmalinguistic factors.

The summary of the entire study is as follows.

First, I answered the question of how Korean hedges can be classified in spoken discourse by providing a summary of Korean hedge classifications in Chapter 4.

Second, I investigated the frequency of individual hedge items after collecting 17 hours of recorded, unplanned, naturally-occurring data, transcribing, and searching hedge tokens by the search engine *hanmalwu* of Secong Corpus in order to determine the frequency of individual hedge item occurrences in Korean spoken discourse in Chapter 4.

Third, in order to answer if there is any correlation between hedge use and sociopragmatic factors (social structural factors and social situational factors), I conducted a sociopragmatic analysis of selected lexical hedge items quantitatively through statistical analysis in terms of social structural factors as well as social situational factors in Chapter 5. In this study, sociopragmatic factors are divided into social structural factors and social situational factors. The social structural factors include gender, gender composition, age, occupation, and region while the social situational factors include number of speakers in conversation, topic of conversation, social power relations between interlocutors, and social distance relations between interlocutors.

Fourth, in order to determine whether there is any correlation between hedge use and pragmalinguistic factors (speech act type and politeness strategy), I selected two interactive sentence enders (ISEs), *-canha(yo)* and *-ketun(yo)* from seven ISEs and analyzed their use qualitatively as well as quantitatively.

Fifth, the implications of the findings of the interdisciplinary analysis between sociopragmatics and pragmalinguistics are discussed below in Section 7.2.

7.2 Summary of Findings

There are several findings reported in this study. First, this book showed the systematic classification of Korean hedges in spoken discourse and identified a total number of 9,962 hedge tokens in Chapter 4. Furthermore, I was able to show the frequency of the individual hedge items as well as the frequency and percentage of each hedge category.

Second, there were twenty-two findings from analyzing 3,445 hedge tokens of seven interactive sentence enders (ISEs) among lexical hedges in Chapter 5 (cf. Summary of sociopragmatic analysis of seven ISEs in Section 5.2). For example, statistical analysis illustrates that *-ketun(yo)* is used more in metropolitan areas than in non-metropolitan areas, used more in two-party conversations than in multiple-party conversations, and used more in conversations with personal topics than in conversations with impersonal topics.

Third, one of the most meaningful findings is that the number of speakers in conversation (two-party conversations vs. multiple-party conversations) affects hedge use. The analysis in Chapter 5 revealed that there were correlations between the number of speakers in a conversation and the use of hedge items such as *-canha(yo), -nuntey(yo),-ketun(yo), -ci(yo),* and *-tay(yo)* among the seven ISEs (interactive sentence enders) examined. Hence, I proposed the hypothesis that hedges are used more in two-party conversations than in multiple-party conversations in contemporary Korean discourse. Furthermore, in Section 5.3 similar results from a statistical analysis re-examining the correlation between the numbers of speakers in conversations and hedge use were obtained. The results of statistical analysis showed that three hedge items such as the auxiliary verbs (AVs) *-kes kath-, -e/ato toy-*, and *-e/a po-*from the six AVs were used more in two-party conversations than in multiple-party conversations. Hence, my hypothesis concerning the number of speakers in a conversation (i.e., More hedges are used in two-party conversations than in multiple-party conversations in Korean spoken discourse.) was not falisified since it is verified statistically both with respect to the use of the seven ISEs and the use of the three AVs. This finding is meaningful in terms of collective psychology and collective dynamism through language use. In other words, an individual is prone to have less responsibility in a group and is more prone to avoid responsibility than in one-on-one conversations.

Fourth, another meaningful finding is that 'the topic of conversation' affects hedge use. The analysis in chapter 5 revealed that there were correlations between the topic of conversation (personal topics vs. impersonal topics) and the hedge items such as the seven ISEs *-canha(yo),-nuntey(yo), -ketun(yo), -telako(yo), -ci(yo), -ney(yo), tay(yo).* According to this result, I proposed the hypothesis that hedges are used more in conversations with personal topics than in conversations with impersonal topics in contemporary Korean discourse. Furthermore, in Section 5.3 similar results from statistical analysis re-examining the correlation between the topic of conversation and the hedge use were obtained. The results of the statistical analysis showed that all six hedge items such as the auxiliary verbs *-kes kath-, -ci molu-, -na po-, -e/a-to toy-, -e/a cwu-, -e/a po-* were used more in conversations with personal topics than in conversations with impersonal topics. Hence, my hypothesis about the influence of the topic of conversation ("more hedges are used in conversations with personal topics than with impersonal topics in Korean spoken discourse") could be valid since it is verified statistically in both seven ISEs and seven AVs. Although a similar claim has been discussed as an intuitive possibility, this study is the first attempt to prove the hypothesis statistically.

Fifth, there were major findings with respect to hedge use in terms of politeness strategies as follows. The results of the statistical analysis reveal that the ISE *-canha(yo)* 'you know' is used more as a positive politeness strategy than as a negative politeness strategy. Furthermore, the ISE *-canha(yo)* is used the most frequently in P-1 speech acts (seeking agreement), followed by P-2 speech acts (informing) and N-1 speech acts (stating an opinion). Similarly, the result of statistical analysis reveals that the ISE *-ketun(yo)* 'you see' is used more as a positive politeness strategy than as a negative politeness strategy. Furthermore, the ISE *-ketun(yo)* is used the most frequently in P-2 speech acts (informing), followed by P-1 speech acts (seeking agreement) and N-1 speech acts (stating an opinion). These results confirm that the function of the hedge is to facilitate the success of interactions between interlocutors and to express the speaker's solidarity with an addressee or a positive attitude toward the addressee. Although hedges were viewed traditionally in terms of a negative politeness in order to mitigate the face-threatening effects, the results of the statistical analysis in this study elucidate that hedges in Korean spoken discourse are employed as a positive politeness strategy as well as a negative politeness strategy.

There are several theoretical contributions. First, the results of this study have criticized the overgeneralizations of previous discussions or claims about hedges which are viewed negatively as gender-specific (women's language) or as an expression of disempowerment (powerless language). The results of the statistical analysis shown in Chapter 5 elucidate the various correlations between hedge use and sociopragmatic factors. For example, there are no gender differences in the use of six interactive sentence enders among the seven ISEs while the ISE *-tay(yo)* was used more by women than men. Also, there is no difference among different age groups in most of the ISEs while the ISE *-ci(yo)* is used more by interlocutors of the age group composed of people over 40 than by interlocutors of the age group of those in their 20s-30s and the ISE -nuntey(yo)is used more by interlocutors of the age group in their 20s-30s than by interlocutors of the age group over their 40s. Therefore, the results of the current study show that previous sociolinguistic views on the correlation between hedge use and social structural factors such as gender have been subjected to overgeneralization and suggest that it is necessary to micro-analyze discourse by each hedge item.

Second, the analysis of the current study proposes the importance of social situational factors such as the number of speakers, and topic of conversation in sociopragmatic analysis. As I mentioned earlier, *sociopragmatics* is the sociological interface of pragmatics, referring to the social perceptions underlying participants' interpretation and performance of communicative action (Leech, 1983). The number of speakers in conversation and the topic of conversation, which chiefly affect hedge use, are all 'situational' or 'contextual' factors. The most influential factors which affect hedge use in Korean spoken discourse are not social structural factors such as gender, age, region or occupation, but social situational factors such as the number of speakers in conversation and the topic of conversation. Thus, the results of this study elucidate that studies on hedge use need to take the sociopragmatic perspective into account.

Third, this study demonstrates the specific conditions for one of the functions of hedge, which is "to express a speaker's concern for the addressee's feelings (softening function)" (Holmes, 1984a). It is assumed that the softening function of the hedge is related to situation or context. However, Holmes does not discuss the softening function of the hedge in relation to the situation or context, which can serve the function of expressing the speaker's concern for the addressee's feeling. Therefore, presenting the specific situational conditions for the pragmatic function of the hedge is one of the major contributions in this study.

Fourth, this study contributes to verifying hedge function in terms of pragmalinguistics. As I mentioned earlier, *pragmalinguistics* refers to the resources for conveying relational or interpersonal meanings and communicative acts. The resources include pragmatic strategies such as indirectness and politeness that both intensify and soften communicative acts. According to the results of the statistical analysis in Chapter 6, there was correlation between hedge use and politeness strategies associated with the use of the ISEs *-canha(yo)* and *-ketun(yo)*. Both *-canha(yo)* and *-ketun(yo)* are used as positive politeness strategies rather than negative politeness strategies. Hence, this study elucidates the function of hedges as an interactive strategy to facilitate the success of interactions between interlocutors, enhance interpersonal rapport, and establish solidarity in terms of a positive politeness strategy extending beyond the negative politeness strategy, which recognize the autonomy of others and avoids imposition.

Fifth, this study demonstrates that both sociopragmatic and pragmalinguistic perspectives are necessary and important when analyzing hedges. According to the empirical analysis of Korean hedges in this book, Korean hedge use is related to situational/contextual factors as well as strategic factors. Thus, it can be evaluated that the interdisciplinary approach is meaningful for analyzing and comprehending the complexity and multiplicity of the hedge.

7.3 Pedagogical Implications

In the field of second/ foreign language education, the focus on grammatical competence is coupled with a focus on communicative competence as a chief pedagogical aim. Second language acquisition research has shown that acquiring sociolinguistic and pragmatic competence is of crucial importance if a language learner is to reach fluency (Ellis, 1994).

Even advanced language learners often lack pragmatic competence, which is the knowledge of what to say, how to say it, and to whom, according to the appropriate social situation. For example, one of my students, who was an advanced learner of Korean, asked me to write a letter of recommendation in an inappropriate manner, as in (1).

(1) *chwuchense taum cwu mokyoil kkaci*
recommendation next week Thursday until
sse-cwu-lswu iss-supnikka?
write-give-can (AUX)-DEF
'Can you write a letter of recommendation by next Thursday?'

Even though the sentence ender is of a deferential level in Korean sentences,[43] it does not sound polite and appropriate. My student should have asked with the appropriate addressee term and pragmatic strategy such as the hedge in (2).

(2) *kyoswu-nim, coysongha-ciman chwuchense* ***com***
professor-SUX (hon.) sorry (hon.)-but recommendation **Hedge**
taum cwu mokyoil kkaci
next week Thursday until
write-give-SH-can(AUX)-SH-ENDER **Hedge**-POL
*sse-cwu-si-l swu iss-usi-n-**ci-yo**?*
'Could you write a letter of recommendation by next Thursday?'

As shown in the above example, hedges are an important interactive strategy in Korean spoken discourse.

Sohn (2001) argues for the necessity of raising student's sociopragmatic awareness in teaching politeness routines. Kasper and Rose (2001) suggest that the first step to enhance pragmatic language teaching in foreign language education is to raise the FL instructor's and curriculum designer's awareness of pragmatic language teaching. Cook (2001) discusses that the enhancement of instructors' pragmatic, sociolinguistic

43 There are six speech levels in Korean: plain, intimate, familiar, blunt, polite, deferential (cf. H.Sohn, 1999, p. 355).

and discoursal knowledge of the target language and culture is the key to effective pragmatic language teaching. Also, as Cook (2001) points out, instructors need to be aware of pragmatic components so that they can bring them to learners' attention. The significant task of language instructors is to raise learners' pragmatic awareness and provide more opportunities for communicative practice in classroom. Hence, Korean language instructors should be knowledgeable about communicative style including hedges in Korean. The challenges in the appropriate use of hedges may partly be due to the lack of teaching of appropriate language use. Moreover, there are some interlanguage studies such as Kasper (1979) that suggest the problems foreign language learners might have in the use of hedges. Thus, teaching the appropriate use of hedges like other pragmatic phenomena can be challenging because hedges bear meaning according to the contexts in which they occur and their use is related to the speakers' attitude. Hence, this study of Korean hedges in spoken discourse will be beneficial in terms of pedagogical implications since it has often been pointed out that teaching pragmatics should be research-based rather than dependent on native speaker instructors. Hopefully, this study will contribute to the area of Korean pedagogy as well as help Korean educators to further understand the significance of Korean hedges in spoken discourse so that they can develop pedagogical materials for Korean language learners to help them acquire appropriate communicative competence in Korean social interactions.

In Korean, hedges are an important interactive strategy in spoken communication.

This study illustrates the importance of hedges in Korean by showing how native speakers use them in real situations. I hope that my study will provide the impetus for a comprehensive analysis of Korean hedges and contribute to helping Korean learners develop their skills associated with the use of them. Scarcella and Brunak (1981) pointed out that native speakers use hedges much more than non-native speakers and low-level students of the target language, who rarely use hedges in their analysis of the politeness strategies employed by native and non-native speakers of English. Thus, it is necessary for KSL/ KFL learners to acquire knowledge of the appropriate use of hedges in different situations. Moreover, it is very important that the appropriate use of hedges, like other pragmatic phenomena, should be taught through the contexts in which they occur. Thus, the findings of this study may have important implications for how KSL/KFL classes may help non-native speakers of Korean to engage in cross-cultural interactions.

7.4 Suggestions for Future Studies

Four points need to be addressed for further studies. First, it is necessary to broaden the hedge items in sociopragmatic analysis for further study. This study makes a contribution to the body of literature as a basic analysis of the hedge for further studies to expand upon. Second, it is suggested that the multiple variables in hedge use be analyzed. For instance, such analyses might include the interactive effect on social structural variables (e.g., gender-social power-social distance, age-gender-occupation, etc.) as well as the interactive effect between social structural factor and social situational factor (gender-topic, age-topic, etc). Third, it is suggested that an in-depth discourse-pragmatic analysis should be conducted in a future study since this study focused on quantitative analysis of Korean hedges in spoken discourse. Fourth, an analysis of Korean hedges in different settings and with different levels of formality (e.g., TV debate, lecture, etc.) would have the benefit of broadening understanding of the use of hedges in Korean, since this study focused solely on informal settings. Furthermore, it is suggested that an analysis of Korean hedges in written discourse should be conducted and compared with those in spoken discourse. Lastly, a cross-cultural analysis should be conducted to reveal the similarities and differences in the use of hedges between languages. Hedges should be examined from the cross-cultural as well as the cross-linguistic point of view.

Bibliography

Adkins, M., & Brashers, D. E. (1995). The power of language in computer-mediated groups. *Management Communication Quarterly,* 8, 289-322.

Ahn, J.-H. (2001). Hankwuke uy mwunpephwa wa yekmwunpephwa hyensang (Grammaticalization versus degrammaticalization in Korean) *Tamhwa wa Inci (Discourse and Cognition),* 8(2), 93-112.

Ahn, J.-h. (2005). A study of the modality and grammaticalization in Korean. *Studies in Modern Grammar* 40, 111-133.

Ambady, N., Jasook, K., Fiona, L., & Rosenthal, R. (1996). More than words: Linguistic and nonlinguistic politeness in two cultures. *Journal of Personality & Social Psychology,* 70(5), 996-1011.

Austin, J. L. (1962). *How to do things with words*. Oxford: Clarendon Press.

Baker, M. A. (1991). Gender and verbal communication in professional settings: A review of research. *Management Communication Quarterly,* 5, 36-63.

Barbiers, S., Beukema, F.&Wurff, W. (Eds.) (2002). *Modality and its interaction with the verbal system*. Amsterdam: John Benjamins.

Bardovi-Harlig, K. (1992). Pragmatics as part of teacher education. *TESOL Journal,* 1(1), 28-32.

Bardovi-Harlig, K. (1996). Pragmatics and language teaching: Bringing pragmatics and pedagogy together. In L. F. Bouton (Ed.), *Pragmatics and language learning* (pp. 21-39). Urbana-Champaign, University of Illinois: Division of English as an International Language.

Bardovi-Harlig, K., & Dörnyei, Z. (1998). Do language learners recognize pragmatic violations? Pragmatic versus grammatical awareness in instructed L2 learning. *TESOL Quarterly,* 32, 233-262.

Bardovi-Harlig, K., & Mahan-Taylor, R.(2002). *Teaching pragmatics*. Retrieved from http://exchanges.state. gov/education/engteaching

Beebe, L. M., & Cummings, M. C. (1996). Natural speech act data versus written questionnaire data: How data collection method affects speech act performance. In S. M. Gass & N. Joyce (Eds.), *Speech acts across cultures: Challenges to communication in a second language* (pp. 65-86). Berlin: Mouton de Gruyter.

Beebe, L. M., & Takahashi, T. (1989a). Do you have a bag? Social status and patterned variation in second language acquisition. In S. Gass, C. Madden, D. Preston, & L. Selinker (Eds.), *Variation in second language acquisition* (pp. 103-125). Clevedon: Multilingual Matters.

Beebe, L. M., & Takahashi, T. (1989b). Sociolinguistic variation in face-threatening speech acts: Chastisement and disagreement In M. R. Eisenstein (Ed.), *The dynamic interlanguage: Empirical studies in second language variation* (pp. 199-218). New York: Plenum.

Beebe, L. M., Takahashi, T., & Uliss-Weltz, R. (1990). Pragmatic transfer in ESL refusals. In R. Scarcella, E. Andersen, & S. D. Krashen (Eds.), *On the Development of Communicative Competence in a Second Language* (pp. 55-73). New York: Newbury House.

Biber, D. (1990). Methodological issues regarding corpus-based analyses of linguistic variation. *Literary and linguistic computing,* 5(4), 257-269.

Bley-Vroman, R., & Ko, H. (2005). *Corpus linguistics for Korean language learning and teaching*. Honolulu, HI: National Foreign Language Resource Center, University of Hawai'i at Mānoa.

Blum-Kulka, S. (1987). Indirectness and politeness in requests: Same or different? *Journal of Pragmatics,* 11(2), 131-146.

Blum-Kulka, S. (1991). Interlanguage pragmatics: The case of requests. In R. Phillipson, E. Kellerman, L. Selinker, M. Sharwood Smith, & M. Swain (Eds.), *Foreign/ second language pedagogy research* (pp. 255-272). Clevedon, UK: Multilingual Matters.

Blum-Kulka, S., House, J., & Kasper, G. (1989). *Cross-cultural pragmatics: Requests and apologies*. Norwood, NJ: Ablex.

Blum-Kulka, S., & Olshtain, E. (1984). Requests and apologies: A cross-cultural study of speech act realization patterns (CCSARP). *Applied Linguistics* 5(3), 196-213.

Bradac, J., Mulac, A. & Thompson, S. (1995). Men's and women's use of intensifiers and hedges in problem-solving interaction: Molar and molecular analysis. *Research on Language and Social Interaction* 28(2), 93-116.

Brinton, L. J. (1996). *Pragmatic markers in English: Grammaticalization and discourse functions*. Berlin: Mouton de Gruyter.

Brinton, L. J., & Traugott, E. C. (2005). *Lexicalization and Language Change*. Cambridge, England: Cambridge University Press.

Brown, P., & Levinson, S. C. (1987). *Politeness: Some universals in language usage*. Cambridge; New York: Cambridge University Press.

Brown, G., & Yule, G. (1983). *Discourse analysis*. Cambridge; New York: Cambridge University Press.

Brown, G., & Yule, G. (1983). *Teaching the spoken language: An approach based on the analysis of conversational English*. Cambridge: Cambridge University Press.

Bussman, H. (1996). *Routledge dictionary of language and linguistics* (translated and edited by G. Trauth & K. Kassazi). New York: Routledge.

Bybee, J. (1985). *Morphology: A study of the relation between meaning and form*. Typological Studies in Language 9. Amsterdam: John Benjamins.

Bybee, J. L., & Fleischman, S. (Eds.) (1995). Modality in grammar and discourse: An introductory essay. In J.L. Bybee and S. Fleischman (Eds.) *Modality in grammar and discourse* (pp. 1-14). Amsterdam: John Benjamins.

Bybee, J. L., & Pagliuca, W. (1985). Cross linguistic comparison and the development of grammatical meaning. In J. Fisiak (Ed.), *Historical semantics and historical word formation* (pp. 59-83). Berlin: De Gruyter.

Bybee, J. L., Pagliuca, W., & Perkins R. (1994). *The evolution of grammar: Tense, aspect, modality in the language of the world.* Chicago: University of Chicago Press.

Byon, A. (2001). *The communicative act of requests: Interlanguage features of American KFL learners.* Unpublished Ph.D. Dissertation, University of Hawai'i at Mānoa.

Byon, A. (2002). Pragmalinguistic features of KFL learners in the speech act of request. *Korean Linguistics,* 11, 151-182.

Byon, A. (2003). The Korean speech act of refusals: Sociopragmatic analysis. *The Sociolinguistic Journal of Korea* 11(1), 241-270.

Byon, A. (2004a). Learning linguistic politeness. *Applied Language Learning*, 14 (1), 37-62.

Byon, A. (2004b). Sociopragmatic analysis of Korean requests: Pedagogical settings. *Journal of Pragmatics,* 36(9), 1673-1704.

Byon, A. (2005a). Apologizing in Korean: Cross-cultural analysis in classroom settings. *Korean Studies,* 29(1), 137-166.

Byon, A. (2005b). Teaching pragmatic competence through speech acts:

American KFL instructional settings. *Teaching Korean as a Foreign Language* 30, 77-112.

Byon, A. (2006). The role of linguistic indirectness and honorifics in achieving linguistic politeness in Korean request. *Journal of Politeness Research* 2(2), 247-276, Mouton de Gruyter.

Byon, A. (2007). Teaching the polite and the deferential speech levels using media materials: Advanced KFL classroom settings. In D. R. Yoshimi and H. Wang (Eds.), *Selected Papers from Pragmatics in the CJK Classroom: The State of the Art* (pp. 21-64). Retreived from http://nflrc.hawaii.edu/CJKProceedings.

Caffi, C. (1999). On mitigation. *Journal of Pragmatics,* 31, 881-909.

Carli, L. L. (1990). Gender, language, and influence. *Journal of Personality and Social Psychology,* 59(5), 941-951.

Cameron, D. (2001). *Working with spoken discourse*. London: SAGE.

Canale, M. (1983). From communicative competence to language pedagogy. In J. Richards and R. Schmidt (Eds.), *Language and communication* (pp. 2-27). London: Longman.

Celce-Murcia, M., & Olshtain, E. (2000). *Discourse and context in language teaching: A guide for language teachers*. Cambridge: Cambridge University Press.

Chafe, W. (1986). Evidentiality in English conversation and academic writing. In W. L. Chafe and J., Nochols (Eds.), *Evidentiality: The linguistic coding of epistemology* (pp. 261-272). Norwood: Ablex.

Chen, R. (1993). Responding to compliments: A contrastive study of politeness strategies between American English and Chinese speakers. *Journal of Pragmatics,* 20, 49-75.

Cho, C.-H. (1982). *A study of Korean pragmatics: Deixis and politeness.* Unpublished Ph.D. Dissertation.

Ph. D. Dissertation, University of Hawai'i at Mānoa.

Choi, S. (1995). The development of epistemic sentence-ending modal forms and functions in Korean children. In J. Bybee and S. Fleischman (Eds.). *Modality in grammar and discourse* (pp.166-204). Amsterdam: John Benjamins.

Choo, M. & Kwak, H.-Y. (2008). *Using Korean: A guide to contemporary usage.* Cambridge: Cambridge University Press.

Clark, H.H. & Schunk, D.H. (1980). Polite responses to polite requests.

Cognition 8, 111-143.

Clark, H.H. (1996). *Using language*. New York: Cambridge University Press.

Clemen, G. (1997). The concept of hedging: Origins, approaches and definitions. In R. Markkanen and H. Schröder (Eds.), *Hedging and discourse: Approaches to the analysis of a pragmatic phenomenon in academic texts* (pp. 235-248). Berlin: Walter de Gruyter.

Coates, J. (1983). *The semantics of the modal auxiliaries*. London. Croom Helm.

Coates, J. (1987). Epistemic modality and spoken discourse. *Transactions of the Philological Society,* 85, 100-131.

Coates, J. (1995). The expression of root and epistemic possibility in English. In J. Bybee and S. Fleischman (Eds.), *Modality in Grammar and Discourse* (pp. 55-66). Amsterdam: John Benjamins.

Cohen, A.(1996) Speech acts. In S. L. Mackay and N.H. Hornberger (Eds.), *Sociolinguistics and Language Teaching* (pp. 383-420). Cambridge: Cambridge University Press.

Cook, H. (2001). Why can't students of JFL distinguish polite from impolite speech style? In K.Rose & G. Kasper (Eds.), *Pragmatics in language teaching* (pp. 80-102). Cambridge: Cambridge University Press.

Coulmas, F. (Ed.). (1998). *The handbook of sociolinguistics*. Oxford: Blackwell.

Crystal D. (Ed.). (1997). The Cambridge encyclopedia of language (2nd Ed.). New York: Cambridge University Press.

Davies, A. (1989). Communicative competence as language use. *Applied Linguistics,* 10, 157-170.

Dixon, J. A., & Foster, D. H. (1997). Gender and hedging: From sex differences to situated practice. *Journal of Psycholinguistic Research,* 26(1), 89-107.

Ellis, R. (1994). *The study of second language acquisition*. Oxford; New York: Oxford University Press.

Faerch, C., & Kasper, G. (1984). Pragmatics knowledge: Rules and procedure. *Applied Linguistics,* 4, 214-225.

Falsgraf, C., & Park, I. (1994). Synchronic and diachronic aspects of complex predicates in Korean and Japanese. In Akatsuka (Ed.), *Japanese Korean Linguistics 4. Stanford: Center for the Study of Language and Information.* (pp. 221-237). Stanford: Center for the Study of

Language and Information.

Faerch, C., & Kasper, G. (1984). Pragmatics knowledge: Rules and procedure. *Applied Linguistics,* 4, 214-225.

Fraser, B. (1974). Hedged performatives. In P. Cole and J. Morgan (Eds.), *Syntax and semantics* 3(pp. 44-68). New York: Academic Press.

Fraser, B. (1980). Conversational mitigation. *Journal of Pragmatics,* 4(4), 341-350.

Fraser, B. (1990a). An approach to discourse markers. *Journal of Pragmatics,* 14(3), 383-398.

Fraser, B. (1990b). Perspectives on politeness. *Journal of Pragmatics,* 14(2), 219-236.

Fraser, B. (1999). What are discourse markers? *Journal of Pragmatics,* 31(7), 931-952.

Fraser, B. & Nolen, W. (1981). The association of deference with linguistic form. *International Journal of the Sociology of Language,* 27, 93-111.

Frawley, W. eds. (2006). *The expression of modality*. Berlin: Mouton de Gruyter.

Fukada, A., & Asato, N. (2004). Universal politeness theory: Application to the use of Japanese honorifics. *Journal of Pragmatics,* 36(11), 1991-2002.

Gass, S. M., & Joyce, N. (1996). *Speech acts across cultures: Challenges to communication in a second language*. Berlin: Mouton de Gruyter.

Gass, S. & Selinker, L. (2001). *Second language acquisition: An introductory course*. Mahwah, NJ: Lawrence Erlbaum Associates.

Givón (1984). *Syntax: A functional –typological introduction,* Vol. 1. Amsterdam: John Benjamins.

Givón (1990). *Syntax: A functional –typological introduction,* Vol. 2. Amsterdam: John Benjamins.

Grob, L. M., & Allen, M. (1996). *Sex differences in powerful/powerless language: A meta-analytical review*. Paper presented at the Central States Communication Association.

Grob, L. M., Meyers, R. A., & Schuh, R. (1997). Powerful/Powerless language use in group interaction: Sex differences or similarities? *Communication Quarterly,* 45(3), 282-303.

Gruber, H. (1993). Political language and textual vagueness. *Pragmatics* 3, 1-28.

Gumperz, J. J. (1982). *Discourse strategies*. Cambridge: Cambridge University Press. Press.

Guo, J. (1995). The interactive basis of the Mandarin modal néng 'can'. In J. Bybee and S. Fleischman (Eds.), *Modality in grammar and discourse* (pp.205-238). Amsterdam/ Philadelphia: John Benjamins.

Hadley, A. O. (1993). *Teaching language in context* (3rd ed.). Boston: Heinle and Heinle.

Haleta, L. L. (1996). Student perceptions of teachers' use of language: The effects of powerful and powerless language on impression formation and uncertainty *Communication Education,* 45(1), 16-28.

Halliday, M.A. K. (1973). *Explorations in the functions of language*. London: Edward Arnold.

Halliday, M.A. K. (1985). *An introduction to functional grammar*. London: Edward Arnold.

Hann, F. (2006). Typological approach to modality. In W. Frawley (Ed.), *The expression of modality* (pp. 27-70).

Harris, S. (1995). Pragmatics and power. *Journal of Pragmatics,* 23, 117-135.

Held, G. (1992). Politeness in linguistic research. In R. J. Watts, S. Ide and K. Ehlich (Eds.), *Politeness in language* (pp.131-153). Berlin: Mouton de Gruyter.

Hellermann, J., & Vergun, A. (2007). Language which is not taught: The discourse marker use of beginning adult learners of English. *Journal of Pragmatics,* 39(1), 157-179.

Heine, B., Claudi, U & Hennemeyer F. (1991). *Grammaticalization: A conceptual framework.* Chicago: University of Chicago Press.

Henstock, M. I. (2003). *Refusals: A language and cultural barrier between Americans and Japanese.* Unpublished Ph. D. Dissertation, Purdue University.

Hinkel, E. (1995). The use of modal verbs as a reflection of cultural values. *TESOL Quarterly,* 29(2), 325-343.

Holmes, J. (1984a). Women's language: A functional approach. *General Linguistics,* 24(3), 149-177.

Holmes, J. (1984 b). Modifying illocutionary force. *Journal of Pragmatics,* 8(3), 345-365.

Holmes, J. (1984 c). Hedging your bets and sitting on the fence: Some evidence for hedges as support structures. *Te Reo,* 27, 47-62.

Holms, J. (1986). Functions of *you know* in women's and men's speech. *Language in Society,* 15(1), 1-21.

Holmes, J. (1990). Hedges and boosters in women's and men's speech. *Language & Communication,* 10(3), 185-205.

Holmes, J. (1993). New Zealand women are good to talk: An analysis of politeness strategies in interaction. *Journal of Pragmatics,* 20, 91-116.

Holmes, J. (1995 a). *Women, men, and politeness*. New York: Longman.

Holmes, J. (1995 b). Soft and low: Hedges and boosters as politeness devices. *Women, men, and politeness*, 72-114. New York: Longman.

Holmes, J. (1998). Signaling gender identity through speech. *Moderna Spark,* 92(2), 122-128.

Holmes, J. (2001). *An introduction to sociolinguistics* (2nd ed.). New York: Longman.

Hopper, P. J. (1991). On some principles of grammaticalization. In E.C.Traugott and B. Heine (Eds.), *Approaches to Grammaticalization* I & II (pp. 17-36).

Hopper, P. J., & Traugott, E. C. (2003). *Grammaticalization. Second Edition.* Cambridge, England: Cambridge University Press.

Hosman, L. A. (1989). The evaluative consequences of hedges, hesitations, and intensifiers. Powerful and powerless speech styles. *Human communication research* 15(3), 383-406.

Horn, L. R., & Ward, G. (Eds.). (2004). *The handbook of pragmatics*: Blackwell Publishing.

House, J. (1996). Developing pragmatic fluency in English as a foreign language: Routines and metapragmatic awareness. *Studies in Second Language Acquisition*, 18, 225-252.

House, J. (2000). Understanding misunderstanding: A pragmatic-discourse approach to analyzing mismanaged rapport in talk across cultures. In H. Spencer-Oatey (Ed.), *Culturally speaking. Managing rapport through talk across cultures*. London: Continuum.

House, J., & Kasper, G. (1981). Politeness markers in English and German. In F. Coulmas (Ed.), *Conversational routine* (pp. 157-185). Hague: Mouton.

Hoye, L. (1997). *Adverbs and modality in English*, New York: Longman.

Hübler, A. (1983). Pragmatics and beyond, Vol. IV: 6. *Understatements and hedges in English.* Amsterdam: John Benjamins.

Hurley, D. (1992). Issues in teaching pragmatics, prosody, and non-verbal communication. *Applied Linguistics* 13, 259-281.

Hwang, J.-R. (1990). 'Deference' versus 'politeness' in Korean speech. *International Journal of the Sociology of Language,* 82, 41-55.

Hyland, K. (1998). *Pragmatics and beyond.* Vol.54, *Hedging in scientific research articles*. Amsterdam: John Benjamins.

Hymes, D. (1972). On communicative competence. In J. B. Pride and J. Holmes (Eds.), *Sociolinguistics: Selected readings* (pp.269-293). Harmondsworth: Penguin Books.

Ide, S.(1989). Formal forms and discernment: Two neglected aspects of universals of linguistic politeness. *Multilingua* 8, 223–48.

Ide, S. (1993). Preface: The search for integrated universals of linguistic politeness. *Multilingua - Journal of Cross-Cultural and Interlanguage Communication* 12(1), 7–12.

Ihm, H. B., Hong, K. P., & Chang, S. I. (2001). *Korean grammar for international learners*. Seoul: Yonsei University Press.

Janny, R. W. , & Arndt, H. (1992). Intracultural tact versus intercultural tact. In R.J. Watts, S. Ide and K. Ehlich (Eds.), *Politeness in language* (pp. 21-41). Berlin: Mouton de Gruyter.

Jeon, H.-Y. (2004). Hankwuke kongson phyohyen uy uymi (On the meaning of polite expressions in Korean). *Hankwuke uymihak (Korean Semantics),* 15, 17-91.

Johnson, M. (2004). *A Philosophy of Second Language Acquisition.* New Haven: Yale University Press.

Jucker, A. H. (1988). Relevance of politeness. *Multilingua,* 7, 375-384.

Jucker, A. H., & Ziv, Y. (1998). *Discourse markers: Descriptions and theory.* Amsterdam: John Benjamins Publishing Company.

Judd, E. (1999). Some issues in the teaching of pragmatic competence. In E. Hinkel (Ed.), *Culture in second language teaching and learning* (pp. 152-166). Cambridge: Cambridge University Press.

Jung, E.-H. (2007). Poco yongen kwuseong uy mwunpephwa wa yeksacek pyenhwa (Grammaticalization and historical change of auxiliary). *Hakwukehak (Korean Studies),* 35, 121-165.

Kärkkäinen, E. (1998). *The marking and interactive functions of epistemic stance in American English conversational discourse.* Unpublished Ph.D. Dissertation. University of California, Santa Barbara.

Kärkkäinen, E. (2003). *Epistemic stance in English conversation: A description of its interactive functions, with a focus on I think*. Amsterdam: John Benjamins.

Kasper, G. (1990). Linguistic politeness: Current research issues. *Journal of Pragmatics* 14(22), 193-218.

Kasper, G. (1994). Politeness. In R.E. Asher and J. M. Y. Simpson (Eds.), *Encyclopedia of language and linguistics* (pp. 3206-3212). Edinburgh: Pergamon and University of Aberdeen Press.

Kasper, G. (1997). Can pragmatic competence be taught? *NFLRC NetWork (6)*. Retrieved from http://nflrc.hawaii.edu/NetWorks/NW06/.

Kasper, G. (1998). Interlanguage pragmatics, In Heidi Byrones (Ed.), *Learning foreign and second language* (pp. 113-129). New York: The Modern Language Association of America.

Kasper, G. (2001). Four perspectives on L2 pragmatic development. *Applied Linguistics,* 22, 502-530.

Kasper, G., & Rose, K. R. (2001). *Pragmatics in language teaching.* Cambridge: Cambridge University Press.

Kasper, G., & Rose, K. R. (2002b). *Pragmatic development in a second language*. Oxford: Blackwell.

Kasper, G., & Rose, K. R. (2002a). Theories of second language pragmatic development. *Language Learning,* 52(1), 13-62.

Kawanishi, Y. (1994). An analysis of non-challengeable modals: Korean *-canha(yo)* and Japanese *-janai*. In N. Akatsuka (Ed.) *Japanese Korean Linguistics* 4 (pp. 95-111). Stanford: CSLI Publications.

Kim, C.-u. (1998). *Wulimal yangthay yongen kwumwun yenku (A study of the Korean modal predicates)*. Seoul: Hankwukmunhwasa.

Kim, H. (2004). Sahoy enehak eyseuy tamhwa yonkwu (Discourse Studies in Sociolinguistics). *Sociolinguistic Journal of Korea*, 12(2), 105-129.

Kim, H. (2008). The semantic and pragmatic analysis of South Korean and Australian English apologetic speech acts. *Journal of Pragmatics,* 40(2), 257-278.

Kim, J. (2000). A pragmatic analysis of *-canh* and *-ci* in Korean: The relationship between informational status and the division of pragmatic labor *Korean Journal of Linguistics,* 28, 237-270.

Kim, M. (2003). *Discourse, frequency, and the emergence of grammar: A corpus-based study of the grammaticalization of the Korean exis-*

tential verb is(i)-ta. Unpublished Ph.D. Dissertation, University of California, Los Angeles.

Kim, M. (2006). *Uysasothong sok uy tayung palhwa (Responses in communicative interactions)*. Seoul: Seycong Chwulphansa.

Kim, M. S. (2005). Evidentiality in achieving entitlement, objectivity, and detachment in Korean conversation. *Discourse Studies,* 7(1), 87-108.

Kim, T.-Y. (2002). Kwuke mwunpephwa uy yangsang (A study on Korean grammaticalization). *Collection of Articles Humanities and Arts,* 24, 1-22.

Kim, Y.-K. (2002). Mwunpepseng uy tankye ey tayhan kochal (A study on the steps of Grammaticalization). *Hankul Hakhoy (Korean Studies),* 256, 45-68.

Ko, Y.-K., & Koo, B.-K. (2008). *Wurimal mwunpepron (Korean Syntax)*. Seoul: Cipmwuntang.

Ko, Y.-J. (1997). *Hankwuke uy munpephwa kwaceng (Grammaticalization processes in Korean: Predicates)*. Seoul: Kwukhak Calyowen.

Koo, J.-N. (2000). Tamhwa pyoci *mwe* uy mwnpephwa wa tamhwa kinung (Grammaticalization and functions of discourse marker *mwe*). *Kwuke Mwunhak* 35, 5-32.

Koo, H.-J. (2005). Conditional markers in speech context: From conditional to politeness. *Tamhwa wa Inci (Discourse and Cognition),* 12(2), 1-22.

Koo, H. J, & Rhee, S. (2001). Coken phyoci-eyse mwncang congkyel phoyci-lo-uy mwunpephwa (Grammaticalization of a sentential end marker from a conditional marker). *Tamhwa wa Inci (Discourse and Cognition),* 8(1), 1-19.

Kramsch, C. J. (1993). *Context and culture in language teaching*. Oxford: Oxford University Press.

Kwon, J. (2004). Expressing refusals in Korean and American. *Multilingua,* 23(4), 339-364.

Kwon, J. I. (2003). Kwue hankwuke eyse seswulmun silhyen pangpep uy kongsithay wa thongsi thay (The synchrony and diachrony of Korean declarative sentences in spoken discourse). *Eoneohag (Journal of the Linguistic Society of Korea),* 37, 25–46.

Lakoff, G. (1972). Hedges: A study in meaning criteria and the logic of fuzzy concepts. *The English Regional Meeting of the Chicago Linguistic Society*, 183-228.

Lakoff, R. (1973). *The logic of politeness: or, minding your p's and q's*. Paper presented at the Ninth Regional Meeting of the Chicago Linguistic Society.

Lakoff, R. (1975). *Language and woman's place*. New York: Harper and Row.

Lakoff, R. & Ide, S. (2005). *Broadening the horizon of linguistic politeness*. Amsterdam : John Benjamin Publishing.

Lee, H. J., & Lee, C. H. (1999). *The study on the Korean sentence enders*. Seoul, Korea: Hankwuk Moonhwasa.

Lee, H. S. (1994). Discourse-pragmatic functions of sentence-type suffixes in informal discourse in Korean. In Y.-K. Kim-Renaud (Ed.), *Theoretical issues in Korean linguistics* (pp. 517-539). Stanford, CA: Center for the Study of Language & Information.

Lee, H. S. (1999). A discourse-pragmatic analysis of the commital *-ci* in Korean: A synthetic approach to the form-meaning relation. *Journal of Pragmatics,* 31(2), 243-275.

Lee, H. Y. (1996). *Hyendai hankuke hwalyong emiuy uymi wa putam cwuliki uy sangkwanseng*. Unpublished Ph.D. dissertation, Ewha Woman's University.

Lee, H. S., & Park, Y.-Y. (1999). Grammaticalization of the Korean connective *-nuntey/(u)nte.* Paper presented at the conference on New Reflections on Grammaticalization: International Symposium (June 16-19).

Lee, J-B. (2006). Kwue kyengepep e tayhan sahoyenehakcek cepkun (On the studies of Korean honorifics from the sociolinguistic standpoint), *Kwuehak (Korean Language Studies),* 47, 407-448.

Lee, K.-d. (1993). *A Korean grammar on semantic pragmatic principles*. Seoul: Hanguk Munhwasa.

Lee, K.-g. (2006). Hankwuke uy yangthay phoyhyen (Modality in Korean). *Tamhwa wa Inci (Discourse and Cognition),* 27, 67-83.

Lee, S.-Y. (2005) A study of the semantic function of modality. *Yenge Yengmwun Kyoyuk (English Language Education),* 11(2), 149-170.

Lee, W.P. (2001). *Tamhwa pwunsek* (Discourse analysis). Seoul: Hankwukmwunhwasa.

Leech, G. N. (1983). *Principles of pragmatics*. London: Longman.

Leech, G. & Svartvik, J. (1975). *A communicative grammar of English*. London: Longman.

Levinson, S.C. (1983). *Pragmatics*. Cambridge: Cambridge University Press.

Locher, M. A. (2004). *Power and politeness in action: Disagreements in oral communication.* Berlin: Mouton de Gruyter.

Lyons, J. (1977). *Semantics*. Cambridge: Cambridge University Press.

Markkanen, R., & Schroder, H. (1997). Hedging: A challenge for pragmatics and discourse analysis. In R. Markkanen and H. Schroder (Eds.), *Hedging and discourse: Approaches to the analysis of a pragmatic phenomenon in academic texts* (pp. 3-18). Berlin: Walter de Gruyter.

Matsumoto, Y. (1988). Reexamination of the universality of face: Politeness phenomena in Japanese. *Journal of Pragmatics,* 12, 403–426.

Maynard, S. K. (1993). *Discourse modality: Subjectivity, emotion, and voice in Japanese language*. Amsterdam: John Benjamins.

Maynard, S. K. (1997). *Japanese communication: Language and thought in context*. Honolulu: University of Hawai'i Press.

McCarthy, M. (1991). *Discourse analysis for language teachers*. New York: Cambridge University Press.

McClanahan, V. K. (1997). *Some interactions of grammar and pragmatics in negation in Korean.* Unpublished Ph.D Dissertation, University of Illinois at Urbana-Champaign.

McGloin, N. H. (2002). Markers of epistemic vs. affective stances: *deshoo* vs. *zanai*. In N. M. A. S.Strauss (Ed.), *Japanese Korean Linguistics,* 10 (pp. 136-149).

McMullen, L. M., & Paslovski, D. D. (1992). Effects of communication apprehension, familiarity of partner and topic on selected women's language features. *Journal of Psycholinguistic Research,* 21(1), 17-30.

Mey, J. (1993). *Pragmatics: An introduction*. Oxford: Blackwell.

Meyerhoff, M. (1992). A sort of something: Hedging strategies on nouns. *Working paper in Language Gender and Sexism: AILA Commission on Language and Gender*, 2(1), 59-73.

Mills, S. (2003). *Gender and politeness*. Cambridge: Cambridge University Press.

Min, H. S. (1997). A study of sociolinguistic features of men's and women's language in Korean. *The Sociolinguistic Journal of Korea*, 5(2), 529-587.

Meier, A.J. (1995a). Defining politeness: Universality in appropriateness. *Language Sciences*, 17, 345-365.

Meier, A.J. (1995b). Passages of politeness. *Journal of Pragmatics*, 24, 381-392.

Morita, E. (2002). Stance marking in the collaborative completion of sentences: Final particles as epistemic markers. In N. M. Akatsuka and S.Strauss (Eds.), *Japanese Korean Linguistics,* 10 (pp. 200-233).

Mulac, A., Wiemann, J. M., & Gibson, T. W. (1988). Male/Female language differences in same-sex and mixed-sex dyads: The gender-linked language effect. *Communication Monographs,* 55, 315-335.

Nittono, M. (2003). *Japanese hedging in friend-friend discourse*. Unpublished Ph.D. Dissertation, Columbia University.

Noel, H., & Gass, S. M. (1996). Non-native refusals: A methodological perspectives. In S. M. Gass and N. Joyce (Eds.), *Speech Acts Across Cultures: Challenges to communication in a second language* (pp. 45-64). Berlin: Mouton de Gruyter

Noh, E. (2002). The Korean sentence-ending suffix *ney*: Epistemicity vs. cognitive effects. *Korean Journal of Linguistics,* 7(4), 27-4.

Nunan, D. (1989). *Designing tasks for the communicative classroom*. Cambridge: Cambridge University Press.

Nuyts, J. (2006). Modality: Overview and linguistic issues. In W. Frawley (Eds.), *The expression of modality* (pp. 1-26). Berlin: Walter de Gruyter.

Nwoye, O.G. (1992). Linguistic politeness and sociocultural variation of the notion of face. *Journal of Pragmatics,* 18, 309-328.

O'Grady, W. D. (1991). *Categories and case: The sentence structure of Korean.* Amsterdam: John Benjamins.

Oh, S.-s. (1998). *A syntactic and semantic study of Korean auxiliaries: A grammaticalization perspective.* Unpublished Ph.D. dissertation, University of Hawai'i at Mānoa.

Olshtain, E. (1985). Crosscultural pragmatics and the testing of communicative competence. *Language Testing,* 2, 16-30.

Olshtain, E., & Cohen, A. D. (1990). The learning of complex speech act behavior. *TESL Canada Journal,* 7, 45-65.

Palmer, F.R. (1986). *Mood and modality*. Cambridge: Cambridge University Press.

Palmer, F.R. (2001). *Mood and modality*. Cambridge: Cambridge University Press.

Park, J.-r. (2001). Politeness: The Korean discourse marker *ceki, Pan-Pacific*

Association of Applied Linguistics, 5(2), 297-319.

Park, J.-r. (2003). A study of selected Korean pragmatic markers: Synchronic and diachronic perspectives. Unpublished Ph.D. dissertation, University of Hawai'i at Mānoa.

Park, M. J. (2003). *The meaning of Korean prosodic boundary tones.* Unpublished Ph.D. Dissertation. University of California, Los Angeles.

Park, M.-J.& Sohn, S.-O., & (2002). Discourse, grammaticalization, and intonation: The analysis of *-ketun* in Korean. *Japanese Korean Linguistics,* 10, 306-319.

Park, Y.-Y. (1997). Teaching authentic conversation: How to incorporate discourse into teaching. In Y.-H. Kim (Ed.), *The Korean language in American* Vol.2 (pp. 27-37).

Park, Y.-Y. (1998). A discourse analysis of the Korean connective *-ketun* in conversation. In B.Park and J.Yoon (Eds.), *Selected Papers from the 11th International Conference on Korean Linguistics* (pp. 861-870).

Park, Y. (2001). *Hankwuke uy sahyo enehak (Sociolinguistics to Korean language).* Seoul: Hankooknumhwasa.

Perkins, M. R. (1983). *Modal expressions in English*. London: Pinter.

Pinker, S. (2007). The evolutionary social psychology of off-record indirect speech acts. *Intercultural Pragmatics,* 4(4), 437-461.

Pinker, S., Nowak, M.A., & Lee, J.J. (2008). The logic of indirect speech. *Proceedings of the National Academy of Science USA*, 105(3), 833-838.

Preisler, B. (1986). *Linguistic sex roles in conversation*. Berlin: Mouton de Gruyter.

Prince , E. F., Frader, J., & Bosk, C. (1982). *On hedging in physician-physician discourse.* Paper presented at the Linguistics and the professions: Proceedings of the Second Annual Delaware Symposium on Language Studies, Hillsdale.

Rees-Miller, J. (2000). Power, severity, and context in disagreement. *Journal of Pragmatics,* 32, 1087-1111.

Rhee, S. (1996). *Semantics of verbs and grammaticalization: The development in Korean from a cross-linguistic perspective.* Unpublished Ph.D. dissertation. The University of Texas at Austin.

Rhee, S. (2000). *Munpephwa uy ihay* (Understanding of grammaticalization). Seoul: Hankwuk Munhwasa.

Rees-Mille, J. (2000). Power, severity, and context in disagreement. *Journal of Pragmatics,* 32, 1087-1111.

Rose, K. R. (1994). Pragmatic consciousness-raising in an EFL context. In L.F. Bouton and Y. Kachru (Eds.), *Pragmatics and language learning* 5 (pp. 2-63). Urbana-Champaign, IL: University of Illinois.

Rose, K. R. (1999). Teachers and students learning about requests in HongKong, In E. Hinkel (Ed.) *Culture in second language teaching and learning* (pp. 167-180). Cambridge: Cambridge University Press.

Rose, K. R., & Kasper, G. (2001). *Pragmatics in language teaching*. Cambridge: Cambridge University Press.

Rounds, P. (1982). *Hedging in Written Academic Discourse: Precision and Flexibility*. Ann Arbor: The University of Michigan.

Preisler, B. (1986). *Linguistic sex roles in conversation*. Berlin: Mouton de Gruyter.

Salager-Meyer, F. (1994). Hedges and textual communicative function in medical English written discourse. *English for Specific Purpose,* 13(2), 149-170.

Samovar, L. A., Porter, R. E., & McDaniel, E. R. (2007). *Communication between cultures* (6th ed.). Belmont, CA: Thompson/Wadsworth.

Savignon, S. J. (1997). *Communicative competence: Theory and classroom practice. Texts and contexts in second language learning*. New York: McGraw-Hill.

Scarcella, R., & Brunak, R. (1981). On speaking politely in a second language. *International Journal of the Sociology of Language,* 27, 59-75.

Schiffrin, D. (1994). *Approaches to discourse*. Oxford: Cambridge.

Schiffrin, D. (1996). Interactive sociolinguistics. In S.L. Mckay and N.H. Hornberger (Eds.), *Sociolinguistics and language teaching*. (pp.307-328). Cambridge: Cambridge University Press.

Schmidt, R. (1993). Conscious learning and interlanguage pragmatics. In G. Kasper and S. Blum-Kulka (Eds.), *Interlanguage pragmatics* (pp. 21-42). New York: Oxford University Press.

Schröder, H., & Zimmer, D. (1997). Hedging research in pragmatics: A bibliographical research guide on hedging. In R. Markkanen and H. Schröder (Eds.), *Hedging and discourse* (pp. 249-271). New York: Walter de Gruyter.

Scollon, R., & Scollon, S. B. K. (2001). *Intercultural communication: A discourse approach* (2nd ed.). Oxford: Blackwell Publishers.

Searle, J. R. (1979). *Expression and meaning: Studies in the theory of speech acts*. Cambridge: Cambridge University Press.

Simon-Vandenbergen, A. (1996). Image-building through modality: The case of political interviews. *Discourse and Society,* 7(3), 389-415.

Skelton, J. (1997). How to tell the truth in the British Medical Journal: Patterns of judgment in the 19th and 20th Centuries. In R. Markkanen and H. Schröder (Eds.), *Hedgings and discourse: Approaches to the analysis of a pragmatic phenomenon in academic texts* (pp. 42-63).

Shibatani, M. (1994). Benefactive constructions: A Japanese Korean comparative perspective. *Japanese Korean Linguistics,* 4, 39-74.

Smith, V., Siltanen, S. A., & Hosman, L. A. (1998). The effects of powerful and powerless speech styles and speaker expertise on impression formation and attitude change. *Communication Research in Reports,* 15(1), 27-35.

Sohn, H.-m. (1978). Contraction as a mechanism of polysemic breeding: A device for speaker involvement in Korean. In C.-W. Kim (Ed.), *Papers in Korean Linguistics* (pp. 197-205). Columbia: Hornbeam Press.

Sohn, H.-m. (1986 a). Strategies of indirection in Korean. In H.-m. Sohn (Ed.), *Linguistic Expeditions* (pp. 266-280). Seoul, Korea: Hanshin.

Sohn, H.-m. (1986 b). Power and solidarity in the Korean language. In H.-m. Sohn (Ed.), *Linguistic Expeditions* (pp. 389-410). Seoul, Korea: Hanshin.

Sohn, H.-m. (1986 c). Cross-cultural patterns of honorifics and sociolinguistics sensitivity to honorific variables: Evidence from English, Japanese, and Korean. In H.-m. Sohn (Ed.), *Linguistic Expeditions* (pp. 411-437). Seoul, Korea: Hanshin.

Sohn, H.-m. (1988). Linguistic devices of Korean politeness. In E. Baek (Ed.), *Papers from the Sixth International Conference on Korean Linguistics* (pp. 655-669). Seoul: Hanshin.

Sohn, H.-m. (1989). Politeness Strategies in Korean. In E. J. Baek (Ed.), *Papers from the Sixth International Conference on Korean Linguistics* (pp. 655-660). Seoul: Hanshin.

Sohn, H.-m. (1990a). Main clause deletion in Korean: Politeness as a cause of linguistic change. *Paper presented at the Panel on Radical Changes in Korean Language of the Association for Asian Studies of America*

Annual Meeting (pp.234-247).

Sohn, H.-m. (1990b). Grammaticalization and semantic shift. In E. J. Baek (Ed.), *Papers from the seventh international conference on Korean Linguistics* (pp. 425-435). Toronto: University of Toronto Press.

Sohn, H.-m. (1999a). Functional transfer in sentence-final positions in Korean and Japanese. *Ene Cengpo (Language Information),* 3, 145 – 185.

Sohn, H.-m. (1999b). *The Korean language.* Cambridge: Cambridge University Press.

Sohn, H.-m. (2001a). Linguistic Politeness in Intercultural Communication. Paper from *5th Conference of the Pan-Pacific Association of Applied Linguistics*, 51-70.

Sohn, H.-m. (2001b). Teaching politeness routines in Korean. In J. Ree (Ed.), *The Korean Language in America* Vol.6 (pp. 25-35). University of Hawai'i at Mānoa: American Association of Teachers of Korean (AATK).

Sohn, H.-m. (2007). Politeness as a cause of linguistic change in Korean. Working paper presented at the Institute for Advanced Study of La Trobe University, Melbourne, Australia.

Sohn, S.-O. (1992). Speaker-oriented and event-oriented causals: A comparative analysis of *-nikka* and *-ese*. *Korean Linguistics,* 7, 73-83.

Sohn, S.-O. (1994a). The development of epistemic causality in Korean. *Korean Linguistics* 8, 67–84.

Sohn, S.-O. (1994b). Phonological reduction and reanalysis in modern Korean: A case of incipient grammaticalization. *Papers from the Chicago Linguistic Society Meeting* 30 (2).

Sohn, S.-O. (1995). On the development of sentence-final particles in Korean. In N. Akatsuka and S. Iwasaki (Eds.), *Japanese Korean Linguistics* Vol 5. (pp. 219-234). CSLI/Stanford University.

Sohn, S.-O. (2005). Corpus-based Analysis of *-ketun(yo)* and *-canha(yo)* and its pedagogical application. In R. Bley-Vroman and H.-S., Ko (eds.), *Corpus linguistics for Korean language learning and teaching* (pp. 25-49). Honolulu, HI: University of Hawai'i at Mānoa, Second Language Teaching & Curriculum Center.

Sohn, S.-O., & Park, M.-J. (2003). Indirect quotations in Korean conversations. In Partricia Clancy. (Ed.), *Japanese Korean Linguistics.* Vol. 11(pp. 105-118). CSLI/Stanford University.

Song, K.-S. (1994). An interactive sociolinguistic approach to discourse analysis: A case of conflict management strategies. *The Sociolinguistic Journal of Korea*, 2(1), 99-127.

Song, K.-S. (1996). Dynamics of gender in English and Korean conversation: Women and men in conflict talk. *Sociolinguistic Journal of Korea*, 42, 113-142.

Spencer-Oatey, H. (2000). *Culturally speaking. Managing rapport through talk across cultures.* London: Continuum.

Spencer-Oatey, H. (2002). Managing rapport in talk: Using rapport sensitive incidents to explore the motivational concerns underlying the management of relations. *Journal of Pragmatics,* 34(5), 529-545.

Spencer-Oatey, H., & Jiang, W. (2003). Explaining cross-cultural pragmatic findings: Moving from politeness maxims to sociopragmatic interactive principles (SIPs). *Journal of Pragmatics,* 35, 1633-1650.

Spolsky, B. (1989). Communicative competence, language proficiency, and beyond. *Applied Linguistics,* 10(2), 138-156.

Stalker, J. C. (1989). Communicative Competence, pragmatic functions, and accommodation. *Applied Linguistics,* 10(2), 182-193.

Stubbs, M. (1983). *Discourse analysis: The sociolinguistic analysis of natural language.* Chicago: University of Chicago Press.

Stubbs, M. (1986). A matter of prolonged fieldwork; Notes towards a modal grammar of English. *Applied Linguistics,* 7, 1-25.

Suh, C.S. (1996). *Kwuke mwunpep* (*Korean grammar*). Seoul, Korea: Hanyang University Press.

Swales, J. (1990). *Genre analysis: English in academic and research settings.* Cambridge: Cambridge University Press.

Sweetser, E. (1990). *From Etymology to Pragmatics.* Cambridge: Cambridge University Press.

Tannen, D. (1984). The pragmatics of cross-cultural communication. *Applied Linguistics,* 5, 189-195.

Tannen, D. (1987). *That's not what I meant!: How conversational style makes or breaks relationships (1st ed.).* New York: Ballantine Books.

Tannen, D. (1996). *Gender and discourse.* Oxford: Oxford University Press.

Tannen, D. (2003). The relativity of linguistic strategies: Rethinking power and solidarity in gender and dominance. In C. B. Paulston and Tucker, G. (Eds.), *Sociolinguistics; The essential readings* (pp.208-230). Oxford: Blackwell.

Tannen, D. (2005). *Conversational Style: Analyzing talk among friends*. Oxford: Oxford University Press.

Thomas, J. (1983). Cross-cultural pragmatic failure. *Applied Linguistics,* 4, 91-112.

Thomas, J. (1984). Cross-cultural discourse as unequal encounter: Towards a pragmatic analysis. *Applied Linguistics* 5, 226-135.

Thomas, J. (1995). *Meaning in interaction: An introduction to pragmatics*. London: Longman.

Traugott, E. C. & König, E. (1991). The semantics-pragmatics of grammaticalization revisited. In Traugott, E. C. and Heine B.(Eds.), *Approaches to Grammaticalization* (pp.189-218). Amsterdam: John Benjamins.

Traugott, E. C. (1995). Subjectificaton in grammaticalization. In D. Stein and S. Wright (Eds.), *Subjectivity and Subjectivisaion in Language*. (pp. 31-54). Cambridge: Cambridge University Press.

Turnbull, W. & Saxton, K. L. (1997). Modal expression as facework in refusals to comply with requests: I think I should say 'no' right now. *Journal of Pragmatics,* 27, 145-181.

Urbanová, L. (1996). Modification of the illocutionary force. *Brno Studies in English,* 22, 63-69.

Wang, H.-S. (1999). Speech acts in Korean language textbooks: Representations and authenticity. *Korean Language Education (Hankwuke Kyoyuk),* 10(1), 195-220.

Watts, R.J., Ide, S. & Ehlich, K. (2005). *Politeness in language: Studies in its History, Theory and Practice* (2nd edition). Berlin: Mouton de Gruyter.

Wesche, M. B., & Skehan, P. (2002). Communicative, task-based, and content-based language instruction. In R. B. Kaplan (Ed.), *The Oxford handbook of applied linguistics* (pp. 207-228). Oxford: Oxford University Press.

Wierzbicka, A. (1991). Cross-cultural pragmatics: The Semantics of human interaction. Berlin: Mouton de Gruyter.

Wolfson, N., & Judd, E. (1983). *Sociolinguistics and language acquisition*. Rowley, MA: Newbury House.

Wood, J. T. (1996). *Gender and personal relationship*. Mountain View, CA: Mayfield.

Wood, J. T. (1997). *Gendered lives: Communication, gender, and culture* (2 ed.). Belmont, CA: Wadsworth.

Wright, J. W., & Hosman, L. A. (1983). Language style and sex bias in the courtroom: The effects of male and female use of hedges and intensifiers on impression information. *Southern Speech Communication Journal* 48, 137-152.

Yoshimi, D. R. (2001). Explicit instruction and JFL learner's use of interactive discourse markers. In K. R. Rose and G. Kasper (Eds.), *Pragmatics in language teaching* (pp. 223-244). Cambridge: Cambridge University Press.

You, S.-H. (2003). Benefactive Verbal Constructions in Korean. *Tamhwa wa Inci (Discourse and Cognition)* 10(2), 75-93.

Yu, K.-A. (2004). Explicitness for requests is a politer strategy than implicitness in Korean. *Tamhwa wa Inci (Discourse and Cognition)*, 1, 173-194.

Yu, K.-A. (2008). The Natural Semantic Metalanguage (NSM) -based approach to a Korean discourse marker: *com. Tamhwa wa Inci (Discourse and Cognition),* 15(1), 85-109.

Yuan, Y. (2001). An inquiry into empirical pragmatics data-gathering methods: Written DCTs, oral DCTs, field notes, and natural conversation. *Journal of Pragmatics*, 33, 271-292.

Yuen, S.-a. (2001). *Socio-pragmatic functions of Korean interactive sentence enders from politeness perspective.* Unpublished Ph.D. dissertation, University of Hawai'i at Mānoa.

Yule, G. (1996). *Pragmatics*. Oxford, Oxford University Press.

Yum, K.-H. (1998). *Congkyul emi uy thongsicek yonku (A synchronic study on sentence enders)*. Seoul: Pakiceng.

Zadeh , A. (1972). A Fuzzy-Set-Theoretic interpretation of Linguistic Hedges. *Journal of Cybernetics* 2(3), 4-34.

Zadeh , A. (1975). The concept of a linguistic variables and its application to approximate reasoning. *Information Science* 8(3), 199-249.